SOUNDS OF SILENCE

... a monk's journey

by

Father Benedict Kossmann

authorHOUSE™

1663 LIBERTY DRIVE, SUITE 200
BLOOMINGTON, INDIANA 47403
(800) 839-8640
WWW.AUTHORHOUSE.COM

First published by AuthorHouse 09/23/05

ISBN: 1-4208-7291-5 (sc)
ISBN: 1-4208-7292-3 (dj)

Library of Congress Control Number: 2005906583

Printed in the United States of America
Bloomington, Indiana

This book is printed on acid-free paper.

Contents

CARTHUSIANS

Through what long heaviness, assayed in what strange fire,
Have these white monks been brought into the way of peace,
Despising the world's wisdom and the world's desire,

Within their austere walls no voices penetrate;
A sacred silence only, as of death, obtains;
Nothing finds entry here of loud or passionate;

From many lands they came, in divers fiery ways;
Each knew at last the vanity of earthly joys;
And one was crowned with thorns, and one was crowned
with bays,
And each was tired at last of the world's foolish noise.

A cloistered company, they are companionless,
None knoweth here the secret of his brother's heart:
They are but come together for more loneliness,
Whose bond is solitude and silence all their part.

(From a poem by Ernest Dowson)

INTRODUCTION

Everyone likes to travel! This work of love will guide you into the intimate life of a Carthusian monk, by an author who has experienced this life. The reader is invited to share his enthusiasm and experience this cloistered life.

Rarely, if ever, does the Carthusian monk write about his life, but our author takes us with him on his interior journey of how to love God and one another in a genuine way.

Many people consider the cloistered life as a useless waste of good talent. They ask, "What do these monks do for the world?" Others, when they hear the words "cloistered monk" have a romantic notion that the cloistered are free of care, experience no real problems, and have used the monastery to escape from the real world. Nothing could be further from the truth. Fr. Benedict clears this myth.

They rise at 11:30 p.m. for prayer while the rest of the world begins their sleep. The Carthusian monastery is alive with the sounds of the monks, chanting their prayers in Latin. They are before God for others who do not take the time to pray, and for those who do not pray enough. The author takes us into the intimate struggle between good and evil and the light and darkness of the human heart. It is a struggle we all have to face.

For once, the doors of the cloister are opened in a live experience. This work will inspire many to enter into a deeper prayer life with God, Who is not satisfied with just Sunday worship. He wants our whole heart in word and work.

After having visited several Carthusian monasteries, I find this book to be a factual representation of the deeply religious experience of the monastic life. You are invited to have this same ultimate experience. This book will remind us of *The Seven Story Mountain* by Thomas Merton, a Trappist monk. Allow yourself to be opened to a new adventure in the spiritual life by one who has been there.

Fr. Jacques DePaul Daley, O.S.B.
Monk of St. Vincent Archabbey
Latrobe, Pennsylvania

the beginning

I will praise your name, O Lord, for it is good. (Ps. 54:6)

I entered this world under the sign of the Gemini in the year of the Serpent, six months before the U.S. was drawn into WW II. I have come to believe that much of my life can be explained by these three facts.

The Gemini is versatile, adaptable, resourceful and changeable. Therein lies a seeming instability, a pull in opposing directions. I wanted to do everything at once, to try everything at least once, and not to be trapped by any one experience. I am a classic Gemini.

Being a Serpent at the same time, I tend to be cautious. The Serpent is wise and cunning, quiet and mysterious; like the Twins, he tends to be changeable. He has a need not to become too involved in any one thing, or with any one individual.

At least one of them, and maybe both of the Gemini, as also the Serpent, tend to be loners, solitary individuals, content to be with their own thoughts and feelings, not particularly wanting to socialize or be bothered by the demands of society.

I believe that I was destined for the solitary, monastic existence from birth by natural forces, or as some might say, by destiny. It might have been my genetic makeup, or the time of year I was born. But beyond these factors and beyond any doubt in my mind, God led me to the solitary, sometimes lonely life of the monk.

As something of a mystery, God led me to the monastic life so that I could try to find Him. After all is said and done, and beyond all that can be intellectualized, I was called to seek God at every moment of my existence. God called me and it has been an obsessive search. As a monk I was obsessed with finding God, with the ever-pressing need to keep searching for Him.

It may take a lifetime of constant seeking and searching for a monk to come even close to finding God. On the other hand, and herein lies a paradox, God wants to be found by those He has called to seek after Him. And He always

3

provides the means necessary to continue the search. Some men seem to be more prepared than others by their very nature to adapt more readily to these means. When God calls, however, He provides the means to follow after the call. After all, how could one follow a true calling without at the same time having the necessary means? We lump these means under the name "grace."

There is only one God. He goes by different names: YHWH, the name He revealed to Moses. He is called Yahweh, Jehovah, Allah, the Great Spirit, the Absolute, and the Truth. God is love and light. He is the energy that formed and keeps in existence the visible universe. He is called the Father, the name He revealed through Jesus Christ, the Son Who is equal to Him in every way. We believe that Jesus is Emmanuel, God with us, the Savior, the awaited Messiah, and the Christ.

A monk is a witness to God's existence and presence in the world. Indeed, the world itself is an outward manifestation of God, created out of pure goodness. The contemplative monk bears witness to this with his life. He is obsessed with God.

The old *Baltimore Catechism of the Catholic Church* answered the question of the *why* of our existence: *to know, love and serve God in this life and to be happy with Him in the next.* The monk takes this whole thing very seriously, making it the center point of his very existence. The monk has an inner need to remain focused on this end or goal of his existence: the quest for the one true God.

There have always been individuals who have found that life is a mystery, that having arrived on earth through no will of their own, they must begin at birth a journey down a path of which the destination is unknown, but which destination must be good, since most of life is good. Therefore, unwilling to trust their futures to chance, they make an in-depth study of this great mystery and seek to ensure that the end will also be good. There is no subject of such over-riding importance, and an answer to it must be sought. Should a man ride with the tide of chaos, tossed and turned about like a twig in the ocean?

I took such questions seriously to heart. I would not be content to waste my life in the pursuit of money, position, or power, and I regarded each of these as a vain quest for the mere temporal things in lieu of the Eternal Good. Even if there were no Eternal Good, I could do better and live more nobly by seeking the One Thing necessary, than those who were not seeking the answer at all.

An old monk used to say that man does not seek God, so much as God seeks man. Such is the key to the monastic life: it is an exercise in patience in order to apprehend God. If one withdraws into a monastery for any other reason, it is escapism and the basest form of self-love. Solitude for the sake of solitude is only a vile sort of misanthropy and narcissism.

The true solitary hermit is one who watches and waits upon God as an obedient servant, ready to perform His every command, anxious to do His bidding. Perhaps paradoxically His commands will generally come through other people, perhaps, again, to keep the solitary in a state of humility. It is necessary to learn the difference between good and evil, to discern the spirits, especially as it is expounded in Scripture. Indeed, unless a person has stamped indelibly upon his soul these rules and unless he has been tested in all of them, he is scarcely able to distinguish between his own good and evil thoughts, much less those that come from the exterior.

In a monastic hermitage, life is slowed down very perceptibly. The sameness, the drabness, the solitude and the rule that the hermit lives by, all combine to make events seem to happen in slow motion before the eyes. It gives a person a certain edge to his reaction to events, which naturally occur more slowly and further apart in time, allowing for preparation for these events beforehand. Some call this edge "meditation," or a form of "contemplation."

As silence surrounded me in the monastery, I became extremely aware of myself. I began to form a true picture of myself. For a time the clamor of my thoughts seemed to scream and chatter like so many birds disturbed in a forest full of trees. I began to think of my true inner self as the only sane inmate in a lunatic asylum, which was the outside world. It was all very confusing for a time as I became more and more conscious that I had little control over the thoughts that bombarded my imagination and memory. I had to take charge of these thoughts if I was going to avoid becoming a raving madman.

5

I learned the difference between a saint and a schizophrenic. A victim of his own dominating thoughts, the schizophrenic reacts to them regardless of how irrational they are. But the saint brings his mind gently back to thoughts of God through the reading of Holy Scripture and pure prayer. He does this gently and repeatedly until it becomes such an ingrained habit that it becomes a part of his nature. Bad habits are replaced with good habits. With the passage of time we forget the past, and begin to live in the present. We learn that the future is in the hands of the God. We abandon ourselves to God.

When I had learned to live comfortably in the present moment, I planned my work carefully and tried to do it in the most perfect manner possible. I considered it my divinely appointed mission of the moment, no matter how lowly it might have seemed. After all, action is but the product of thought, and if my actions were not good and holy, then how could my thoughts be dwelling upon God?

The Christian monk seeks God with Jesus ever as his model. Jesus is the perfect man, the perfect model, and the living way. The monastic tradition based on the lives of the "Desert Fathers," those third and fourth century hermits of the Egyptian desert, speaks about seeking God, about union with God. The tradition rarely specifically speaks about Jesus, though it is obvious that the utterances of those men (and women) mirror and paraphrase the teachings of Jesus in the Gospels. They were obsessed with finding God and living in constant union with God. In the later Christian tradition seeking union with God speaks of union with Jesus as "the Bridegroom of the soul."

Man's quest for the One True God through solitude has its roots in antiquity, from Elijah's cave on Mount Carmel and the monks of Qumran, through the hermits of the Egyptian and Syrian deserts, to the modern quest for answers to the eternal question in Eastern and non-Christian religions. Oneness with God has always been the principal goal of the monk.

In the Christian tradition it is attained by following after Jesus, by imitating Him who is the very image of God. By following the example of Jesus, therefore, the seeker-monk logically arrives at union with God. Man can only return to his Maker, short of dying, by the solitary search into the depths of his own soul.

I lived the life of a cloistered monk for almost twenty years. There are various orders of cloistered monks in the Catholic Church, and I was a monk of the Carthusian Order. My life experience will differ from that of other monks just as I am a unique individual among other unique individuals. But the essentials of my Carthusian monastic journey will be similar to others who have been called to make the same journey. It can be summarized in these words taken from the rule of life that I was called to follow:

To the praise of the glory of God, Christ, the Father's Word, has through the Holy Spirit, from the beginning chosen certain men, whom he willed to lead into solitude and unite to himself in intimate love.

The founding Fathers of the monastic life were followers of a star from the East, the example, namely, of those early Eastern monks, who, with the memory of the Blood shed by the Lord not long before still burning within them, thronged to the deserts to lead lives of solitude and poverty of spirit.

Accordingly, the monks who seek the same goal must do as they did; they must retire to deserts remote from men and to cells removed from the noise of the world, and even of the monastery itself; and they must hold themselves, in a particular way, alien from all worldly news.

Just like those men living in the early Christian era rejected "the world" of their time to embrace a life of solitude and silence in the deserted wildernesses of Egypt and Syria, I too rejected the world in my search for the living God. They were rejecting not only the moral corruption of the early centuries after the birth of Christ, but in a positive and all consuming way, seeking an experience of God. They were thirsting after a spiritual reality. As a means to living in this spiritual reality, they were disciples of Jesus, the Way, the Truth and the Life.

The Carthusian rule of life, *The Statutes*, explains that:

this same Lord and Savior of mankind deigned to live as the first exemplar of the Carthusian monastic life, when he retired alone to the desert and gave himself to prayer and the interior life; treating his body hard with fasting, vigils and other penances; and conquering the devil and his temptations with spiritual arms.

Jesus, whose virtue was above both the assistance of solitude and the hindrance of social contact, wished, nevertheless, to teach us by his example; so, before beginning to preach or work miracles, he was, as it were, proved by a period of fasting and temptation in the solitude of the desert; similarly, Scripture speaks of him leaving his disciples and ascending the mountain alone to pray.

Then there was that striking example of the value of solitude as a help to prayer, when Christ, just as his Passion was approaching, left even his Apostles to pray alone -- a clear indication that solitude is to be preferred for prayer even to the company of Apostles.

The need to follow Jesus as the first exemplar of the Carthusian monastic life generates other needs that will help the monk remain focused on the goal: celibacy, solitude, silence, detachment, and stability. It is very important to keep in mind that these "other needs" are the means to remain faithful to the inner calling of this search for God. They are not and should not be ends in themselves. Solitude, for example, is not lived for its own sake, but as a privileged means of attaining intimacy with God. Nor is the monk defined as "the celibate." Celibacy is another of those means necessarily associated with the unhindered seeking of the Absolute.

The monk is always alone before the living God, a solitary seeker of the Truth, a man intent on only one thing: finding the Truth. This was my calling. The journey itself was in a real way the end of my existence as a monk. I came to this awareness as I traveled the journey, always seeking the truth, ever seeking God in a real way.

The Truth shall make you free, if you have been true to your calling. You will experience a true inner freedom of spirit, a spiritual fulfillment, as I have. To know oneself - to be true to oneself: this is the nature of the journey. As you progress toward the truth, you tend to become a spiritual being. Truth is a spiritual reality, and the pursuit of a spiritual reality (or Spiritual Being, if you will) entails becoming a spiritual person.

In many obvious ways, spirituality is a fulfillment of religiosity. Being "religious" means following a set of binding rules, rules usually placed upon us by a respected religious authority. Professional religious people live the greater part of their lives in monasteries and convents under rules by which they publicly vow to abide. True religion, if practiced with a sincere and pure heart, should eventually lead to spirituality, a spiritual fulfillment of the human person, and a union of sorts with the Spiritual One. Religion will almost always be the necessary and preliminary framework, but may sometimes tend to take a secondary place as we advance in the spiritual life.

Grandparents in the Country

Mom and Dad

In the Country

The Little Admiral

Mike, Marilyn, and Me

First Communion

the calling

The Lord said to me, "I chose you before I gave you life, and before you were born I selected you." (Jer 1:4-5)

Our parents and our early upbringing form us to a great extent into what we will be in later years. I was fortunate to have parents who were not only dedicated to each other, but also entirely devoted to their children. Growing up in an atmosphere that was at once loving and genuinely religious influenced my later life choices.

Everyone who knew my Dad called him "a good man." He was a devout Catholic, worshipping the Lord with a strong and simple faith. He always went to Mass with his prayer book: *Key of Heaven: A Manual of Prayers and Instructions for Catholics*. Inside the front cover he had written his name and the words, "Got May 28, 1923." As the oldest son of his family, he had a chance to get only a rudimentary education and went out to work early in his life. He was always interested in the automobile, and I am told that he would spend hours working on his cars. Mom once told me that he was almost late for their wedding because he was tinkering. Whatever else he had worked at before I was born, his occupation is listed as "automobile mechanic" on my birth certificate.

My impression is that Mom had a stronger personality than Dad. She also was a devout Christian, having been raised in the German Lutheran tradition. I remember her as the disciplinarian. She had control of the family finances and did the shopping, in the beginning of her marriage under the watchful eye of her mother-in-law.

Mom and Dad seem to have experienced a jolt of love at first sight. I don't know how they met, but I think it was a kind of blind date arranged by mutual friends. Dad was five years older and had a good job. Mom was so good looking that she could have become a movie star. She became a Catholic for Dad and Dad's family. When growing up she had entertained thoughts of becoming a missionary, and probably would have, had it not been for Dad. I had the impression that Dad's parents and sisters didn't like Mom much because of her Lutheran background. But after I was born, their first grandchild, they became more accepting of Mom.

Dad's father, my grandfather, was a carpenter and building contractor. His father, my great-grandfather, had come to this country from Germany in the 1860s with two of his brothers. My grandfather married a girl whose parents had come from Ireland. They settled in what was then the German-Irish section of Queens County on the Brooklyn-Queens border.

My grandparents had five children. Aunt Frances was the oldest, and always the most independent. Aunt Mae was next after Dad in age, and always had a close relationship with Dad. I remember that she was always asking Dad to look at her car or to do minor repairs on her house. She became my favorite Aunt, the typical spinster aunt common to most families. She married later in life and after Dad passed away. Uncle Jack was Dad's only brother. He was the typical uncle, always ready to take us out crabbing in his rowboat, or showing homemade movies at Christmas when we were kids. Aunt Carole was the youngest sibling, the baby of the family. They were a pretty close-knit group in a loving and devout Catholic family. When they grew up, married, and had families of their own, we used to get together for the big holidays.

When I was born Mom and Dad lived in a small apartment or "flat" in Glendale, Queens. There wasn't anything unusual about the place that would be worth remembering, even if I did remember it. The one and only memory I have is of trying to chase a roach. The roach went into an electrical outlet. When I stuck my little finger into the socket I remember a bright flash and must have received a strong electrical shock.

On the next street over was St. Pancras Roman Catholic Church, where I was baptized two weeks after my birth. Aunt Frances and her husband, my Uncle Walter, were my godparents. Mom and Dad were both devoutly religious, and must have taken me to Mass every Sunday. Whether Mom or Dad attended daily Mass I don't know. But I suspect that Mom often stopped at the church for a visit during the day when she took me out in the baby carriage. In general I can only surmise that living so close to the church had an important influence on my life.

From photographs that I still have, I know that there was a park nearby complete with swings and a slide. Mom and Dad would have me dressed in a sailor outfit when they took me to the park. Mom told me later that people used to call me "the little Admiral." I vaguely remember going down the slide one day and promptly rolling off the edge, right onto the hard concrete. I fell right on my head. Mom used to say, always with a half-smile, half-scowl on her face that she must have dropped me on my head when I was a baby because of some of the unusual things I thought and did when I was growing up.

Mom frequently walked over to her mother's apartment with me in the baby carriage. Her mother was always "Nana" to us. Nana was not my Mom's biological mother, and I don't know much about Mom's biological family. Mom never talked much to us children about it out of respect for Nana. From what she related to us in bits and pieces, my maternal grandfather's name was Bridgeman. He, or perhaps his parents, had come to the U.S. from England. My grandmother was a Carlsen whose origin was in some Scandinavian country. Mom must have resembled her mother, because she looked like she would have fit in well with Norwegians, Swedes, or Danes. She had a touch of what you might call the "Viking spirit," adventurous and courageous.

From time to time Mom would mention that she had two sisters. She told us that when she was born, her parents decided they couldn't support all three children. Mom was the youngest and was left in the care of their friends, Nana and her husband, Bill. Mom's parents later wanted their daughter returned to them; but Nana had grown so fond of her that she went to court for a formal adoption. I don't know the details, but that was the story Mom always told. Mom would like to have found her two sisters, but she gave up trying and never did.

It was always said that Nana's husband was something of a legend in his own time. He was a physically imposing man, a pool shark, a member of the Polar Bear Society, and had been an amateur prizefighter. When he passed away prematurely, Mom went to live for a time with Nana's mother in the Bronx. She went to grammar school there, and visited with Nana from time to time. Nana had several sisters and brothers, so she had plenty of company in the household. Two of Nana's brothers and sisters used to frequent our home while we were growing up. We called them Uncle Leslie, and Aunt Elinore. She and Mom were about the same age, and used to spend a lot of time together enjoying each other's company.

Apparently Mom was happy living with her grandmother. She did well in school, took piano lessons, and participated in sports as much as was permitted to girls in those days. Sometime later after Nana had remarried, she went back to live with Nana and her second husband, whom we called "Uncle Charlie." A quiet, unassuming, and intelligent man, he provided well for Mom and Nana. He worked as a mail carrier in Manhattan until he retired in the 1950s.

I never knew any of my grandparents, and I feel to this day that it was a great loss to me. Dad's mother and father both died in 1942, when I was a baby. My grandmother died on Good Friday in April, 1942, when I was less than a year old. If there ever is a fitting day to die, this was it for one so devout in the Catholic faith. My grandfather died about five months after my grandmother from burns he had received from a fire at his bungalow on Long Island.

Grandfather had built a small weekend house about twenty-five miles from the city in Nassau County. He loved to go there with family and friends for relaxation and just plain fun. Being the proud carpenter that he was, he loved to keep the place neat and in good repair. One Saturday he and Uncle Jack were painting the interior walls. It was a chilly day and they had a small kerosene stove burning. Uncle Jack's wife was warming a bottle for their newborn daughter when the stove somehow tipped over, starting what could have been a disastrous fire.

Grandfather in his paint-covered clothes courageously rushed over and picked the stove up with his bare hands, carrying it outside. Uncle Jack was right there to help and their clothes went up in flames. Both of them were taken to the local hospital, burned over ninety percent of their bodies. My grandfather died within a week, but Uncle Jack remained in the hospital for almost a year. I was told that Uncle Jack didn't know that his father had died, and only found out when Aunt Mae came to visit him dressed in black.

After grandfather passed away, none of my Dad's siblings wanted the weekend bungalow. They all thought it was too far out in "the country." But Mom and Dad thought it would be a good place for my brother Mike and me to grow up. And so, when I was around three years old we moved into the house that my grandfather had built. This move away from the city into the country had a profound influence on the rest of my life.

Far removed from a city-like atmosphere, and at that very early age, I began to perceive city life as complicated and intimidating. Although I did not either feel or understand all of the consequences of living in a rural area, I nevertheless began to develop a sense of contentment living far from the noise, arrogance, and smuttiness of the city. Once in a while Nana would have me stay over at her apartment. I remember looking out the front window of her apartment and wishing I were home again playing in the open fields, away from the people and noises of Brooklyn.

Dad had no trouble finding a job with the Pontiac automobile dealer in Hempstead, about ten miles from where we lived. He was already a good automobile mechanic. The dealer sent him to school in Detroit for further training, and he became the top specialist in the shop. Then the owner of the Shell gasoline station on the corner up the road also wanted Dad to work for him, and Dad thought about it for a long while. But he seems to have been happy working for the dealer, and so he declined the offer.

My younger brother Mike had been born in 1943. We did everything together while we were very young. As his big brother, I taught him, much to Mom's chagrin, how to get out of his playpen. I probably taught him other tricks that I would have denied any knowledge of. Though he was intelligent, Mike was never fond of school, and gave the teachers a hard time. He developed a reputation among the teachers, many of whom compared him to me.

Mike would sometimes be accused of mischievous things that I actually had done, like the time another student's mother called to say that one of us had ripped her son's shirt during a game of tag. Mom immediately thought it was Mike who had done it and punished him instead of me. As we grew up, our personalities and interests developed in very different directions. He was more inclined to work with his hands, and was interested in automobiles. I was more inclined to work with my mind and interested in books. Mike had his own group of friends, and I had mine.

Mom was a good mother to both Mike and me. She was happy to be a housewife and homemaker. She belonged to a card club with some of her friends. They played at night, taking turns at each one's house once a week. When it was Mom's turn to play hostess, Dad went out for the evening, and Mike and I were sent off early to bed. Mom joined the PTA when we were in elementary school, taking the responsible job of treasurer.

When Mike and I were old enough we joined the Cub Scouts and Mom acted as a den mother. She enjoyed cooking and baking for her family. Dad bought her a sewing machine, which she used for a while and kept with her for the rest of her life as a nightstand next to her bed. On Friday evenings Dad would hand over his pay envelope, and Mom would have her grocery list ready. Friday night was our family night out.

Living where we did in the country, we kept chickens in a big old chicken coop out back. Dad also kept pigeons in another small coop. We had a dog named Jeff and a cat named Knobby. There were chores to do, including keeping our room clean and neat. One Easter Nana gave me a rabbit. A neighbor that lived around the corner and in back of us kept a cow, a goat and a pig. The cow and the goat were tethered in the big open field behind the chicken coop.

Across the street was a florist with several long green houses. The florist lived in a big house up the road next to the greenhouses. Behind the florist was what we called the "sand pit," which was adjacent to a cement block factory. Cranes dug the sand out and put it on a conveyor belt sending it into the factory. The cranes created a huge hole that promptly filled with water. Mike and I were told to stay away from the sand pit lest we fall in and drown. Sure enough, one summer evening a neighborhood teenager went swimming in the sand pit, couldn't get out, and drowned.

Before we started school, Mom would have Mike and me lie down for an afternoon nap. I think Mom was more in need of a nap than we were. The blue jays squawked in the trees while we pretended to sleep. The Hempstead bus passed in front of our house, and Mom often took us into Hempstead on the bus to the movies and to see Dad on his lunch hour. At Christmas we went into town to see the arrival of Santa.

On most Sundays and holidays we went to Nana's for dinner. It was always a treat. We usually stopped around the Belmont Raceway where street venders sold big salted soft pretzels. Dad bought us one each. Nana was an excellent cook. She sometimes invited Uncle Les and Aunt Elinore for dinner. Uncle Les was fun to be with, until he started to drink too much. Then sometimes he became violent, but was always good with us kids. He would give Mike and me a five-dollar bill sometimes. That was a lot of money in those days, and we appreciated it.

There weren't many other kids my age in the neighborhood to play with. Mike and I used to look forward to visiting with our cousins, especially with Uncle Jack's daughters, Judy and Carol. For as long as I can remember Judy and I were mutually attracted to each other both physically and psychologically, almost as twins. We were friends and sometime "kissing cousins." We talked about getting married when we grew up and of having horribly deformed children. I was born on the day Uncle Jack and Aunt Shirley were married. Judy was born in April of the following year, five days after our grandmother passed away.

Next to our little house was a bar and grill, appropriately named "The Pines" because of the silver and green pine trees surrounding the property. My brother and I used to sneak around the place at night peeking in the windows pretending we were spies or commandos on a mission. Sometimes I would rub soap on the windows before disappearing into the darkness. On Saturday and Sunday afternoons, when groups from the city rented the grounds for outings and picnics, we would wander over for a hot dog and a soda, pretending to be with the group. Sometimes we were successful; sometimes we were chased away. For our part, we always chased those unfortunate individuals who happened to wander over into our territory.

On many pleasant summer days I would sit outside under the big maple and elm trees in our front yard, working through the Math and English books Mom had bought for me. Before I started school I could read, write, and do simple arithmetic.

My parents were keenly interested in my having a good education. They bought a set of *World Book Encyclopedia*, and a big encyclopedic dictionary that I have to this day. In addition, Mom took Mike and me to the local lending library every Saturday. I became a voracious reader.

For many years on warm summer days I liked to sit on our open porch reading my books. Even in the winter, I sometimes sat outside on the open porch with a blanket or old carpet over my legs and read. I had a collection of books, all well known classics that Mom bought at Woolworth's in Bellmore. When we went there on Saturdays, the first place I headed for was the book section. Along with my many books, I had a complete collection of *Classic Comics* and was very familiar with all the stories.

I loved to walk, and as I grew older extended my range. Down the road about a half-mile was a large peach orchard with a small pond that dried up in summer. In the early spring I would go to the pond to catch tadpoles in jars, bringing them home and watching them turn into frogs. When the pond started to dry up, I would sit and watch the dragonflies swoop over the mud that was emerging. We called them "darning needles" and had to stay away from them lest they sewed our mouths shut.

On snowy winter mornings Mom would bundle us up in our snowsuits and boots, and Mike and I would rush out into the newly fallen snow. The winter of 1947 was a particularly snowy one. We took our sled out, and we trudged through the knee-deep drifts. After the snowplows had cleared the road we took turns pulling each other on our sled. Mike usually got tired of being outside long before I did. I could stay outside entertaining myself making snowmen or sliding on the icy road with my rubber boots. Sometimes I would just watch the cars go by, though there weren't many in those days.

Those were some of the happiest times of my life. Dad had a good job. We were comfortably well off. Mom was happy. My brother and I had just about everything we wanted in the way of material things, and were sheltered in the midst of a loving, safe and secure family life. Dad came home one day with a new car. Santa was very good to us at Christmas. We always woke up to a multitude of presents, including new bicycles, wagons, and books. I had no concept of what it might mean to need something; I already had all that I ever needed and didn't want for anything.

We were among the first in the neighborhood to have a TV. We watched the *Pixie Playhouse* on WPIX, Channel 11, from New York, or the *Howdy Doody Show* with Buffalo Bob Smith and the Peanut Gallery. I inherited the old family radio and would retire to my room to listen to the *Shadow* or *The Lone Ranger* many nights instead of watching TV. I liked to be alone. I felt comfortable being with myself and could always find something to occupy my time. When I wasn't reading, I made model airplanes. When I wasn't watching TV or listening to the radio, I would be walking or playing with the dog. I listened for hours at a time to the record collection that Nana gave me.

The day that I started school in North Bellmore was a memorable one. As was the custom in our neighborhood, Mom took me that morning. Soon after arriving I informed her that she didn't have to stay around, that I wanted to be on my own. When she came to pick me up in the afternoon, I proudly told her that I already knew more than the teacher! Apparently the teacher had said something that I knew was incorrect. I went to this school, which was about two miles from our home, for several years, riding the big yellow bus.

One day, when I supposedly was mis-behaving while in line for the afternoon bus, a teacher-monitor made me wait out of line. I didn't put up any fight, submissively stepping out of the bus line. One by one I watched the busses leave, until, lo and behold, I was left behind. I had to walk home that day. Mom wasn't at all pleased that a six-year old was made to walk home. She went right down to school to find out why it had happened. The teacher gave some lame excuse that she had thought I was on the bus. The next day the teacher made sure that I was on the bus.

The end of WW II had ushered in a time of change. The number of school-age kids began to increase, the suburbs where we lived began to grow, new "housing developments" mushroomed out of farm fields, and new elementary schools began to spring up. A new school was built closer to our house. We had to walk the distance every day because the school bus only transported kids who lived beyond a certain distance from the school. Our house was within the non-rider distance, less than a mile and a half from the school. We walked the distance on opening day and most days thereafter, weather permitting. I began the fourth grade in the new school. Many of the friends I had made during the previous four years continued in the old school.

I wasn't fortunate enough to attend a Catholic elementary school. St Raphael's didn't have one in those days, and I would have had to travel a relatively long distance every day to the nearest school in Bellmore. There was no school bus for the Catholic school; and my parents would have had to pay tuition, which was more than the family budget could bear. Later on I was offered a scholarship to a Catholic high school in Brooklyn; but for the same reasons of finance and distance, I stayed with the public schools in the area.

Once a week through elementary school I attended Catechism class. Initially they were after the Sunday Mass; later we were released from school during school hours for "religious education" classes in preparation for First Holy Communion and then for Confirmation. The Sisters of Charity who were stationed at St. Barnabas in Bellmore taught the classes. Though the Sisters were strict, I never had any problems with them, maybe because I never caused them problems.

I was happy to attend religious instructions classes. In fact, I looked forward to them. I liked to read and study. I faithfully memorized the tenets of the *Baltimore Catechism*, and received awards in the form of holy cards and stars on my test papers for my efforts. Mom hung them in the hallway outside my bedroom. All this provided a great and solid religious and moral foundation for the rest of my life.

Otherwise, I was a happy-go-lucky student, usually competitive, and sometimes aggressive child. At times I would "talk back" with impunity to my teachers or any other adults who bothered me in any way. But as a rule I was respectful toward my parents and teachers. Once in a while, when I was "bad," Mom would threaten to tell Dad when he came home from work. This meant that Dad would "get the strap out." In reality, I do not remember a single instance when Dad actually did punish us physically. Dad was easygoing, and he was usually too tired when he came home from work to think about anything but having supper and relaxing.

I had a group of friends that I hung around with, and was not immune from getting into occasional fistfights with kids I did not like. I developed crushes on some of the girls in my classes, and would ride my bicycle around the neighborhood after school, checking where they lived. I sometimes visited with friends at their houses, playing chess or talking over recent happenings. My life was pretty normal.

School was my life at that time. My social, intellectual, and physical life was developing. I didn't put on any acts or masks -- what you saw was what you got, like it or not. I was sometimes shy and most always reluctant to raise my hand to answer questions in class. I felt jittery if I had to give an oral report. I was a good student generally, but sometimes the teacher would put me out of the classroom (a common practice in those days) for being what she called a "cut-up."

I learned my school subjects pretty quickly and easily, spending little time on homework or study for tests. Sometimes I would complete homework assignments during class time or after school on the day the assignment was due, handing the assignment in late on that particular day. I didn't see much purpose in going to school, certainly not for the social interaction it afforded. Nor was I interested in striving for 'A's, although I would accept them, making Mom and Dad proud of me. I usually tried for a more naturally attainable B or B+. I didn't think going to school was very exciting, and I wasn't at all concerned about getting into the best colleges, or any college at all for that matter.

One of my greatest anxieties in those years was contracting infantile paralysis, or polio, which was at an epidemic stage in our area of Long Island, and I think the whole nation, in the late 1940s. I saw the "iron lungs" and leg braces, and was scared that I might need them. Every day a number of new cases were reported over the radio. For whatever reason, many cases were reported in the Levittown housing development, which was only a mile or so from our house. We were told to avoid crowds, and to stay away from Levittown, and especially the community swimming pool. It was enough to terrorize any young child. I used to pray fervently every single day, "Dear God, please don't let me get polio."

I prayed in my room, but mostly at St. Raphael's Church, and with my family. From the beginning of our life on Long Island the whole family had attended St. Raphael's. It was a small, single-aisled white building, holding maybe a hundred and fifty people at most. Mom and Dad took us faithfully every Sunday. From time to time I would go to church by myself, especially on Saturdays for Confession. In my immature way, my prayers, outside of Mass and the Stations of the Cross, were prayers of petition, requesting favors from God.

One of my earliest memories in church is when I said to Dad during a low point in Father Connolly's sermon, "Hey, Dad, let's go home and have a glass of beer." Father Connolly, who was said to be fond of his beer, replied from the altar, "That sounds good to me too!" What brought on that utterance I would never know. Perhaps I was already becoming bored with sermons. In later years I would hear many of them. Later I too would give some talks that I even thought were boring. Whenever I felt that there was a general boredom in the air with my sermons, I thought back to that incident with a sense of resigned acceptance.

Somewhere along the way I was chosen to be an altar boy, which in those days was considered a privilege. Though many were called, few were chosen. You had to show certain qualities of reliability and intelligence to be chosen for the job. In those days being an altar server was often a prelude to a vocation to the priesthood. It was definitely a rite of passage to be chosen as an altar boy, to study the Latin responses and the ceremonies. When did you ring the bell at Mass? What was the signal for bringing up the water and wine after Communion? *Ad Deum qui laetificat juventutem meum.* It was my first close encounter with Latin. Little did I know that in later life, the "dead language" would become very much alive for me. Dad came to the first Mass that I served. It was the feast of St Agnes.

I loved being in Church. Mom used to say, "I lived in Church." Did she recognize a calling to live in the Lord's house even in those days? I would sometimes serve the early Mass before going to school, but most of the time I would serve a Saturday Mass and one or more of the Sunday Masses. Once I was a veteran server, I was chosen to swing the censor at Monday night Miraculous Medal Devotions and Benediction of the Blessed Sacrament. I would swing the incense burner with great fervor and devotion. *O Salutaris Hostia -- Salve Regina Mater Misericordiae--* the Latin tunes stuck in my mind.

In the meantime, the changes never stopped. New housing developments continued to spring up in the neighborhood. They were populated by refugees, not only from the City, but also from parts of Europe, by some who had escaped the War. Fisher's peach orchard down the road with its beloved pond was one of the first open areas to disappear. The vacant lot where I used to play next to our house made room for a new house. The field behind our house where I used to build cardboard and wooden huts served as a building spot for two or three new houses. The one lane roadway in front of our house had to be widened to two lanes. The local school board decided that a junior-high school was needed.

When a baby sister joined my brother and me on January 2, 1952, Dad built an extension onto our house, creating a separate bedroom for our sister. Mike and I had to be very quiet during the day so as not to wake the baby. It was a novelty for both of us to have a little sister, and we enjoyed playing with her. Dad was ecstatic at her birth. He had wanted a girl to complete his family. Mom and Dad named her Marilyn. We were a happy family of five.

The happiness was about to come to an abrupt halt one gray day in November, 1953. Dad came home from work early. I heard him tell Mom that he didn't feel well. The next day Mom took Dad to see a Doctor who had recently moved into the neighborhood. Not knowing Dad, he diagnosed a touch of rheumatism, and maybe a case of the flu, prescribing a mustard plaster and antibiotics. Dad didn't respond. Mom called our longtime family doctor, who immediately put Dad in the hospital for tests, stating that he had "an unknown illness."

While Dad was in the hospital Mom took us to visit him, but we weren't allowed to enter the hospital building since he was "in quarantine," until his illness could be determined. He always had a smiling face while he waved to us through the window. It must have been extremely painful and lonely for Dad. He had never been away from us for days at a time. I think it was his faith that carried him through the ordeal. I was happy to see him at all, but I didn't realize the extent of the situation. None of us did, not even Dad.

Tests finally showed that Dad had blood cancer, but the doctors claimed that he could live for another five or ten years with this type of leukemia. Dad came home for a while, but continued to lose strength. Although Mom took good care of him and was happy to have him at home, he was becoming too weak to stay at home and had to return to the hospital. For the next several weeks he was in and out of the hospital, so much so that I didn't know whether he was in or out, unless I thought about it. He was rapidly becoming a shadow of his former self, but always showed a smiling face and cheerful demeanor. He didn't seem to be in any great pain, but he knew that he was dying, wasting away from the inside. He told Mom that she should "do her best" to carry on without him.

The last time I saw Dad in the hospital a few days before he died he weighed about a hundred pounds. He was unshaven and showed us his legs where the blood vessels had broken leaving black and blue marks. I'll always cherish the last kiss Dad gave me on the cheek before we left the hospital that Sunday afternoon. Together with Mom and Mike, Aunt Mae and her fiancé, Artie, were there with Dad. I remember that someone said that Dad had too many visitors in his room. But it was the last time we would be with him.Dad and I had just started doing things together, getting to know each other. As it turned out, I didn't have the opportunity to know him as well as I would have liked to. Although I was conscious of his paternal presence in my life, I don't remember any strong personal rapport between him and me at that time. Dad had been devoted to his work; he was devoted to the automobile. I trust that we would have had a wonderful relationship had he lived, and I miss him terribly to this day.

On a rainy afternoon in February, 1954, Mom was getting ready to go to visit with Dad, when a call came from the hospital that Dad had just passed away. Dad's chronic leukemia had really been acute. When Mom broke the news to us, I looked at myself in our big dining room mirror in disbelief and shock. Dad was gone. He was forty years old. He died alone in the hospital. None of the family had been with him.

When Dad died, Mom died too. Her life would never be the same. She would rely on me more and more for support. I knew that the course of my life was forever changed. Almost thirteen years old, I was now "the man of the house." Would I be up to the task? Could I handle this new responsibility? I could not begin to fathom all the consequences.

My sense of security vanished in an instant. I realized that life was short, that sooner or later everyone would leave me. Perhaps it would be better not to get too close to anyone. I had to insulate myself from my feelings to avoid disappointment and suffering later on. I began to construct a shell around myself, perhaps a prelude to a desire for a monastic life. I experienced a sense of guilt that somehow I had caused Dad's death. Perhaps I should punish myself in atonement for the rest of my life. As the saying goes, "God writes straight on crooked lines." What seemed like purely natural forces were forcefully and steadily directing and shaping what would be my response to monastic calling.

Life took on the nature of a very serious business; it had to be lived in a serious way. Although for the most part I continued to "hang out" with my friends and do the things most teenagers do. I continued to go to the school dances. I continued to have an interest in girls. At the same time I began to take a greater interest in religious activity. Religion began to give meaning to my life and to life in general. *What did it profit a man if he gained the whole world and lost his soul?* (Mt. 16:26)

I began to pray the rosary every day. I spent even more time in Church. I began to sense within myself a calling to a life of service, maybe to the priesthood or to the religious life. Because this life was a brief and serious business, I had to do the best I could. I began to withdraw ever more deeply into myself searching for answers.

One Saturday morning after serving Mass at St Raphael's, I was inspired to approach Father Pat with the question, "How could I become a Jesuit, or something?" Maybe he sensed a yet veiled calling. Father gave me some books to read. One of them listed religious communities and diocesan seminaries. I had not thought about religious communities, so that this alone was something of a revelation. I felt an immediate attraction to several of the religious orders and contacted some of them for more information. At the same time, I asked Father for whatever spiritual guidance he might be able to offer.

Father Pat might have sensed in me a vocation to a monastic form of life, because he introduced me to the writings of a young Trappist monk, Thomas Merton. I was amazed by what I read with my idealistic eyes. I took an immediate interest in the Trappists. I read *The Seven Storey Mountain*, *The Waters of Siloe*, and *The Sign of Johas*. I felt a calling to give myself entirely to the Lord, to do the most I could, just like the Trappist monks that I read about.

In his writings Merton made mention of a small and obscure group of hermit monks called Carthusians. Few in number, they were said to be the most solitary and silent of all monks. A true Carthusian calling was said to be a rarity in the Church. Apparently, many aspired to what they thought was a Carthusian calling, but few were chosen to enter the Order. It was said that the life was so difficult that even those very few who entered the Order ever persevered until the end. But I thought living the Carthusian life would be out of my reach. Besides, I really didn't want to go overboard in my zeal. But God had planted a seed. I kept the thought of a Carthusian calling in the back of my mind.

I began to pray more frequently, fervently and deeply, asking God to make His will known to me. I felt more and more that I had a calling to the religious life. I didn't feel particularly called to the priesthood as such. I was pretty sure that I was not called to the diocesan priesthood, but I had not ruled out being a priest in a religious order. At the same time I wasn't particularly looking for a life in community, since the strong loner traits of my personality were already formed to a large extent.

Through all the searching, I often thought back to that day when I was sitting alone upstairs in our house reading. Dad came by and I heard him later say to Mom, "He's upstairs reading. He looks like a priest." Maybe Dad had a sense of my future. Maybe it was wishful thinking on his part. I know Dad would have been proud to have a priest for a son. I think I smiled when I heard him. Had the seed been planted at that time?

Soon after Dad passed away, Mom started to think about moving away from Long Island. There were too many memories of Dad for one reason. For months after he died, she used to talk to him across the kitchen table as if he were still physically present. Then again, she had a hard time financially making ends meet with three children to support. Though she received Social Security payments, the cost of living kept rising faster than she could keep up with. She took baby-sitting jobs and did housework. I don't know how she did it, but she managed. She must have had very dark moments, because she would often say to us that she wanted us to stay together as a family if anything happened to her.

Both the rising cost of living and the population growth had already prompted two families from the neighborhood to relocate to a rural area in the Finger Lakes region of Upstate New York. Mike and I had all started school together with their children, we had been in the Scouts together, and we visited each other socially from time to time. Many a day I would ride my bicycle to the Johnson's little house after school to play a game of chess with their oldest son, Arthur, who was my age. We had gone to Boy Scout camp together several summers. We were friendly with the Warings and visited with them from time to time. Mr. Waring operated a plant nursery. I always liked their son Jay and his sister Ellen.

Mom started to take road trips upstate, visiting with the Johnsons and the Warings. She left us in the care of Uncle Charley who stayed with us and cooked his beef stew for our supper. I think it was the only dish he knew how to make! Upstate in the wilds of the mountains Mom liked what she saw and felt comfortable with what she experienced. She felt more comfortable in the slower and friendlier atmosphere. With support coming from both the Johnsons and Warings, she began making serious plans to relocate. She came home from her visits each time glowing with prospects. Mike and I were not so sure, and Nana didn't like the idea at all. She pointed out to Mom that she would be taking us away from our family and everything that we knew. But Mom refused to listen.

The following summer she took us to visit the Johnson's upstate farm for a week. The experience was not pleasant. The surrounding area of rolling hills and forests was beautiful, but the farmhouse was old and not only looked like a dump, but was a dump. The place was dirty and smelled of urine. There was no indoor plumbing. My brother and I slept with the two Johnson brothers in the unfinished attic. The bed sheets were filthy, and the attic smelled of rotten wood, smoke and tar. From the kitchen ceiling hung a dozen fly strips. After I muttered some uncomplimentary words at the misery of the situation, Mom asked us not to complain. We were put to work each morning taking cow manure from the barn and spreading it on the fields under the orders of a drill sergeant!

The only pleasantness I remember was spending time with my friend Artie. Having similar interests, we passed long afternoons waking along the dirt roads, engaged in philosophical conversation. We tried to impress each other with our extensive vocabulary of big words. We played chess and talked about our school subjects. He took French classes, while I preferred Spanish. We both did well in school.

My brother Mike had interests similar to the Johnson's second son, Don. Both were less inclined to intellectual pursuits and more interested in things mechanical. They talked about tractors and the farm animals. All the while we were there Mike tried to stay close to his older brother, looking for acceptance, guidance and support. Unfortunately, I think I was more interested in myself than in helping my brother.

That trip to Newfield was a test run in Mom's eyes. Although I think she had already made her decision to relocate, she wanted to see how her two sons would react to country living. My sister Marilyn was still a baby, having just turned four. Mom was pleased with the experience; but neither Mike nor I wanted to leave Long Island. To our dismay, shortly after our return to Long Island Mom contacted a real estate agent near Newfield. Two years after Dad died she made the decision to relocate.

She put our house up for sale. Mom took it as a sign from heaven and Dad when a buyer appeared in less than a month. An upstate realtor found ninety-six acres of land in the hills between the towns of Newfield and Van Etten for her to look at. There was a three-bedroom house on the land. Mom liked it. She was able to purchase it at a bargain price, using most of the money that had come from the sale of the house on Long Island.

I was fourteen, going on fifteen. It was very hard to leave the life I had known on Long Island, my friends, my school, the church, the beaches, our family. But Mom seemed to take none of this into account. She had never been close to Dad's family anyway and had not been to church since Dad died. Completely on her own, she hired a moving company. They packed our household items, and we packed everything else into our car and headed for the wilds of upstate New York on a cold March evening in 1956. It would be a six-hour drive. I sat in the front while Mom drove. She was so tired that more than once she almost fell asleep at the wheel.

We drove through the Bronx and headed north on the New York State Thruway. Mom always got off at Harriman and followed Route 17 through the Catskills toward the Finger Lakes. We made a brief stop in Binghamton and headed west to Owego. Then we took Route 34/96 the rest of the way to Newfield, turning off at a big red barn. That was the landmark we looked for. It was a shortcut to the dirt road that passed by the Johnson's. We must have arrived late that night at the Johnson's. I don't remember.

The next morning we went looking for our moving van. Though it had left Long Island before us, the drivers were nowhere to be found. When we finally located them, the one driver told us that they would be unable to take our furniture and belongings directly to the house. A local farmer had told them that the muddy spring road was impassible for the truck. They would unload our belongings two miles away. The farmer where the moving van was parked used his hay wagons and tractor to take everything the rest of the way to our place.

The one-lane dirt road was indeed muddy from the spring thaw and full of deep ruts. The large moving van would definitely have sunk into the mud, perhaps never to get out. You could approach our house from two directions, each connecting with a fairly good paved road. From the south or Van Etten side, you had to cross a narrow bridge over a shallow creek. You made a sharp left turn and climbed and climbed, about a mile, passing the first farmhouse, until you came to a plateau of sorts. Another half mile further and you reached our place -- a one and a half story farmhouse, typical of the area.

Just past the house, on the other side of the road, was a large two story wooden barn with a small cinderblock building at one corner that had been a milk house. At one time the farm had been a dairy farm and the milk had been collected and placed in containers at the "milk shed," to be picked up by the milk buyers who took it to the dairy processing plants. Just past the barn and the milk house, the road continued to rise to a height of two thousand three hundred feet above sea level. On the hottest summer days, there was usually a breeze blowing across the top of the hill. If you continued along the road, you reached Lane's big dairy farm, where our worldly belongings had been parked. This was the Newfield side.

Our mail came through Newfield, but we went to school in Van Etten. Newfield was in Tompkins County, Van Etten in Chemung County. Oddly enough the road we lived on started in Chemung County and passed through a little sliver of Schuyler County on its climb toward the Newfield side and Tompkins County.

On that first memorable day on the hill with the help of the neighbors, we literally carted everything we owned down the muddy road to the house we were to call home. Besides helping to put a few nicks and scratches in our furniture, the neighbors got to see just about all of our belongings. I don't think the whole thing bothered me. I was already feeling numb and quite helpless. All the while, Mom remained brave and courageous, leading us into this "Promised Land" all by herself.

Mike and I were not happy. In the course of two days we had gone from the modest and comfortable dwelling my grandfather had built to a run-down farmhouse that had no central heating and a bathroom that had been added as an afterthought. As a consolation, the outhouse was still in useable form if we needed it. I began to feel angry and resentful.

The first time I entered the house I pushed open the side door and stepped over the broken floor boards and assorted pieces of garbage into the big country kitchen. The place smelled musty and was dirty. When we turned the house water on, a flood came pouring down through the kitchen ceiling tiles. The water pipes had burst during the preceding winter when the house was empty.

The wooden wall behind the sink faucets was rotten and full of ants enjoying the moisture. It was a discouraging disappointment and a mess to clean up. I was getting upset and feeling very resentful at this point, blaming most of the predicament on the Johnsons. I refused to go to their house for a meal that day, spending the first of many solitary times outside on top of the hill that looked over the valley.

There was an old-fashioned cast-iron stove in the kitchen, which we used for a time before Mom bought a new electric range. There was no central heating other than a wood-burning stove in the living room that provided heat to the rest of the house. In the meantime, the upstairs rooms where Mike and I slept were cold at night. The wind whistled through the spaces around the crude window frames. During the following summer, Mom was able to have an oil-burning furnace and a central heating system installed. In time we became accustomed to using the bathroom, which was usually cold because it didn't have any pumped in heat. We had to keep the door open during the day when not in use; but the cold indoor bathroom was better than the smelly and much colder outhouse.

Although we had telephone service, the system was not what we had been accustomed to on Long Island. You had to call a central operator for every call you wanted to make. We were on a "party line," so that anyone in the area could listen in on your conversation. TV reception was just as poor. There was no cable or satellite dish in those days. Even with an outside antenna we could receive clear reception from only two channels.

Around the house was a partially wooded six-acre plot of land. About an acre of open area had been used for a vegetable garden. We planted corn, potatoes, peas, and carrots that first year; but raccoons destroyed the corn, and rabbits ate the carrots. The potatoes didn't grow well, and the peas didn't mature. In the following two years, having gained valuable experience, I successfully planted potatoes and peas, and even melons.

We kept a goat, a cow, a bull and two pigs in the barn. The animals were to provide milk and meat for the table. They were not meant to be pets, but soon they did become pets to us. I played with the little goat for hours at a time. And she became so attached to me that when we left the farm for a brief trip to Long Island, the poor animal felt she had been abandoned and wouldn't eat. When we returned from our trip, she was so weak that she died. I told Mom that I didn't want any more animals. Thereafter my brother Mike became the animal man and I became the gardener. Even so, I did take care of two little pigs that would join me while I worked in the garden whenever they managed to burrow under their fence. When they became bigger pigs, they converted to pork roasts and chops.

When we moved upstate Mom bought us a German Shepard puppy that I named Rex. I loved the little puppy in my own imperfect way, taking care of him as best I could. I wanted to train him to bite intruders. Mom didn't like the idea, especially after he went to bite one of our neighbors. Rex would follow me as I hiked through the fields, his tail wagging all the way. Sometimes we saw deer, and I had to restrain him from running off after them.

Rex followed me when I walked down the hill to meet the school bus, especially on winter days when our shuttle didn't make it through the drifts. I still feel guilty over not being as affectionate with the dog at that time as I would have been today. Even so, he wanted to be close to me, and he was one of the few joys in my life on the hill. After I left home, Mom told me that Rex attacked one of the neighbor's children and had to be destroyed.

Across the road from the house were ninety acres that belonged to us also. It was partially wooded. Several acres had been used for growing wheat, rye, and alfalfa. The land was divided into smaller plots by rows of trees and stone fences. Some of the fields were open and free of brush, while others were overgrown with brush and small trees. The previous owner had planted Christmas trees in one of the fields. Some of the fields were flat. Remnants of alfalfa and rye were still growing in some of them. Using some ancient and rusting farm machinery in the field behind the barn, we cut hay for the cows and goats. Mom bought a used tractor, which I came very close to tipping over when cutting and raking the hay.

The cleared and open fields were closer to the one-lane dirt road that separated the property into two parts. Further back into the fields the ground sloped down through dense trees into a narrow valley. I used to imagine that I was the "first white man" to see the forest. In the valley was a stream or creek. One of my "special places" was a grassy spot along the bank of the creek, where I would sit and pray and pretend that I was a hermit.

I spent many pleasant summer and fall afternoons exploring the fields and forests. Sometimes I would hike into the valley and climb the facing hillside. I would see deer and raccoons and beaver. I would sit in a corner of the highest open field to admire the beautiful valley stretching out before me. In late summer and early fall I gathered wild blackberries and raspberries for our supper dessert. All the while, and most of all, I enjoyed the silence and beauty of the hills and fields. It was God's country and I felt close to Him.

I was still angry, but began to feel more peaceful in this beautiful, though rustic environment. There were difficult times when I would react to simple things by slamming doors or throwing furniture. I was confused. My teenage problems of coping with a changing body and new emotions added to everything else. There were periods of calmness and alternating periods of upheaval.

From the beginning of our life on the hill I had desperately wanted to get out, to get away, to return to what I had known for fifteen years on Long Island. Living eight miles away from the nearest town in whatever direction you went, I felt isolated and helpless. I had no car, and there was no bus or taxi service. We had gone from the hustle and bustle of Long Island to the wilds of upstate New York in the space of a single day in March.

Unable to escape the situation, I looked forward to the time when I could be on my own. In the meantime I tried to find consolation in long and solitary walks. I gradually learned to enjoy the beauty of God's physical creation. I began to love the silence and solitude of the hills and valleys more and more. I was becoming a contemplative, starting to look at the world in a more loving and non-threatening, accepting way. Was this a foretaste of what was to come?

The Van Etten Central School, so called because it was in a more or less central location, was a disappointment. I went from a very large, grade ten through twelve high school to a school where you began in Kindergarten and graduated twelve years later. The academic program was below the standards I was used to on Long Island. Spanish was not offered; but I was able to take the Spanish II Regents exam and passed it for full credit. I continued with Latin. My interests outside of school were different from those of my new classmates, who were interested in hunting, cars, and girls.

I found the classes easy, and I had extra time to devote both to outside readings and to sports. I was more attracted to the solitary type sports, not being much as a team player. I didn't feel that I could rely on anyone else as much as I could on myself. I gained varsity letters in Track and in Football. I was pretty good in track, running the half-mile and holding the school record at one time. I had to stay in town longer for practice, taking the "late bus," which left me off at the bottom of the hill. I had extra exercise walking the two miles up to the house. I don't think Mom was too happy that I got home later than I usually would have; however, I was never in any great hurry to get home.

I went to some of the dances sponsored by the school. I had a few friends that I felt comfortable with, but never on an intimate enough basis to spend time at their homes. I did have a steady girlfriend, who was the sister of one of my classmates. She and I spent many happy Saturday afternoons together. Because I did not have a car during high school, I walked the eight or nine miles to her house both summer and winter. During the winter months we ice-skated; in the spring and early summer we picked wild strawberries and spent time together. At times I felt drawn in opposing directions. My mind and heart still drawn toward a life dedicated to religion; but I felt the normal attractions toward having a wife and family.

Though I felt the normal teenage passions, I kept myself from anything that smacked of what I thought might be sinful and immoral. I went to confession at least once a month before the Sunday Mass. I never used drugs, nor drank alcohol, although both were available. Though I felt the urges and had opportunities, I kept my sexual inclinations in check. I remained a virgin. It was years later in the monastery when I studied theology that I learned about sexuality in depth.

I faithfully attended the little missionary church in Van Etten on a regular basis, sometimes walking the eight miles on Sunday mornings when Mom didn't want to drive me. At first Mom went to Mass on Sunday; then later she stopped, mainly because she didn't care for Father Michael, the elderly Capuchin priest who came from the friary near Ithaca. He was of "the old school," rough and gruff, conservative and serious, but kindly and considerate at the same time. He was well known to the townspeople.

More or less on my own as far as spiritual guidance, I started to read the lives of the saints for guidance and inspiration. I felt a special attraction to St. Therese of Lisieux, the Little Flower. She was my big sister. Her "Little Way" of love was attractive to me, and I would deny myself in many little ways out of love for God. I would give up a dessert or deny myself some other little pleasure out of love. I read about St. Benedict Joseph Labre, an eighteenth century wanderer who had tried the monastic life with both the Trappists and the Carthusians. He found that both Orders were not austere enough for his austere tastes. I began to feel that I had a particular and peculiar calling, outside of the mainstream of traditional religious or monastic life.

I found books that helped me. One was *The Imitation of Christ* by Thomas a Kempis. It became the cornerstone of my spirituality. *Vanity of vanities and all is vanity but to love God and serve Him alone.* The book became my constant companion. I also read a book about a priest-hermit who had lived on an island in the Bahamas. He had constructed a hermitage on Cat Island, and I would dream of living there alone among the flowering hibiscus. I continued to devour the writings of Thomas Merton. I was especially fond of a little book of meditation paragraphs called *No Man is an Island.* I used to have the book open behind my school texts, especially when classes were dull and I felt bored, as I sometimes did in high school classes.

I began to distinguish between the different religious orders and congregations in the Catholic Church. I learned about meditation and contemplation, active orders and cloistered contemplative orders. As I learned more and more, I tried to model my everyday life after the saintly examples I read about. Outside of school I spent a good amount of time in my room, practicing solitude and silence, praying and meditating. During the summer months I rose early, worked in the garden and prayed during the day, fasted and abstained, and made time for spiritual reading and study.

Without human guidance, Divine Providence guided my readings. From a little book of lives of the saints, I learned that St. Anthony of Egypt, regarded as the "Father of the monastic way of life." Upon hearing the Gospel passage about the rich young man, he sold all of his possessions and withdrew to the desert to devote himself to a life of prayer and manual labor. Others followed his example. While Anthony lived the life of a hermit, Pachomius, who was also Egyptian, proposed a "cenobitic," or communal form of religious life. It was a way to practice charity as well as to live a life of prayer and work in the desert. I felt the attraction of the desert, to give up everything, to follow in the footsteps of Jesus.

Through my studies and readings I learned that the religious lifestyle was as old as Christianity itself. I knew that all Christians were called to a "religious life" in the sense that they accepted and professed belief in the Triune God: the Father, the Son, and the Holy Spirit, not only as a living reality, but as something having supreme value in their lives. This profession of faith was not simply to be with one's lips, but carried with it certain obligations like attending religious services and obedience to religious authorities. It was a response with one's whole being -- with actions as well as with words -- leading the committed Christian to bear witness both by offering worship and by giving service in the name of Jesus Christ.

While all Christians were called to imitate His way of life, to "follow in His footsteps," not all Christians were called to follow Jesus in the same way. Faith was an invitation and call from God. It found its visible expression above all in Christian Baptism and in the personal acceptance of Jesus Christ as Lord of one's life. It would involve the development of an "interior life" and a spirit of prayer; and for most Christians, this following of Christ was done in solidarity with other Christians traveling on the same pathway toward God.

Besides the "ordinary" Christian life, there would be a more formal way for some Christians to follow Christ. This was "religious life" in the strict sense of the term. The public profession of the "evangelical counsels" -- poverty, chastity, and obedience -- was at the heart of the religious life. Like every Christian vocation, the calling to the religious life was a specific call to holiness. It was normally lived within the framework of an institute or community recognized by the Church. Among the various institutes and communities there were contemplative communities and institutes of active life. There were institutes whose members lived and worked in monasteries, and there were active communities of men who lived and worked in the outside world.

I felt an attraction to the more enclosed and contemplative groups. Among these I learned that the communities of Benedictine monks were the most common. They followed the *Rule of St. Benedict.* After living as a hermit for some years, with the disciples who had gathered around him, Benedict founded the monastery of Monte Cassino in sixth-century Italy. His way of life, as written in the Rule, was soon widely adopted by other monastic communities throughout Europe. By the tenth century he was considered to be the "Father of Monks" in the Western Church.

Like Pachomius before him, Benedict focused on the idea of living the religious life in a community. He discarded the more strict physical asceticism of the early desert fathers in favor of the asceticism of humble and willing service to the brethren in the monastic community. He pointed out the need for a strict enclosure where the noise of the world would not disturb the monk. Then again, since it was often easier to run to the world for comfort in the guise of helping others, a strict rule of enclosure would help prevent this. In the monastery the monk was to face up to his failings with firm courage.

To my surprise I learned that religious institutes followed a general pattern of starting out with great zeal for a strict lifestyle toward a gradual lessening of zeal for strict observance of the rules, ending in a sort of decay or breakdown. At this stage someone would step in to reform the community in an attempt to return it to the "primitive observance." During the early Middle Ages, for example, the Benedictine Order gave rise to a reform by the Cistercians in an attempt to return to the original inspiration of St. Benedict. Several centuries later the Cistercian Order was reformed by the Trappists. The Trappist Order was able to keep the strict observance of the rules; they appealed to my spirit because of their austerity and no-nonsense approach to life.

The name Trappist came from the Abbey of La Trappe, where the reform was initiated. Outside of the time of community prayer called the "Divine Office," and when not engaged in manual labor, the monks devoted themselves to personal prayer, study and pious reading. Their devotional exercises always took place in common, never in private rooms. In fact, they did just about everything in the company of their fellow monks.

They rose at 2 a.m. on weekdays, and retired to bed around 7 p.m. In summer they took a siesta after dinner. The monks had seven hours of sleep during the course of the twenty-four hour day. About seven hours were devoted to community prayers, including the daily Mass. At least five hours of the day were devoted to manual labor. The monks were obliged to live by the labor of their hands, so the tasks appointed for manual labor were seriously undertaken, and was of such a nature as to render the monastery self-supporting. Most of the work was fieldwork. Living on the hill, with my garden work experience, I was attracted to this aspect of their lifestyle.

Their meals were simple. There was no breakfast. Dinner was taken at 11:30, with a light supper in the evening. Their food consisted of bread, vegetables, and fruits; milk and cheese were omitted at certain times of the year and on most Fridays. Meat, fish, and eggs were forbidden at all times, except to the sick. This didn't concern me in any particular way. I was always careful about what I put in my stomach. I liked good and simple fare, and that in moderation.

The monks slept in a common dormitory, the beds divided from each other by a partition and curtain. The bed itself consisted of a straw mattress and a pillow stuffed with straw. The monks slept in their clothing, which consisted of underwear, a habit or robe of white wool, and a scapular of black wool with a leather belt. They were never allowed to speak among themselves, though the one in charge of a work crew could give necessary directions using a highly developed sign language. All this had a kind of romantic attraction for the idealistic and austere teenager that I was.

I was searching, and I trusted God to guide my search. I wanted to do something with my life that would "make a difference." Service to others was a high priority; but at the same time I felt drawn more and more toward a life dedicated solely to God in a monastic environment. I began to understand that service to others did not necessarily mean being physically present in a helping way. I could help and serve others by praying for them, by interceding for them with God. While being useful to everyone by going directly to God in prayer and intercession, I could be of service to others within a religious community at the same time.

As I read, studied, and prayed, I began to realize that there was solitude in every type of life. With this in mind, and desirous of exploring every possibility before making a commitment, I did not rule out entering a community with an active lifestyle. I wrote, for example, to the Maryknoll Missionaries, whose magazine I received every month. Serving as a missionary in South America was somehow a distinct possibility in my mind. Upon expressing my interest in their community, I received an invitation from the Maryknoll Fathers to finish my high school courses at their minor seminary in Clarks Summit, PA. The high school seminary wasn't too far away from Newfield, and I liked the idea of getting out of what was the unpleasant home environment. But Mom persuaded herself and me that she needed me at home.

I was experiencing a strong calling to the religious life, and I continued to be open to all possibilities. But with so many possibilities open to me, I was a little confused and uncertain. The Internet did not exist in those days, but somehow I found out about the Order of Recollects of St. Augustine. The Recollects advertised themselves as "the Order of Fraternal Charity." They were a Spanish reformed community of a group of hermits who traced their origin to St. Augustine. They lived in monasteries and followed a rule of life that combined prayer and action.

Father Bob, the Recollects' Vocation Director, sent me information about their community and lifestyle. He drove up to our farm from Suffern to meet me. After administering some kind of aptitude test, he invited me to a weekend vocation retreat at the monastery. A few weeks later I took the bus from Ithaca for the weekend retreat. It was my first contact with a real religious community. Several other candidates were there, and I met some of the young students in training. Although I felt a little confined by the enclosed atmosphere, I was generally impressed with the place and with the young friars I met. Best of all, I was given the indication that I would be accepted as a candidate. I felt that I was on the right track.

Back home from my weekend retreat, I began to read the *Confessions*. I wanted to model my life after St. Augustine. I still had internal conflicts, trying to live a good Christian life in a place I did not like with people I did not want to associate with. I conversed with God in prayer as I took long solitary walks. I prayed the rosary every day. I recited the "Litany of Our Lady" and made a personal consecration to the Immaculate Heart of Mary. I withdrew to my room in the evening to pray and recite the beautiful prayers in a book Fr. Bob had given to me.

As time passed, it was becoming clear to me that my vocation was to more of a strict monastic and contemplative lifestyle than to an active or missionary community. I knew that the decision I would reach had to be in response to a true inner calling rather than to an intellectualization of my own. I didn't have anyone to talk with about my inner feelings and contradictions. I tried to converse with God as with a trusted friend. During the spring of my senior year in Van Etten, I used to walk to the local Church at school lunchtime, where I would lie prostrate before the Sacramental Presence of Jesus, asking for guidance.

By the time I finished high school, I had definitely decided to pursue the religious life. I had felt the invitation to come, to follow. *If you want to be perfect...come follow me.* I relinquished several scholarships and turned a deaf ear to suggestions that I enter the diocesan seminary in Rochester. I was certain that I had a calling to the religious life as opposed to the life of a diocesan priest. I was strongly attracted to the Augustinian Recollects and decided to join them. To my relief and delight, I was accepted as a candidate. The attraction of a balanced life of prayerful contemplation and active service within a monastic setting had won me over.

I graduated from high school in June, 1959. I had just turned eighteen, and was ready to launch out on my own. I could hardly wait to get away from Newfield. Mom knew it. Mike and Marilyn understood it to a degree, but were not happy with the idea of my leaving home. My brother Mike was especially concerned, partly because my leaving home meant that he would now be the "man of the house."

At the very least, I think Mom accepted my leaving. She had always told us that we should do what we wanted to do and what we had to do. She would not interfere with our decisions, and she did nothing to discourage me. I was required to have a physical exam and dental checkup. Mom laid out the money. She paid for my train trip to Kansas and bought me some clothes for the trip. I think that in her heart she was proud of me.

I was required to be in Kansas City by mid-August, since the clothing of novices was to take place on St. Augustine's feast day at the end of that month. The day before I left, Mom invited the Johnsons and Warrings over for a going-away party. Due to the train schedules, Mom drove me to the train station in Ithaca late that night. I had started on my journey. When I boarded the train I realized that this would be the first time I would be away from home by myself. This is what I had been waiting for during the past three years. Now that the time had come, I felt very much alone and lonesome. I prayed the rosary for comfort and soon fell asleep.

By early morning I was in Buffalo, where I bought some breakfast. From Buffalo I took the train toward Chicago, and from Chicago I caught the Santa Fe to Kansas City. I finally arrived late at night, about twenty-four hours after I had set out from Ithaca. Father Luis, the Novice Master, met me at the train and drove me to the Monastery of St. Augustine, where he showed me to my room. I was happy to have arrived, but was already feeling homesick. I was on my own, but it was a different feeling than I thought it would be. I didn't have family, friends or familiar places to rely on.

A dozen of us eager young candidates for the religious life came together in Kansas City that summer in 1959. I was happy to be among young men who had the same outlook toward life that I did. None of us had any doubt about our calling to the religious life; or, at least we didn't express it to each other at that point in time. One or two left the Monastery after only a few days. I guess they were disappointed, thinking they would find something else than what was there. I more or less kept to myself.

After a couple of weeks of orientation and observation on the part of the superiors, those of us who had not left the program were accepted into the novitiate on the feast of St. Augustine. We were given the title "Frater," and were required to add a saint's name to ours. The saint would be our patron to help us through the novitiate, and to distinguish us from other members of the Order who might share the same first name.

I was known as Frater Joseph of St. Therese of the Child Jesus. I called upon St. Therese to be my patroness and guide during the course of my religious life. Mom sent me a statue of Therese when she heard the news. She was happy that I was where I wanted to be.

By the time I began the novitiate, I had gotten over most of my homesickness. I was happy to be where I felt I belonged. Though we had lost a few, those of us who stayed seemed to share the same ideals and aspirations. Along with my companions, I followed a set daily schedule with fixed times for prayer, Mass, classes, and work. We lived a monastic life that was just austere enough. Some of my companions thought the life was a little too strict; but I thought it was comfortable. I had been used to "roughing it" on the hill. Generally, the food was good, all of our needs were cared for, and we were in a safe and secure environment.

As a novice I wore a black habit that consisted of a long robe with a belt and a separate hood that fit over the head and shoulders. We had a large rosary that was hung from the belt. Under the robe we wore a pair of black pants and a tee shirt. I wasn't used to anything like this, and removed the habit whenever I could, until the Novice Master told me that I had to keep it on. Likewise, I was required to stay on the monastic grounds at all times. We spent free time in the novitiate common room, and were allowed to walk outside on the grounds. Once a month we were allowed to walk together off the grounds.

During the week classes in Church Latin and the Rules of the Order were held morning and afternoon. We had a novitiate conference everyday before Vespers in the novitiate room. We took turns reading from a spiritual author, after which the Novice Master made comments and other announcements that pertained specifically to the novitiate. Once a week, usually on Friday, we had a mini-chapter of faults. After the conference, we went to the church to pray Vespers with the entire community.

When we were not in class or studying in our rooms, we were given tasks and chores to do. Because I had some experience in farm work, I looked after the chickens and drove the tractor cultivating the apricot and peach orchards. During the work periods I wore ordinary street clothes. During one of our afternoon novitiate conferences we wove little cord whips to be used for self-flagellation, always in moderation. We were allowed to use the whip in our rooms whenever we felt the need. Once a month, always on a Friday evening the entire community assembled in the large entry hall for a common self-flagellation.

We recited our prayers with the entire community in the monastery church and had choir practice once a week. We were taught the rudiments of Gregorian chant and modern musical notations. We had our meals in the big refectory three times a day with the entire community, although the novices had a table reserved for us. As novices we were not allowed to communicate freely with the professed friars and priests. I had met several of the younger religious in Suffern, and it was hard to refrain from speaking with them.

There was a lot of time for study and solitude in my room, and silence was strictly observed after supper until after Mass the following day. When I finished my studying I would often turn the light off in my room and pray in silence. We were allowed to visit the Blessed Sacrament, and I made use of this permission frequently also. The autumn and winter passed quickly. When spring came I was already a veteran novice, and candidates were being accepted for the next class. We were being advised that our philosophy and theology courses were to begin in the fall.

Our number had been reduced to three or four by that time, and I was beginning to have doubts weather the

Recollect Augustinians were strict enough for me. Was the life austere enough? Would it remain so after the novitiate? I saw that the lifestyle of the students was quite different from that of the novices. Although still in the monastery, the students were in more of a college setting. They lived in a separate building and had more freedom of movement. It seemed to me that we novices were living a true monastic life. I was candid about my feelings with the Novice Master and spoke with some of the students about it. No one thought my objections or feelings were unusual. I would get used to it.

I loved the novitiate lifestyle and continued to be more and more uneasy about the students' lifestyle and that of the priests. After ordination, most of the priests either taught at the seminary or worked in parishes. I did not want to be a parish priest. Why would I want to be a Recollect and work in a parish? If I wanted to be a parish priest, why would I want to bind myself with religious vows? I interpreted the continued uneasiness as a sign that perhaps I should not remain with the Recollects. I prayed in earnest for light and direction. I spoke with some of my fellow novices about my feelings. Some of them felt the same as I did and told me that they were about to depart.

I began to think once more about the Trappists and Carthusians. In my mind they both formed an elite corps, the best of the best. With either of them I felt that I could follow Jesus to the fullest. I had a fighting chance of saving my soul and of serving others through a life of prayer and sacrifice. I didn't want to settle for anything less. I continued to browse through the books in the little novitiate library on a daily basis, desperately searching for guidance.

Then something extraordinary happened. One day while I was paging randomly through a number of books about the religious life, I picked up a little book by Thomas Merton -- *The Silent Life*. I came upon a passage that pointed out that the Carthusians did the most, or went the furthest in devotion to God. Their members sacrificed the most. Over the centuries they had remained closer to their original calling than any other group. I saw for the first time the quotation attributed to Pope Innocent XI, *Cartusia numquam reformata, quia numquam deformata.* (The Carthusian Order was never reformed because it was never deformed.)

Carthusians were hermits who lived within a community. They were devoted to silence, solitude, contemplation of the human condition, and the personal quest for grace. They lived in solitude and followed a style of life similar to that of the Desert Fathers who had left the preoccupations and distractions of the world to seek God in the Egyptian desert. Their life was held to be one of purest contemplation. I felt like I was hit with a bolt of lightning. I saw a flash of light. I knew in an instant that I was called to be a Carthusian monk.

I had already known about the Carthusians; but as I read on, I learned more details about the Carthusian charisma. In the year 1084 Bruno of Cologne established the Carthusian Order in the valley of Chartreuse in the French Alps near Grenoble. Carthusians did not follow the Rule of St. Benedict, as the Trappists and Benedictines did. They had their own book of rules called *The Statutes.* Their sole occupation was to cultivate and maintain a direct and immediate contact with God. Within the Carthusian monastery the community aspects of religious life were minimal.

According to Merton, the Carthusians lived almost wholly cut off from the outer world, each one in almost complete isolation. They had introduced into Western Europe a life resembling that of the early Egyptian monks modified with an element of common life. They lived a basically eremitical lifestyle within a community framework. They observed an austere simplicity in the ceremonies of the liturgy and Divine Office. Poverty and strict silence were observed with great diligence. The Carthusians kept to the solitude of their cells within a strict enclosure. All this was exactly what I was looking for and wanted!

I went to the Novice Master that same day and told him that I didn't want to go to the Trappist monastery after all. I think he expected me to say that I wanted to remain with the Recollects. I had been approved for making my profession of the vows, and there were no other problems that might exclude me from remaining with the Recollects. Father Luis was visibly shaken when I told him that I wanted to be a Carthusian! As a last ditch attempt to persuade me, he brought out a page of psychological test results that seemed to show that I was confused and did not know what I really wanted. But I knew that I had been called and was unshakable in my resolve.

A calling comes from God, but it is left to the freedom of man to respond. God offers, He does not impose. It is sometimes difficult to hear this calling. Rarely known and seldom held in esteem, the purely contemplative cloistered life is so far from what the modern world holds valuable, that few are ready to take the challenge seriously enough to experience the call, much less to accept it. This calling is quite contrary to what the modern world holds dear.

Carthusians have traditionally believed that St. Bruno himself has a hand in choosing who is to live the life he founded. The calling of those who are chosen to live the Carthusian life often parallels his calling in general and particular ways. Sure enough, some aspects of Bruno's own calling to the solitude of the Chartreuse were similar to what I had experienced. Above all, however, I knew in my heart even at that time -- and through the coming years would become more and more convinced of it -- that Bruno had chosen me personally to be one of his sons.

Born in Cologne in present-day Germany around 1030, Bruno began a course of studies at the school of the Cathedral of Reims at an early age. Eventually he became a Doctor of Theology and Rector of the University. According to his contemporaries, he was one of the most remarkable scholars and teachers of his time, known as "a prudent man whose word was rich in meaning." A man of simple tastes and totally alien from political intrigue, he found himself ill at ease in a city where scandal was widespread among the clergy and touching the Bishop himself. After having protested and fought against the disorders for a time, Bruno felt ready to give up the struggle as useless. He wanted to devote himself to a life completely given to God alone.

He made several attempts at a solitary form of life with the Benedictines, but without finding the peace he wanted. In June 1084, as a last resort he entered the region of "Chartreuse," near Grenoble in the French Alps, where Bishop Hugh offered him a solitary site to build a monastery. Bruno seemed always to have like-minded companions in his attempts to find a life of solitude.

According to tradition, Bishop Hugh had seen Bruno and his companions in a dream the night before Bruno arrived. In the dream Hugh had seen himself leading Bruno and his companions into a primitive and solitary mountain valley. There they built a hermitage consisting of a few log cabins opening onto a covered walkway that allowed them access to the communal areas of a small church, refectory or dining hall, and chapter house (so called because a chapter of Holy Scripture was read there on communal days). With Bishop Hugh's help, Bruno found the solitude he had been searching for.

After six years of solitary life, however, Pope Urban II asked Bruno to leave his solitude for service of the Holy See. With regret, but without hesitation, he submitted to the wishes of the Pope. Without Bruno as their leader, the members of his community at the Chartreuse thought of disbanding; but later they convinced themselves to persevere in the life they had developed under Bruno's guidance. As a trusted advisor to the Pope, Bruno was ill at ease at the Pontifical Court. He lived in Rome for a few short months until with the Pope's blessing, he established a new hermitage in the forests of Calabria in the south of Italy. There he died on October 6th, in the year 1101.

At his passing, his Carthusian brothers praised him for being "a man of even temper, always joyful, and modest of tongue." He is said to have led his community with "the authority of a father and the tenderness of a mother." No one found him too proud, but "gentle like a lamb." Bruno was buried in the little cemetery of the hermitage in Calabria, and miracles were worked at his tomb. Pope Leo X authorized his cult for the Carthusian Order in 1514, and it was extended it to the whole church by Gregory XV in 1623.

A genuine call to the Carthusian life almost always manifests itself by a strong and continuous desire for that particular and specific kind of solitary, silent, and enclosed life. The desire might suddenly appear following a significant spiritual experience, or it might develop slowly over time. It is a genuine calling, not merely an inclination to work at a particular job, or even a calling to the religious life in general. There will be a strong accompanying desire for solitude and silence, since these provide the framework in which the Carthusian monk's contemplative life takes place.

I knew this was my calling. *He called us not because of what we have done, but because of His own purpose and grace.* (II Tim 1:9) I believe that Dad's death, living in the country, moving from Long Island, and living in relative poverty and rustic conditions on the hill had prepared me in a human way to accept the calling. My initial experience of the religious life with the Recollects had added to that preparation. God was preparing me gradually, and would continue to lead me and guide me.

It was time for me to leave. There were only two others of the original group of candidates remaining in the novitiate at this point in time. They went on to take their vows as Recollects. The others had left before the year of novitiate was completed, and I too made arrangements to leave the Recollects forever. Mom had to wire me the train fare for my return trip to Ithaca, and she met me at the train station when I finally arrived. Everyone was happy to see me. I knew being "home" was merely a temporary thing. It was only a side road on my journey. When I left for Kansas, I knew that I could never return to what had been.

I had been away for almost a year. During that time life went on as usual on the hill without me. My brother had taken over my room, while my sister had taken over his smaller room. Though I don't think they expressed any concern, I assured both of them that I did not intend to reestablish my claim to my old room. Mom informed me in a nice way that I would have to find a job if I expected to live there with them. But I knew what I had to do.

Almost as soon as I returned to Newfield, I wrote to the Carthusians in Vermont. I knew they were in Vermont because of what I had read in *The Silent Life.* In 1950 the Order had been given some property by a young woman who was planning to enter a convent. The five hundred and fifty acre piece of land she donated to the monks was known as the "Sky Farm," and was located not far from a big hydroelectric complex in southern Vermont. In response to my letter of inquiry, I received an informative brochure with an invitation to visit the Carthusian Foundation in Vermont at the Sky Farm.

It did not take me long to respond to this invitation. In late August I took the Greyhound bus from Ithaca to Bennington, Vermont. It had been arranged that Brother Paul would meet me at the bus station and drive me the twenty miles to the foundation. I didn't know quite what to expect, or if I would recognize the Carthusian Brother. I was surprised that a Carthusian would be able to meet me at all, since they were supposed to remain in silence and solitude.

It was Brother Paul, however, who had some difficulty recognizing the young retreatant he was to meet. Brother was dressed in brown robes and had a beard. As he drove he told me a little about himself and the Carthusian Foundation. He was from Belgium and was a Donate Brother. He encouraged me to endure what might seem like hardships to persevere in my vocation. I don't know if he felt that I had a true calling, or if he was expressing a total dedication to his own calling He asked me a few questions and advised me to study philosophy, recommending a book by Maritain. He gave the impression of leaning toward the severe, but I felt comfortable in his presence. I was happy to be on my way to an experience of the Carthusian lifestyle, and I felt pretty much open to whatever God might throw my way.

When we arrived at the Sky Farm, Brother Paul introduced me to the acting Superior, Father Stephen Boylan, after which he dutifully disappeared into his world of silence. Father Stephen was at that time "the only Irish Carthusian," according to his own testimony. His brother was a Trappist Abbot in Ireland and his sister was a cloistered nun in New York City. He related that the "black sheep" of the family was an attorney who practiced in Dublin.

Father Stephen gave off an immediate impression of sanguine congeniality. He was much more talkative than I had expected a Carthusian monk to be. He exuded an aura of austerity that redeemed any possible negative impression I may have had. I liked him and felt comfortable in his presence as I had with Brother Paul. I had a feeling that I would eventually be a member of this family, that I would fit in very well as a Carthusian.

After a brief interview at the small, rustic farmhouse, Father Stephen informed me that I would not be staying there, but rather in one of the isolated cabins similar to where the three or four other monks lived their Carthusian calling. I was a little disappointed at not staying in the farmhouse, but at the same time eager to experience the authentic life of the cell. After showing me the impressively simple and rustic wood-frame church where the monks prayed and had Mass, he led me along a well-trodden path from the church to my cell.

The "cell" was a one-room, not so impressive, very rustic cabin hidden among the trees. It was small and dark. There was no running water or electricity. Toilet facilities consisted of a bucket in the corner of the room with a shovel to be used for disposing of the contents. In another corner I saw a small wood burning stove and a pile of firewood. Against one wall was a wood-framed bed with a straw mattress, and in the center of the room were a table and chair. The whole place smelled musty with a hint of smokiness.

A flashlight was provided for making one's way to the church for the night prayers. The only light came from two small windows from which you could see nothing but trees if you looked out. Father told me that in winter the snowdrifts were sometimes so deep that they rose above the windows, cutting off all light. The last monk who had lived in the cell had to dig his way out in the winter.

Before leaving me to experience a taste of Carthusian solitude and silence, Father explained the daily schedule and showed me how to use the book of day prayers that was in the cell. The prayers were in Latin. I had studied Latin for three years in high school, and taken a good Church Latin mini course with the Recollects. I was proud to recognize just enough words and phrases to get along reasonably well to be able to pray the psalms.

The Carthusian Foundation at the Sky Farm was very primitive, even though it had been in existence for ten years. Perhaps noticing my apprehension, my fear that this might be too hard for me to handle, Father Stephen explained that this was only a beginning, a foundation for things to come. He told me that they were negotiating for a more suitable, permanent place to build an authentic Charterhouse, as the Carthusian monastery was called. I knew that the word "Charterhouse" was an English corruption of the French "Chartreuse," the place St. Bruno had founded the Carthusian Order.

I was disappointed and feeling a little discouraged, for I had expected something less primitive and rustic; but I accepted Father Stephen's words at their face value. At least some of my apprehension and sense of disappointment disappeared. I had, after all, just recently left a fairly comfortable monastery, totally convinced that I was called by God to be a Carthusian. I had no other thought in my mind. It was almost an obsession; and I was determined to pass through fire and water if necessary to achieve my goal. Little did I suspect at that time what perils life in the cell would hold. My experiences would lead me to fear that I was losing both my physical health and my mental sanity.

I was allowed to stay at the Sky Farm for a few days. The day began around 11:45 p.m. when I rose from the bed of straw to recite the prescribed prayers in the cell in preparation for what was called the "night office." I lit the oil lantern, and used it and the flashlight for reading. Although it was August, the nights were cool and often damp. I could smell the dampness of the cabin and the woolen blankets mixed with the smell of the kerosene lamp.

My first experience at the night office was one of confusion and very little prayerfulness. At the sound of the church bell I grabbed the flashlight and managed to find my way along the forest path to the church. Father Stephen was at the door to meet me, and led me inside to what was to be my place. I watched as the hooded, white-robed monks arrived one after another in surreal fashion. They lined up in their assigned places, standing facing toward the altar with their hoods raised.

I was assigned a place next to Father Stephen, who prompted me through the ceremonies and guided me through the prayers. The monks were divided into two choirs of two or three on either side of the narrow church. They faced each other while chanting alternate verses of the Psalms in a slow, monotone Latin. Large choir books, one for each two or three monks, were set out on the long stands in front of their places or "choir stalls," as they were called.

After the night prayers, which lasted about two hours, I was directed toward my cabin. Once safely back and inside, I attempted to follow the rest of the required prayers before getting into the now cold and still damp bed. It took a little while, but I finally fell asleep. The alarm woke me at 6:30 a.m. for morning prayers, which I attempted as best I could in the cabin. At around 7:00, I stumbled toward the little chapel in the farmhouse for Mass. Father Stephen had instructed me to do this the previous day. After Mass, another young man and I were offered a small breakfast of coffee and bread, which we consumed in silence. Then we walked back in silence to our assigned cabins for the rest of the day.

At around noon, a Brother brought the one meal of the day to my cabin in a wooden box. Inside the box were three metal containers, stacked one on top of the other. Brother Bede instructed me to start from the bottom container with the soup, and work up through the vegetables to the top container that held the main dish, which was either fish or eggs. There were several pieces of fruit and a jar of apple juice in the box, along with a loaf of bread and piece of cheese. I was hungry, and found the food well prepared. There was certainly enough of it -- almost too much.

On finishing the meal I re-stacked the containers, set them back inside the food box, and put the box outside the door for the Brother to collect it. I kept some bread and a piece of fruit to eat with the evening meal, as the Brother had recommended. I walked in the woods and explored one of the open fields on the edge of the trees, returning to the cabin when I heard the church bell signaling the time for afternoon prayers.

The time passed quickly. At the same time, I had a sense of the isolation and emptiness that the hermit life could provide. I had experienced the solitude and silence of a desert environment. My experience was eerily similar in its broad outlines to the description of Carthusian life by an anonymous Benedictine Abbot about the first Carthusian community more than seven hundred years earlier:

Warned by the negligence and lukewarmness of many of the older monks, they adopted for themselves and for their followers greater precaution against the artifices of the Evil One. As a remedy against pride and vainglory they chose a dress more poor and contemptible than that of any other religious body, so that it is horrible to look on their garments, so short, scanty, coarse and dirty are they.

In order to cut out avarice by the roots they would not accept a foot of land more if you were to offer them. For the same motive they limit the quantity of their cattle, oxen, sheep and goats. In order that they might have no motive for augmenting their possessions, they ordained that in every one of their monasteries there should be no more than twelve monks, with their prior the thirteenth, eighteen lay brothers and a few paid servants.

To mortify the flesh they always wear hair shirts of the severest kind, and their fasting is well nigh continuous. They always eat course bread, and take so much water with their wine that it has hardly any flavor of wine left. They never eat meat, whether in health or illness. They eat cheese and eggs only on Sundays and Thursdays. On Tuesdays and Saturdays they eat cooked vegetables. On Mondays, Wednesdays and Fridays they take only bread and water. They only eat once a day.

They live in separate little houses like the ancient monks of Egypt, and they occupy themselves continually with reading, prayer, and the labor of their hands. They recite the prayers of the minor canonical hours in their own dwellings when warned by the bell of the church; but they all assemble in church for matins and vespers. On feast days they eat twice, and sing all the offices in the church, and eat in the refectory.

Had I not been accustomed to the silence of the fields and forests in the hills of Newfield, I might possibly have lost any desire to spend the rest of my life in such a solitary setting. Perhaps he sensed my continuing discouragement, for Father Stephen once more assured me that Sky Farm was merely a very primitive beginning.

Once a permanent Charterhouse was established, the life would be more tolerable and seem less brutal. He explained that even some of the experienced professed monks who had lived at the Foundation had found the life there both too difficult and too different from what they had known in the European Charterhouses. They were accustomed to an established monastic community with all its necessary supports and comforts, including a Sunday community meal, a community recreation, and a weekly walk.

In Vermont the number of monks was yet too small for any kind of real community life. Some of the monks who had been at the Foundation left the Order, while others asked to return to their European monasteries. As I later was to find out, being in a long-established community might make all the difference between persevering in the monastic life or having to leave it against your own will and preferences. In any case, at that time I was consoled by all that Father Stephen had to say. I realized that the Carthusian monks were just as human as I was. It had been difficult to imagine anyone living in those conditions for the rest of their life, calling or no calling. All candidates had to go to Europe for training at that time to become true Carthusians. Presumably they would return to the United States once they were formed in the observances of the Order and a permanent monastery was ready. No one was certain how long all this would take, since it was a question of a great deal of money and planning. "A Carthusian monastery costs about a million dollars to build. It has to last at least nine hundred years," Father Stephen explained.

I supplied some basic personal information and filled out a short application form. Influenced by the examples of saints like Francis, John of the Cross, and Benedict Joseph, who out of humility considered themselves unworthy of the priesthood, I told Father Stephen that I was more inclined toward the Carthusian Brother's life than the priesthood. Besides, I enjoyed working with my hands, and did not want a life of continuous reading and study.

Monks in the Roman Catholic tradition have traditionally been divided into two classes: choir monks and lay brothers. Although all monks in the monastery were brothers, the choir monks were destined to be ordained to the priesthood. The lay brothers never became priests; they did most of the material work of the monastery. During the early years of monasticism, only a handful of monks were ordained to the priesthood, the idea being that many priests in a monastery were superfluous. Only a few were needed to say Mass, hear confessions, and administer the other sacraments.

There was little or no social mobility in pre-Reformation Europe. A person died in the same social caste to which he had been born. Peasants, mostly illiterate, were allowed to enter monasteries and to partake of all its benefits. However, they could never move up into Holy Orders, nor were they required to pray the Divine Office, which was sung in Latin. Lay brothers did not know Latin. They had their own set of prayers consisting mostly in 'Hail Mary's and 'Our Father's.

I already knew a little about the general organization of the Carthusian monastery, that there were really two communities of monks living slightly separate lifestyles within the same monastery. It was a symbiotic relationship, both Fathers and Brothers forming the unique Carthusian monastery. The slightly different lifestyles of the Fathers and Brothers corresponded to the different aptitudes and aspirations of those who wished to lead a Carthusian life. Both tended toward fulfilling the same unique ideal, lived in two different manners.

The Fathers were referred to as "cloister" or "choir" monks. Priests, or destined to be priests, they were bound by the laws of the Church to recite or sing their prayers together in choir. Their life was very nearly eremitical, except on Sundays and holidays. They met only three times a day in the monastery church: for prayers at midnight, for morning Mass, and for evening prayers called Vespers. Once a week, usually on Sunday, they shared a meal in the common refectory, followed by a time for recreation, when they could get together and talk freely.

All the rest of their time was passed in strict solitude in their hermitages, which were separated from one another, but joined by a common covered walkway called "the cloister." The cloistered monks did not leave their cells other than for community prayers. They occupied their time with prayer, reading, and work compatible with their life in the cell. Work might include cutting wood, gardening, transcribing books, and making pottery.

The Brothers were called "Converses" due to their "conversion" from the world to a religious life, and "Lay Brothers," due to the fact that they were not considered members of the clergy. They took the same monastic vows as the choir monks, but were not required to sing their prayers in choir. Brother Bede was a Converse Brother.

In the Charterhouse there was another group of Brothers called "Donates." They lived the Carthusian lifestyle, but were not obligated to take vows, although they could do so if they wished. For love of Christ, they "donated" their life to the Carthusian Order by mutual agreement. They had their own set of customs, which differed slightly than those of the Converse Brothers. In addition, they could continue to own and dispose of their belongings at will; and after seven years, they could be fully incorporated into the Order. Their gift to God was no less than that of the other monks. Their position, however, was unique in that they were free to tackle tasks and duties less compatible to the obligations of the professed lay brothers. I was attracted to the Donate life. Brother Paul was the first Donate Brother I ever met.

Both the Converse and Donate Brothers needed five or more hours of manual work a day for their human and spiritual equilibrium, in addition to time in the solitude of their cell for prayer, spiritual reading, and study. The Brothers ensured that the varied needs of the monastery were met by their work outside of their cells. They worked in as much silence and solitude as possible, yet their obligations in this regard were less demanding than the Fathers'.

Given my experience and liking for manual work in the fields, the Brothers' lifestyle continued to attract me. When asked if I aspired to the Priesthood or the Brotherhood, I replied that I was more inclined toward the more simple life of the Brother. But Father Stephen thought I should be directed toward the Priesthood because of my education and intellectual ability. He also told me that I was still too young to enter the Order, and would have to wait "a year or two."

Speaking from his experience with other candidates, he told me that this waiting period would give me a chance to test my vocation. He also pointed out that when a man entered a Carthusian monastery "everything stopped." What you had when you entered was generally what you would remain with for the rest of your life. He advised me to get as much culture as I could before entering. I should become acquainted with the great classical music, the great works of art, and to study French in the meantime.

Although I was disappointed that I could not enter the Carthusians immediately, I recognized the wisdom of his words. I hadn't been rejected outright; rather I was given hope that I would be accepted into the monastery. Years later I would learn that the treatment I had received was standard practice; for entering a Carthusian monastery was a very serious move for both the one entering the Order, and the Order that would be responsible for the monk. The Order had to be careful that the candidate had the proper intentions and aptitudes; and the candidate had to be as sure as possible that he was being called and that he was up to the sacrifices involved.

A certain level of personal and spiritual maturity was obviously required. Although I thought I had a high degree of maturity at that time, I didn't have the degree of maturity required for taking such a serious step. The candidate who presented himself in self-surrender had to have a profound desire to consecrate his entire life to prayer and the search for God in love. To experience that desire required a high degree of self-knowledge and spiritual maturity. Anyone who wished to join a Carthusian monastery must already have achieved a fairly high degree of prayerful relationship with God.

I had done my part by contacting a monastery and explaining in as great a detail as possible my attraction to the Carthusian life. I had supplied personal information and had been offered a retreat at the monastery in order to experience the life. As I later was to learn, even if the results of the retreat were positive, the candidate normally would be asked to wait a little longer before entering. The burden of the decision rested more on the judgment of the superiors involved than with the candidate. Only in rare cases would the superiors let the aspirant enter without delay.

My experience at the Sky Farm was an initial contact, a first retreat. Although I was ready to join the Carthusians then and there, I was told that I would have to wait at least another year to test my calling. During that time I would hopefully gain a greater amount of personal and spiritual maturity. To enter the Carthusian monastery and persevere there until death, one had to start out as mature as possible.

When he learned that I had relatives in New York City, Father Stephen suggested that I go there and "work in a bank" for a year. Why he suggested a bank I do not know. Perhaps he felt I could have interaction with the public in a profitable way and that this would contribute to my maturing process. He certainly thought that the cultural life of the "big city" would round me out; and I could earn money for my trip to Europe. At that time all the candidates who were sent to Europe for training were required to pay their own way there. Father Stephen also wanted me to join the Legion of Mary and to learn the rudiments of Gregorian chant.

With feelings of disappointment mingled with positive hope for the future, I returned to Newfield. Mom had not been sure when, or even whether, I would be returning. She was happy to see me, but again disappointed when I announced that I would be going to New York to stay with Nana for a year or so. I was always Nana's favorite, and she was ecstatic when I asked if I could spend time with her. Though Mom was disappointed that I would not be staying in Newfield, I think in her heart she understood that I had received a calling that I had to follow. I was determined to become a Carthusian monk, and equally determined to follow Father Stephen's advice as best I could.

And so, I went to live with Nana without any regret about leaving my family in Newfield. When I expressed my desire to get a job in a bank, Uncle Charley took out the newspaper and pointed out one of the best employment agencies in Manhattan where I might go to look for that type of work. After several false starts, I was hired as a teller at a Savings & Loan Association in lower Manhattan.

Before being hired I had two interviews at other banks. I would have been hired by either of them, but when asked if I planned to return to school, I candidly answered, "yes." I didn't tell the interviewers that I was planning to enter a monastery, but my candid answers excluded me from the available positions. It soon became clear to me that I would do better to be less candid. On my next interview I answered "no" to the further schooling question. To my surprise I was told that the Savings & Loan encouraged their employees to return to school! Father Stephen's suggestion for me to work in a bank then became a reality. Was this due to his prayers? Was God providing me with the means to prove my vocation?

I kept up my prayer life while living with Nana. Every weekday morning I attended Mass before taking the subway to Manhattan. At lunchtime I went into the local Church and recited the rosary. On Saturdays and Sundays I went into the City to the art and history museums. I was particularly attracted to The Cloisters in upper Manhattan, close to the George Washington Bridge. I spent many Saturday afternoons happily roaming through the French monastery that had been transferred stone by stone to the New World. I would imagine that I was already a monk, pretending that this was my personal hermitage.

I purchased a French record course and found a Gregorian Chant group. On Friday nights a group of us young Catholics would meet at a small apartment in downtown Brooklyn for chant instruction and practice. I developed some close and deeply satisfying relationships with some members of the group. They were intrigued and impressed when they found out that I was planning to become a Carthusian. Several of my best friends started to consider entering the religious life after my example.

I joined the local church's chapter of the Legion of Mary. We met once a week to recite the rosary and to discuss our apostolate. The Legion operated a small storefront lending library, providing books that were mostly religious in nature. Each member of the Legion spent several hours a week at the library, signing books in and out, arranging the shelves, and keeping the place clean and neat. I loved books, and I took pleasure in being in the library to the point of volunteering to work extra hours.

After a few months in Brooklyn, I felt good about my life and was happy. I learned a lot about myself and about human relationships. But through it all I kept my goal in mind. While I could very well have stayed where I was, doing what I was doing for the rest of my life, I was conscious of having received a calling to something else. I was absolutely convinced that God was calling me to the religious life; and I was stubbornly determined to follow the calling. I knew in my heart that I was destined to be a Carthusian monk. I did what I could to follow the calling and left everything else in God's hands.

As far as keeping in contact with the Carthusians, I did not want to impose upon their solitary existence by writing to them, much less by calling them on the phone. However, after being in New York through the fall and winter, I thought it time to try to contact the monks at the Sky Farm. When spring came I sent several letters to the Foundation, but to my dismay the letters were returned. The monks had moved, and I didn't know where they had gone. How could I contact them to relate my progress and continued desire to join them? I telephoned the Post Office in Vermont where they had been, but couldn't get any information. Finally I sent a letter with a specific forwarding request. It worked. After a few weeks of anxious and anguished waiting, I received a very kind reply from Father Stephen. Shortly after I had visited them, the community had moved about fifty miles to a place called Mt. Equinox, which was a few miles north of Arlington, Vermont. As I learned later on, the Equinox-Carthusian connection had its beginning when Brother Paul paid a visit to a certain Dr. George Davidson. Brother Paul held a degree in civil engineering and had hoped to utilize a small stream on the Sky Farm property to generate electricity for the community. He had heard about Davidson's ability to develop hydroelectric power on Mt. Equinox -- how he was able to produce electric power using only gravity and waterpower.

On examining the situation at Sky Farm, Dr. Davidson concluded that there was insufficient waterpower for setting up a turbine. However, in the course of several visits, he and his wife Madeleine became fond of Brother Paul and began to develop a relationship with the Carthusian community. Significant to this relationship was the fact that the Davidsons had no children. As the relationship deepened, the Davidsons suggested that it might be ideal for both them and the Carthusians if they offered their land on Mt. Equinox for the site of a Carthusian monastery.

A chief problem for the Sky Farm community had been the lack of the quality seclusion the Carthusian lifestyle required. A Carthusian monastery would ideally be situated in a secluded mountain valley, within a large plot of land that would provide a buffer from both noise and unwanted guests. Such sites were difficult to find. The Sky Farm site certainly failed to fit the ideal description. A state highway brought traffic distractingly close to the monks whose purpose it was to remain far removed from contact with the exterior world. The noise of two or three cars passing by an hour was too much!

Upon examination of the Mt. Equinox property, the Order found that several sites would make an ideal location for a Carthusian community. And so, the monks moved to Mt. Equinox on a trial basis during the summer of 1960. The experiment worked to the mutual satisfaction of both the Carthusians and the Davidsons. In fifty-acre parcels, the Davidsons began transferring the property to the Carthusian Order. The eventual gift would total seven thousand acres. By the time Dr. Davidson passed away in October, 1969, the new monastery would be substantially completed.

All that was still in the future when I found my monks in the spring of 1961. At my request I was able to make a brief weekend visit to Mt. Equinox in the fall of that year. I related to Father Stephen my work in progress, together with my continuous desire to enter the Carthusian Order. While on retreat, I had time to hike for the first time many of the dirt and gravel roads that Dr. Davidson had carved out through the trees and fields on Mt. Equinox. The weather was cool and pleasant, and the leaves were starting to show their true autumn colors. I was at peace.

Father Stephen seemed pleased with my reports of activities; but he thought that I was still a little too young to enter the Order at that time. He told me that I should "wait another year." Yet another year! It was a disappointment, but this time I was not discouraged. Father Stephen assured me that if God were indeed calling me, everything would work out. A little more time in the world would only serve to strengthen me for the rigors and trials of my Carthusian life.

By that time I had begun to appreciate the patient cautiousness so typical of the Carthusians when it came to admitting new members. If my calling were authentic, there would be little danger of its leaving me. It was in God's hands, and that is where I would leave it. Father Stephen encouraged me to continue with my human and spiritual development. I expressed my feelings of wanting a closer relationship with my family, and he encouraged me in this. We decided that it would be particularly beneficial for me and for my family if I lived closer to them in upstate New York.

After the short retreat I returned to Brooklyn and made arrangements to leave my job. The bank manager was surprised at my decision to leave and tried to dissuade me. Since I started at the bank, I had been transferred to a much busier branch in Rockefeller Center. Although I was happy there, I found this office too busy for me; and so, I left it with no regrets. Besides, the whole purpose of my working at the bank was to gather some experience in working with the public, and also to earn enough money for a plane ticket to Europe. I had gained some maturing experience and had saved some money.

It was, however, with some regrets that I left the friends I had made through the Gregorian chant club. Nana and Uncle Charley were both surprised and disheartened at my decision. They had graciously accepted me as a boarder in their apartment. I contributed to the household expenses, but they lost some of their privacy. On a Saturday morning they drove me and my few belongings back to Newfield.

Mom was pleased at my return, and I stayed on the hill for a short time. At that point, returning to Newfield was okay. I had no negative feelings, probably because I knew I would not be there for very long. About a week after I arrived, I bought a car for sixty dollars, and found a job at a bank in Elmira. Within the space of a few weeks I was working again in a bank, and had settled into a small attic apartment in Elmira.

The apartment was furnished and Mom helped set me up with some dishes, curtains, sheets and blankets. My first few days of living in my apartment left me feeling lonely to the point of desolation. But it was something I knew I had to endure. I had to have a job and I couldn't drive the distance from the hill to Elmira every day, especially in the winter when the roads were icy and snow-covered.

I continued to be faithful to my prayer life. I attended Mass everyday on my lunch hour. I read and studied the Bible in Latin, and prayed the rosary every evening. I had no social life to speak of, nor was I interested in developing one. I gave up eating meat as much as possible in an attempt to prepare my body for the Carthusian dietary regime. I learned to live on eggs, sardines, and vegetables. Within a short time -- and after some trial and error -- I became a pretty good cook.

On weekends I drove to Mt. Savior Monastery, just a few miles outside of Elmira, where the monks attempted to follow the Rule of St. Benedict in its original form. They operated a thriving farm and were in the process of building a permanent monastery. Their round church, with the altar in the center and the monks seated around it in a semi-circle, was something of a novelty in those days. It attracted many visitors to their prayer services. In addition to having a weekly retreat experience, I found excellent monastic reading material in Mt. Savior's little bookshop that nourished my spiritual life for years to come.

Though I visited them on many weekends, I never felt I had a calling to join the community. I found a friend and spiritual advisor there in the person of Father Benedict. He heard my confessions, offered valuable advice, and consoled me when I needed consolation. One of the friends I had made in Brooklyn entered the Mt. Savior community while I lived in Elmira, and I was able to visit with him also. I usually joined the community for their evening meal, and sometimes stayed the night in the monastery guesthouse.

On most Saturday mornings, even when I stayed over at Mt. Savior, I drove to Newfield to be with my family on the hill. On Sundays I went to Van Etten for Mass, and returned to Elmira on Sunday evening. I did not enjoy living and working in Elmira as much as I had living and working in New York. I found consolation in being able to escape to the solitude and silence of the hills on the weekends. It was good for me and for my family. We were strengthening our relationship in preparation for our more easily dealing with my eventual departure to the charterhouse.

In the spring of 1962, I made arrangements to pester the Carthusians once more about my entering the Order. Through the winter I had come to the conclusion that I had waited long enough to enter the religious life. I didn't want to wait any longer. I wanted to get on with my life. I was ready for a final answer from the Carthusians. I had accomplished all that they had asked of me. I felt that I was wasting my time working in the bank. I knew that I did not belong in

65

the world. I felt that I had gone as far as I could with my spiritual development, and that my human development was becoming stagnant.

During the time I was in Elmira awaiting the Carthusians' decision, I had written to a group of Camaldolese Hermits, who had established a foundation in Ohio. I was convinced more than ever that God was calling me to a type of solitary, eremitical lifestyle. The Carthusians continued to put me off, and I had to be prepared for a possible negative from them. I had learned from other sources that it was not easy to gain admittance to this exclusive brotherhood. I told myself that I needed an alternative plan. Perhaps the Camaldolese would receive me into their incipient community.

I had learned about the Camaldolese hermits from Merton's book *The Silent Life*. At Mt. Savior I found the book, *Alone with God*, about the hermit life of Paul Giustiniani. Blessed Paul had experienced a deep religious conversion and turned to a life of solitude, seeking God alone. He started a reform movement within the hermit branches of the Benedictine Order, culminating with the establishment of a separate religious congregation in the sixteenth century. Members of his group had recently come from Italy to establish a foundation in Ohio. They were a much smaller and less well-known group than the Carthusians, who had come to the United States at about the same time.

The literature I received from the Camaldolese foundation in Ohio described a life that seemed less appealing than the Carthusian life. The Camaldolese lifestyle seemed less solitary and silent than the Carthusian. They were more Benedictine in their customs, and were consequently more community oriented. The Carthusians, who were decidedly not Benedictine, put more emphasis on the hermit aspect of their life. The Camaldolese were headquartered in Italy and seemed generally to be less austere than the Carthusians. I was attracted to a life that would be as simple and austere as possible.

The Camaldolese foundation in Ohio was further in distance from Newfield than the Carthusian Foundation in Vermont. It would have been more difficult for me to visit the Camaldolese for a retreat. However, despite the distance and my reservations about their lifestyle, the Camaldolese became my second best choice. I decided that I would formally apply to the Camaldolese if the Carthusians told me to wait another year. If God were really calling me to the Carthusians, the reception would be positive; if the Carthusian response were negative, I would take it as a sign that my vocation lay with the Camaldolese hermits in Ohio.

In May of 1962, anticipating a positive retreat, but prepared for a showdown, I drove my 1952 blue Chevy to Vermont. I arrived at Equinox Mountain after the five-hour journey from Newfield. The people at the tollhouse called the monks to announce my arrival, and I drove the next two and a half miles up the mountain. I already knew my way. As I had done a year earlier, I passed the guesthouse and followed the private road down the steep slope toward the temporary monastery. I was excited about finally arriving, but didn't know what to expect. I took it as a good sign of positive things to come that my old car had climbed the mountain with no difficulty.

Father Stephen met me at the door of the temporary monastery, seeming happy to see me once more. The first thing he asked me was whether I was "fasting." I thought he was referring to my general eating habits and physical appearance, and replied negatively. Actually, as I later realized, he was asking me if I had had anything to eat that day. I looked hungry, or he was being hospitable -- probably both were true.

This was my second visit to the temporary Carthusian monastery on Mt. Equinox. The "wagon shed," as it was called, was already familiar to me from my first visit. I was given a longer and more thorough tour of the facility this time. The building, once intended for use as a ski lodge, was a long, two-storied wooden structure. On the second floor were two suites of several rooms, kitchen facilities, and smaller rooms under twelve gables, six off each side of a long central corridor. The gabled cubicles, originally designed as rooms for transient skiers, were now cells for solitary monks and retreatant candidates. Each cubicle contained a bed, small closet, a desk and bookshelf, and a sink for washing. On both ends of the central corridor was a bathroom complete with shower stalls.

The cubicle that I was given was again on the backside of the building, but it wasn't the same one I had been in on my previous visit. When I looked out the window, I saw the tree-covered slope of the mountain. I could see a dirt road running through the forest. Once or twice a day a car passed along the road. Had I been in a room at the front side of the building, I would have had a spectacular view of the mountain valley; but I also would have been more aware of the comings and goings associated with the community business.

The ground floor of the wagon shed was a big garage for the trucks and snow plows necessary for maintaining the property's roads in summer and winter -- hence the name of the building. Dr. Davidson kept a converted fire engine-pickup truck in the garage. Just about every morning he took it out for a survey of his seven thousand-acre piece of property.

Besides Father Stephen, the two Carthusian Brothers, Paul and Bede, were still in residence. A young American, whom I had not met before, had recently been sent from Europe to assist in the details of the construction of a permanent monastery. This was my first meeting with the man who would be my friend and mentor in the years to come, as well as the first Prior of the new Charterhouse. Father Raphael's mission was a complex and delicate one. He had to choose an architect who would design and build a monastery that would last "at least nine hundred years," as Father Stephen continuously told visitors.

Father Raphael lived in a suite of rooms at one end of the building; at the other end was a similar suite that belonged to Father Stephen. Each end of the building had its separate entrances. Adjacent to Father Stephen's rooms was a small and sparsely decorated chapel where the Blessed Sacrament was kept and where the monks gathered for community prayers and Mass.

On the door of the simple wooden tabernacle were the Greek letters *NI/KA*, which they told me referred to the "Son of God, Risen King." This was particularly appropriate, since the Carthusian monks were sometimes referred to as "sons of the Resurrection." The main altar faced a window of opaque glass. Through it you could make out the outlines of the distant green mountains. It was beautiful and inspired devotion!

Those days of my retreat in May of 1962 were warm and sunny. I followed the daily schedule of night prayers, morning Mass, and spiritual reading. Both Fathers Stephen and Raphael visited me in my room for short conferences. On several mornings I worked outside digging in a garden that was under construction at one end of the wagon shed. Father Raphael asked me to plant Easter lily bulbs in a little garden he had started. For free time after the noonday meal I walked along the country roads that Dr. Davidson had hewn out of the forest. One evening I walked down the road to the man-made Lake Madeline where I sat on the dam and meditated. The site for the eventual Charterhouse was close to the lake. It was a happy time. I felt relaxed and very much at peace. I felt confirmed in my vocation. I would be able to live the Carthusian life in its entire rigor. I was totally willing to go to Europe for training, though I would much rather have stayed in the United States. My experience of the Carthusian lifestyle thus far was everything I had expected it to be and more, with its almost total silence and positive solitude. I had time and opportunity to really be alone with God. I had absolutely no reservations about leaving my family and my country to follow my calling.

My perseverance in knocking at the door along with my comportment during the weeklong retreat had apparently impressed both Father Stephen and Father Raphael. Toward the end of my retreat Father Stephen came to my room and asked me if I would prefer to go to England or to France. I had been accepted! I had anticipated this moment for a long time. Without hesitation I answered that I would like to enter the Order in Spain. I had studied Spanish for the past five years; and my research had found that the Spanish houses were the strictest in Carthusian monastic observance. I explained that I wanted to do the most I could in the strictest environment. More than anything I wanted to be a well-formed Carthusian.

Father Stephen was somewhat surprised at my answer, but he related that one other American had preceded me to the Spanish Charterhouse of Miraflores, which was in North-central Spain. Thomas Verner Moore was a trained psychiatrist and former member of the Paulist Fathers and later a Benedictine monk. He had been somewhat reluctantly accepted by the Order in 1947 because of his age. Although he was not the first American to enter the Order, he was the first to make it all the way to solemn vows. As a professed monk, he had been instrumental in convincing the Order to establish a foundation in the United States in 1950.

Some of the European Charterhouses did not have provisions for the accepting and training of candidates. Most of the American candidates thus far had gone to either England or France. And not all Charterhouses were willing to accept candidates from America, since it was widely felt within the Order that Americans were much too active for the totally contemplative and cloistered Carthusian lifestyle. Father Stephen told me, however, that the Charterhouse of Our Lady of the Defense (Nuestra Senora de la Defension) at Jerez in the South of Spain was accepting candidates for their Novitiate.

The Prior of the Charterhouse of Jerez spoke English. He had accompanied Father Moore to the United States in the 1950s to investigate the Sky Farm property. Later on I heard a rumor that he had been attached to the Spanish Diplomatic Corps in Washington before entering the Carthusian Order. I never verified this; but it was well known that he was a nobleman with the title of *Marques*.

Father Stephen contacted the Prior of Jerez, and it was now my turn to be surprised when I was told that it was okay for me to go to Jerez to test my calling. I was ecstatic! My calling was verified and confirmed by God's representatives. Up to that time I had experienced all those doubts and insecurities that a candidate for a job has during and after an interview. But now I had really been accepted as a candidate; and I was going to Spain. Father Stephen was willing to pay part of my plane ticket, but I told him I had saved enough for the one-way fare.

Spain

The Lord said to Abram, "Leave your native land, your relatives, and your father's home, and go to a country that I am going to show you... there I will bless you." (Gen 12:1-2)

I wanted to arrive in Jerez for the Feast of the Assumption of the Blessed Virgin on August 15th to enter the monastery on that day. I felt that my calling and my keeping faithful to my calling had been in the hands of the Mother of God. I wanted to honor her and remain under her patronage by initiating my Carthusian career on her feast day.

I returned to Newfield with the good news. Mom received it with mixed emotion. She questioned why I wanted to leave the country and "live among foreigners." I told her that it was something that I had to do, that I was ready to risk my health and life to follow what I believed was my calling from God. The Carthusians had confirmed it by giving me the green light to enter. I don't think my brother or sister understood what I was doing or why I was doing it.

One of the first things I did was to make arrangements to quit my position at the bank. I gave my two weeks' notice. The manager was surprised that I wanted to leave, and offered me a good management position in Binghamton, and then another in Watkins Glen when I turned that down. He was disappointed when I declined both offers. I didn't explain why I was leaving, because I knew that I would not be returning under any circumstances. And so, with no regrets I left the world of banking. I purchased a one-way plane ticket to Madrid, and bade a last farewell to my apartment in Elmira and to my friends at Mt. Savior.

I spent a few weeks with my family on "the hill." I continued to take long, solitary walks, practiced mortification in small ways, and consumed as little meat as possible. I practiced what I thought was the monk's life, rising at 6, and working in the garden until 7 or 7:30, when I had breakfast with the family. Then I spent some time in reading until dinner, after which I worked in the fields for a few hours. After supper I retired to my room where I prayed the rosary and read before going to bed when the sun went down. I wanted to prepare

71

myself as much as possible. I was going to sacrifice as much as I possibly could for the love of God. I was going to dedicate my life exclusively and completely to God.

Before leaving for Spain I wanted to spend a few days with Nana in New York; and there were relatives and friends I wanted to see, perhaps for the last time. The night before I left Newfield, Mom gathered together a few of our friends for a sort of going-away party. Mom was always thoughtful in ways that I could never fully appreciate at the time. The next morning on August 8ᵗʰ, I went to Mass at the Immaculate Conception Church in Ithaca and set out for New York by bus.

I spent a couple of days at Nana's in Brooklyn. I visited with Aunt Mae and met with a young Jesuit Priest who intended to go to Jerez later that same year. He was stationed at Fordham in the Bronx. I would see him again in Jerez. I said my farewells to New York as I had to Elmira and Ithaca. I felt no pains of separation. I accepted all of it as what I was supposed to do, and it was what I wanted to do. Devoid of emotion perhaps, I was fulfilling God's will in my life, and that was that.

Aunt Mae drove me to the airport. I was excited about flying to Europe. It was my first flight anywhere, and I was anxious with anticipation. I left on the 7 p.m. flight for Madrid, arriving in the early morning. I had intended to stay in Madrid for a day or two; but finding that my Spanish was not as perfect as I thought it was, and anxious to get to the monastery, I decided to go directly to Seville by train, arriving around 3 o'clock in the afternoon.

I decided to stay overnight in Seville, splurging at the best hotel in town, the Alfonso XIII. Before settling in for the night, I sent a telegram to the Charterhouse telling the Prior that I was in Seville and would be arriving the following day. I had been so tired from the trip and the jet lag that I slept well. The next morning after breakfast I caught the train for Jerez, which was about fifty kilometers to the south.

At the train station in Jerez I asked about *"la Cartuja."* Did I mean *"el barrio de la Cartuja,"* or *"el convento de la Cartuja?"* It turned out that there was a subdivision of the city of Jerez called *"la cartuja,"* and that the monastery (*"el convento"*) was within the subdivision. When the monastery was built in 1473, the city of Jerez was a small walled town about two miles away. A Spanish nobleman in what was then a deserted area gave the monks some fifty thousand acres outside of the town.

By the twentieth century, through political and cultural upheavals, including being chased out of their monastery by Napoleon's troops during the Peninsular Wars, the monks were left with a very large monastery and only a few acres of surrounding land. Much of the monastery had been destroyed or was in decay. The farmland surrounding the monastery was equally in decay from disuse. In the meantime, the city of Jerez had expanded beyond its original walls and grown to a large city with a suburban population.

I took a horse-drawn cab to *"el Convento de la Cartuja."* I was surprised and somewhat disappointed that the monastery was so close to the city of Jerez. We drove along the main road from Jerez toward Gibraltar, passing several villas and some farmland. I had pictured the monastery as being in a "wilderness," as all Carthusian monasteries were supposed to be. After spending time at the Carthusian Foundation in the Vermont mountains, an ideal location for a Charterhouse suited for the Carthusians' love of solitude and silence, I felt a deep disappointment in the pit of my stomach.

When we arrived at *"la Cartuja"* the cab driver asked me if I was there for a visit, thinking that he might have to wait for me. I replied in my best Spanish, *Voy a vivir aqui.* However, I took one look at the seventeenth century grandiose entrance to the grounds and thought to myself, "I really don't like this at all. I don't know if I'll be able to adapt. Maybe I should take the cab back to Jerez and return to the States." What I saw obviously didn't measure up to my ideals of religious poverty and simplicity, even as the nearness to the city had raised doubts about the monastic solitude and silence.

On the other hand, I already had come this far and should try to "stick it out" in the hope that I would get over these initial reactions. I knew without a doubt that I had a calling. I told myself that things would get better with time. I knew I was called to an apostolate of prayer and sacrifice -- to be a living sacrifice of praise. I was doing this so that those I loved most in the world might have a good life. I was sacrificing my life for them and their salvation. I felt emptiness in the pit of my stomach.

While all this was going on within me, Brother Agustin appeared at the gate to meet me. He had a long black beard and looked almost scary in his austerity. Carthusian Brothers were permitted to grow beards, while the choir monks remained clean-shaven out of reverence for the celebration of Mass and the reception of the Precious Blood during the Eucharist. Communion was given to the Brothers in the form of bread only. They did not receive the consecrated wine.

The monks had been expecting me. Brother Agustin showed me to the guesthouse. While showing me my room, he warned me about the "*mosquitos.*" There were no screens on the windows, and he told me that I should close the windows at night or be bitten. When he spoke the word "mos-qui-to," his facial expression was such that he reminded me of a mosquito. And in true European style, he spoke his words about two inches from my face. Not used to this, I was taken aback. I began to experience the Spanish culture that I realized I knew so little about.

I didn't know that Carthusian monasteries had a guesthouse, and again I was surprised and a little disappointed. I was feeling impatient too. I thought I would be going directly into a cell, as I had when visiting in Vermont. While I waited at the guesthouse for Brother Agustin to notify the Prior and the Novice Master of my arrival, I looked around the guesthouse. It had two reception rooms, nicely decorated in a simple Spanish style, and two small bedrooms, each furnished with a bed, nightstand, table and chair. Each bedroom had a small separate bathroom. To my added surprise, there was a chapel attached to the guesthouse. I learned later that the chapel was open to passersby who wished to attend Mass services.

Father Gerardo, the Novice Master, was the first to come to meet me at the guesthouse. I was favorably impressed from the moment I saw him. He was welcoming and warm in his bearing towards me. As I learned later, he had been a Jesuit and university professor before joining the Carthusians. Father Gerardo knew a little English, and I communicated with him as best I could in Spanish. We managed to exchange pleasantries and have a light conversation. As a welcoming gesture Brother Agustin had brought out a bottle of *Chartreuse*, and Father Gerardo took a shot of *Chartreuse* with me. Again I was somewhat surprised at the ease with which he swallowed the strong yellow liqueur. My idealistic image of the solitary, austere Desert Father, Carthusian monk, was tarnished, but still unshattered.

After a while I met the Prior, Father Luis. Carthusian monasteries do not have Abbots. The Prior is the head of the community; and as the title suggests, he is the first among the brethren. The Prior's seat in all places and his clothes did not differ by any kind of dignity or luxury from those of the other monks. He did not wear anything indicating that he was Prior. Following the example of Christ, he was among his brothers as one who served, guiding them according to the spirit of the Gospel and the traditions of the Order. From his humble demeanor I did not realize that he was the Prior until he introduced himself.

Even the Prior of the Grande Chartreuse, who is always the General of the Order, wears no insignia. I was to learn that he was the only one in the Order who received the title of "Reverend Father." All the other choir monks were known as "Venerable Father." As an example of solitude, the Reverend Father never leaves the confines of the Grand Chartreuse in France for any reason whatsoever. When I was in Jerez the story was told of Dom Ferdinand, the previous Father General, who had a serious heart condition. Whenever he felt an attack coming on, he would lie on the floor of his cell until it passed rather than go to a hospital.

As I was to experience in Jerez, Father Luis was an ideal Prior. By word and by example he strove to be of benefit to the cloister monks from whose number he had been chosen. He always offered us an example of peaceful repose, stability, solitude, and all the other observances of our Carthusian life. Above all, he was conscious of mirroring the love of our heavenly Father, uniting the monks into a family. He once confided to me that "something happened" when he was chosen to be Prior -- he felt that "he was given the heart of a father."

A Carthusian monastery has often been called "a church within the Church." As I too was to experience, almost all Carthusians had a feeling of belonging to a "Carthusian

Church" as part of the "mystical body" of Christ. When outside of the Carthusian monastery, the monk may be aware that he is a Roman Catholic; but he feels a sense of alienation from everything he experiences in a Catholic church. But all this knowledge and experience was yet in the future for me.

On that first day of my life in an established Carthusian monastery, the Prior and the Novice Master and I conversed briefly. I was very positively impressed with both of them, almost in awe. Along with Brother Agustin, they were the first Carthusians I had met in Spain. Neither of them ate anything with me, although Father Luis joined us for another sip of *Chartreuse*. I was more comfortable knowing that I would not be sharing a meal with either of them. As I was later to learn, as a rule the Prior does not eat with guests.

After both Fathers had left me for their midday meal in cell, Brother Agustin brought some lunch. By this time I was feeling hungry. I was served cold gazpacho soup, which I had never tasted before, but enjoyed as something different. There was an egg and potato omelet, bread, and some fruit. Brother poured me a glass of sherry wine, and there was also water to drink. After lunch I felt sleepy and had time to relax in the guest room. It was a hot August afternoon. I took a short nap. I felt comfortable in that I had at last arrived at the Charterhouse; but I was beginning to feel impatient anticipation about going into a Carthusian cell.

That afternoon Father Gerardo came to fetch me and show me around the cloister, the community places, and the community church. The church had been abandoned for many years and was under reconstruction and renovation. This was to last for the first three or four years that I was there. The churches in Carthusian monasteries were usually small in size, since Carthusian communities were small by design. But this church was very large, due in part to the wealth given by the original benefactor in the fifteenth century. I learned that he was buried beneath the floor of the church at his death.

Following the European monastic tradition, the church was without aisles or pews. A solid screen divided the church into two parts. The choir monks occupied the front part, nearest the main altar. A door and two altars on each side of the opening separated the choir monks from the lay brothers' choir. The church had no organ according to Carthusian custom; but it did have one statue, and one statue only, that of the Virgin Mary. There were no stained glass windows, or Stations of the Cross. There would be no visitors.

The monastery in Jerez had been empty for about a hundred years, when in the 1940s the Carthusian Order decided to reopen it and restore it to its original beauty. It had been declared a Spanish National Monument. Funds came from the Order in France and from the Spanish government for the restoration of the monastery and its church. Several monastic cells had been restored, and work on the remaining cells was to continue for most of the years that I was in Spain.

During the time the church was being restored, the community met for common prayers and daily Mass in a smaller chapel that became the "chapter house," where community meetings were held. For several years, we were crowded together in the small chapel. In warm weather I could smell the odors coming from beneath the heavy woolen robes of my neighbors in the choir. On especially warm nights, the doors were kept open, letting mosquitoes and bats into the community prayers.

On that first day of my arrival, I attended Vespers in the chapel in a place of honor next to the Prior. It was my first encounter with the entire community of choir monks, my first taste of a Carthusian community gathered in prayer. I followed the chant as best I could. I noticed the different voices, some of the monks obviously singing better than others. I'm sure the monks listened to me, although I sang rather reservedly, more in a silent voice. More than listening to me, I suspect they were more interested in looking me over out of the corner of their eyes, just as I furtively glanced at each of them from time to time. At that time the community numbered around nine. After Vespers I retired once more to the guesthouse where I was served a small supper of soup and bread.

That evening I had a visit from one of the young Spanish monks who knew English. Dom Jose Maria would be my "Guardian Angel" during my first few weeks in Jerez. When I asked him how I should address him, he told me that all Carthusian choir monks, from the last novice to the Prior, had the title "Dom." He was very pleasant and informed me in good English that he would be my shadow for a time while I adapted to the Carthusian regime. He was designated to teach me the proper way to recite my prayers in the cell, and I would be stationed beside him in the choir during community prayers.

Dom Jose Maria informed me on the part of the Novice Master that I was not obliged to attend the night prayers that first night. I could sleep in, and this was welcome news, although in my initial fervor I would gladly have gone to the night office that night. I might just as well have gone to prayers when the big church bell started to ring at 11:30. It continued to ring for a full half hour, and I was fully awake when it finally stopped. The next day I learned that the ringing of the bell for such a long period of time served to wake the monks and provide them with enough time to prepare for the night prayers.

Within the next few days I would officially begin my career as a Carthusian monk. Upon entering the monastery, the candidate began a period known as the postulancy. It can last from three months to a year, depending on the judgment of the superiors. If my vocation were confirmed, I would then receive the Carthusian habit and begin my Novitiate training. I was anxious to get on with the process.

Over the years I have heard some secular people, and even some religious ones, suggest that Carthusians are escapists -- cowards who are running away from the realities of the world. I would challenge anyone who thinks so to try the life of a Carthusian monk for a month to see if they are not faced with a harsher reality than they will ever meet in the world, outside of dying. Indeed, dying to oneself -- dying to every natural desire that the flesh is heir to -- was what life in the monastery was all about. *Unless the grain of wheat falling into the ground die, it remains alone; but if it dies, it brings forth much fruit.* (Jn 12:24)

Everyday a monk dies to himself. The Carthusian monastic life was a life of dying to oneself, of self-mortification, of turning away for love of God from all that was easy and natural. I entered the Carthusian monastery with the express intention of dying to myself. I wanted to embrace the life of austerity. At every moment of my monastic life I embraced this life of mortification. I did it out of love for Jesus, the Church, and all of mankind.

Through all the dying and self-sacrifice, my monastic life had its lighter moments, and from the beginning I could sense an underlying abundance of joy among my fellow monks. As I was able to experience within myself, there seemed to be a subtle correlation between the mortification and the joy: the more severe the mortification, the more abundant and strong the sense of joy.

Candidates who wanted to enter the Carthusian monastery were examined in accordance with the warning of the Apostle John, *Test the spirits, to see whether they are of God* (I Jn 4:1). Just as Father Stephen had done when I visited the Foundation in Vermont, the Novice Master and the Prior in Jerez inquired about my family, my past life, and my fitness of mind and body for the rigors of Carthusian life. I knew that only those candidates were accepted as postulants who, in the judgment of the Prior and of the majority of the community, were sufficiently gifted with piety, maturity, and physical strength, to bear the burdens of the Order.

It was the Novice Master who had the task of examining and testing the candidate's vocation. He had to be careful that the candidate decided his vocation with complete freedom. Just as it happened in other places, the Novice Master could possibly have been interested in acquiring warm bodies to populate the monastery, rather than in getting good and true vocations. When he visited with me, we spoke of my sense of a calling, of my motives, and my expectations; and as we spoke, he came to be convinced of my calling to the Carthusian life just as I was. God was asking me for a sacrifice.

My situation as a candidate was a slightly different, because the Superior in Vermont had already accepted me as a candidate. If I had remained in Vermont, I would have no other questions to answer. But because I was to be a member of the community in Jerez, the community had to know as much as they could about my background. There was no problem with the language. I preferred to speak nothing but Spanish, and we were able to understand each other perfectly well.

Dom Gerardo questioned me on my education, whether it was sufficient for a monk destined for the priesthood. I had not taken any college courses, but my high school education was considered sufficient. Could I sing? I had belonged to the Gregorian chant club. Did I have any canonical impediments? Was there anything in my background that would clash with the Church's law concerning admission to either the religious life or the priesthood? I had already been a novice with the Recollects. I answered in Spanish to the satisfaction of the Novice Master.

Did I have a sufficient knowledge of Latin? I could not begin the novitiate without a sufficient knowledge of Latin. A good working knowledge of Latin was necessary for getting into the Charterhouse as a choir monk. Latin was used everywhere and exclusively in the Charterhouse in those days. The prayers in church and cell, the studies, including textbooks, classes and oral exams, the community conferences and sermons -- all were in Latin. I had studied Latin in high school for three years, studied Church Latin both with the Recollects and on my own. Even so, and I suppose to be on the safe side, the Novice Master had me take a brief course in Latin during the several months before I received the habit as a novice.

According to monastic custom, I knew I would be required to choose a religious name when I began my Carthusian monastic life. I knew that I couldn't keep the name Joseph, since there was already a Joseph in the community. Being known by a new name meant that the "old you" was now dead, and a "new you" was coming alive. Because entering the religious life was considered a "second baptism," just as I received a name at the first baptism, so it was also at the second baptism.

It was recommended that new monks choose names consistent with monastic usage. Names like Bruno, Anthony, John the Baptist, and Benedict were especially popular. Someone once pointed out, probably in jest, that it would be interesting to know what they plan to do with all those like-named people in Heaven -- somebody yells Bruno or John or Benedict and eighty million souls stand up!

Before leaving for Spain I had thought about what name I would want to take. When the Novice Master questioned me on this point, I replied without hesitation: "I would like to take the name Benedict." In Latin, Benedict means "blessed one," and I felt particularly blessed by having been given a calling to the Carthusian life. In addition, I wanted to honor my friend and spiritual advisor at Mt. Savior. The Novice Master thought this was a good choice.

I had read somewhere that at the beginning of the postulancy, the Novice Master washed the feet of the candidate and placed stockings on his feet, and a black mantle on his back over his street clothes. All this would be symbolic of leaving the world behind to begin a new and hidden life in the monastery. I asked the Novice Master about the washing of feet, and he said they didn't do it any more.

To my surprise, however, on the 13th of August, just before First Vespers of the Assumption of Mary, Dom Gerardo came to the guesthouse with a basin of water and a towel. He washed my feet and clothed me with the woolen stockings that I would wear from that time on, both day and night. He also gave me the black cape that I would wear at all community functions for the next two and a half years. If by chance I had to leave the cell during the day, he told me that I had to carry the cape over my arm as a sign that I was a postulant.

From that time on, I was a postulant under the watchful care of the Novice Master. The process had begun! I was shown to my place in the choir, between Dom Jose Maria and another experienced novice, who would guide me through the proper ceremonies, and point out how to use the big choir books. Along with the *Psalter*, which was always used for chanting the Psalms at the night office and at Vespers, another different set of books was used for other parts of the night office and Vespers. It would be several weeks before I learned to use the books by myself.

I was beginning to feel uncomfortable with the heavy black woolen cape on my back and the heavy woolen stockings on my legs. After all, it was the middle of summer in the south of Spain! After Vespers, Dom Gerardo led me without any particular ceremony to the hermitage cell that would be mine. It was late in the afternoon, but the day was still bright and the heat was intense. I was happy to remove the cape and hang it on the hook on the inside of the cell door. I took a few minutes to look over my cell, about five minutes later Dom Gerardo came in to visit with me with the purpose of introducing me to the cell's secrets.

The cells were known by letters of the alphabet, not by numbers. Cell M was a particularly large and recently renovated cell. The walls were made of stone, three feet thick and covered with stucco. The rooms were very large. The interior walls were unpainted, in some places black with age and mold. The bed was in an upstairs room that was windowless. The floors were of clay tile, and although the cell had been swept, it still seemed dingy and dark.

The inner downstairs room where I was to eat my meals was very dark. Near the door of my cell was a "hatch" through which a Brother delivered my food each day. The Brother opened the outside hatch door to put the food in. On the inside was another hatch door where I could access the food. I noticed that there was another wooden door on the wall near the hatch door. It swung down to form a table where I could set food at mealtime. I called it the "eating station."

The wooden door or table covered a space that had been hollowed out of the thick stone wall. The space was big enough to store my bottle of wine, leftover bread and fruit, and eating utensils. I had a wooden fork, a wooden spoon, and a stainless steel knife. I saw a very large napkin and a smaller cotton cloth. The Novice Master informed me that the napkin served double duty as a tablecloth. He showed me how to set it on the table in a diagonal way. I put my food containers on it, and tucked a corner of the napkin into my collar.

I had always suspected that the Carthusians were almost ashamed to have to eat anything at all -- ashamed to have to provide the body with nourishment. But the necessity was sanctified by the lengthy prayers said before and after the meals. During the meals I was taught to keep in mind the Divine Providence that provided the food and to offer prayers for all those persons who had any part in providing the food -- from the farmers to the cook. There were more after meal prayers followed by the *"Miserere"* Psalm (*Have mercy on me, O Lord, have mercy*) as I walked upstairs to my little oratory to finish the prayers there.

The first meal I received in my cell was an unforgettable cold almond soup with a rice dish that resembled rice pudding.

Although considered a delicacy in the south of Spain, I found the soup to be entirely unpalatable. I ate a little of the rice dish and sent the leftovers back to the kitchen with some peach peelings in it. Soon after dinner that very day, the Novice Master visited me with two admonitions: I was to try to consume all the food that was served; if I returned any food to the kitchen, it had to be in good enough condition to be served again.

Fortunately, the cold almond soup never re-appeared. Generally the main meal of the day consisted of a container of soup or cereal, a fish or eggs dish, some vegetable, and cheese, just as I had eaten in Vermont. A small loaf of bread was put in my food box each day. If I needed more than one loaf, or if I needed more bread for the evening meal, I put a note in the food hatch. In fact, if I needed anything from the kitchen or pantry, I put the proper note in my food box. It took several tries to get toilet paper because the phrase in my Spanish-English Dictionary was different from what they used in southern Spain.

Dom Gerardo, the Novice Master, told me that I was not to wash the wooden eating utensils, but rather wipe them clean with the small cotton cloth. I was to roll them up in the large napkin that was provided and put them in the eating station. I could send both the cleaning cloth and the napkin to the wash once a month. Because black and red ants tended to get into everything, I had a thin, foot-long plank of wood with four nails, one at each corner, inside the eating hollow. Around the nails I put white ant repellent powder to keep the ants away. I had to sprinkle the same powder around the legs of my bed so as not to be awakened during the night by ants biting on my legs and arms.

For dessert on most days there were several pieces of whatever fruit was in season. Sometimes there were four or five large naval oranges, or maybe a whole plate of purple plums. I learned to appreciate the taste of pomegranates and persimmons, green figs and black figs. Sometimes, especially in the hot summer days, I had to be careful to remove the little white worms that were present inside the fruit. I don't remember ever having anything that resembled cake or pastry. There was never anything like pudding or ice cream -- no butter or margarine for the bread.

83

A small bottle of wine was available with each meal. Since I rarely drank the wine, a bottle would last for weeks at a time. When I needed more, I put an empty bottle and a note inside my food hatch. The quality of wine varied with the season, lighter wine being served in the summer, and heavier, sweeter wine during the winter. Whenever I drank wine I mixed it with a copious amount of water, as was the Carthusian custom.

At least once a week we had fresh fish from the Atlantic. Cheese made in the monastery was usually served with the main meal, while milk was given only to sick monks. It was always warm with sugar in it. The monks said the local farmers sometimes mixed their milk with water and chalk to make it go further when they sold it to the monastery. As part of our abstinence program, during the liturgical seasons of Advent and Lent, and on all Fridays, milk, cheese, and eggs were not served. No meat was ever allowed, even for the sick. I never missed eating meat -- no hamburgers or chicken, or bacon with your eggs.

I never had any breakfast -- no coffee and toast or oatmeal or eggs. Supper consisted of a cup of wine and a crust of bread from mid-September until after Easter. At other times of the year the kitchen served a light supper of greens, bread and fruit. I could drink water at any time during the day; otherwise, eating and drinking outside of mealtimes was forbidden. The water was good and could be taken directly from the faucet. It flowed from a well on the hill overlooking the monastery. I drank a lot of water.

I also developed a great liking for the protein-rich chickpeas and lentils that were a substitute for meat. I looked forward to their being served several times a week in different fashion. Beans had always given me a lot of intestinal gas, and Spanish beans were no exception. It began to get so bad in choir that some of the monks must have complained. The Novice Master gave me a little pamphlet about the proper way to go to the toilet. I was supposed to push in on and massage my lower abdomen while sitting on the toilet.

All this helped keep me "regular," but did not stop the flow of grossly smelly gas from escaping now and then. Once in choir during the night prayers, when all the lights were out and the monks were praying piously, I let out a real stinker.

84

It was so bad that my neighbor monk actually turned the light on for a few seconds while he turned to me and let out a hardy, very audible, "ugh...!" That poor, stupid American! Not a very good start of my monastic career!

I found the meal portions to be copious enough, but I had difficulty adapting to the Spanish style of cooking. The abundant olive oil that Brother Cook smothered on everything continuously bothered my stomach. Many a day I had a stomach ache that lasted all afternoon and into the evening. When I spoke to the Prior about this, he told me that I would get used to it.

After I had been in Jerez a few months, the Prior asked me if there was any particular food that I liked or wanted. I suppose he had seen my loss of weight. At that time I was having nightly dreams of mashed potatoes, actually waking up chewing my dream potatoes. I told him of this, and without any hesitation, he replied that they didn't serve mashed potatoes. So much for his asking!

Once a week, normally on Fridays or on the eve of a major feast day like Christmas, I fasted on bread and water. I could have as much bread as I wanted, but that's all I ate -- just plain bread, no margarine or jelly or peanut butter. In fact, I never saw butter or margarine, jelly or peanut butter at any other time either. I don't think the cook knew what those things were. I did receive a small portion of honey or a piece of jellied guava from time to time, but that was as a dessert and not as a bread spread.

We postulants and novices were supposed to become accustomed to the fasts and abstinences of the Order gradually so that we could "prudently and safely" tend towards the rigor of complete observance. I was enthusiastic about trying the Friday bread and water abstinence, and Dom Gerardo had me try it once a month. I always felt weak and shaky in the afternoons of those Fridays. I was not accustomed to eating so much bread at one time. On those Fridays when I did not observe the fast and abstinence of bread and water, I had a one-course meal, usually of eggs or a piece of fish -- nothing else.

Fasting and abstaining from food in general had as its goal to chasten the flesh for its past and present misdeeds. The idea was that by carrying in one's body the death of

Jesus, the life of Jesus might also manifest itself in the body. You first had to die before you could live. Everything to do with mortification had as its goal the future resurrection. I learned that the mortification of the flesh was as necessary for an ascetic -- a man of prayer -- as it was for Jesus, who fasted for forty days in the desert.

But it wasn't only the food that was material for mortification. Cleanliness, or the lack of it, also entered into the concept. On the second floor of my cell was a bathroom with a shower, a concession made to the monks of Jerez due to the warm climate. I soon found out, however, that the water was hot in the summer and cold in the winter. The water pipes ran along the roof and were heated by the sun whenever the sun shone.

The lack of hot water for morning showers was one of many mortifications I was yet to endure. I had been accustomed to the daily bath or shower; but when I showered in my cell during those first few days, I found that my one small towel I had did not dry well. When I asked for another towel, I was informed that the linen was changed once a month, and, in the meantime I should hang my towel outside in the garden to dry. I could also rinse it myself before I hung it to dry. I got used to it and did what I was told with a joyful heart.

Once a month a notice on the community bulletin board informed us that the "linen" would be collected the next day for washing. Any articles of cotton or linen, like the dinner napkin and utensil towel, were set in the cloister beside the cell door in the morning when I went to Mass. A Brother would collect them and return new items before the end of the day. Woolen items were sent to the wash a week after the linen. Since I wore my own clothes during the postulancy period, I didn't have anything to send to the wash except the woolen stockings. I washed the napkin myself when it needed washing.

When I became a novice, I had two sets of woolen garments, so that I might have something to wear while the other was in the wash. My cell's letter was printed or sewn onto my clothes. Everything went directly from the wash to a Brother who looked it over and mended or repaired anything that was ripped or wearing too thin. If the article of clothing was beyond repair, he issued a replacement. The replacement was often a recycled garment from a deceased monk, or a monk who had left the community.

I was overwhelmed during those first few days and weeks by many new and unexpected things. There were many details of daily monastic life to learn. I had to get used to the enormity of the cell and the monastery. Then there was the food and the climate. I had to pray in Latin, and learn the chant. Continuously using the Spanish language and living in the Spanish culture affected me more than I had anticipated.

While I made an effort to understand the proud Spanish character, the sometimes fiery temperament, and the extraordinary culture, being surrounded by nothing but Spanish and more Spanish, I sometimes felt hostility and contempt. I grew tired of speaking Spanish all the time, and felt sick and tired of living in a Spanish culture. When I mentioned this to Dom Gerardo, my good Novice Master was very understanding, and did not think I should be concerned about any of these things.

Still, I thought back, with some nostalgia, to the simplicity of the wagon shed in Vermont. The books and articles I had read about Carthusian life began to appear different and more idealistic than what I had begun to experience. I began to realize that I was living in an institutionalized setting. Perhaps I had made a mistake. Perhaps I should have entered the Order in England. Perhaps this -- perhaps that. After a while I became sick and tired of dealing with all the "perhapses!" Were these thoughts and feelings temptations?

As Father Stephen had tried to explain to me, I began to find the reality of the established European monastery quite different from the rusticity of the American Foundation. I felt a little disillusioned and disappointed during those first days and weeks. My ideals had been fixed on strict solitude and silence, rusticity and barrenness. This was my primary vantage point of the Carthusian ideal. In the recesses of my mind I began to wonder whether the whole idea of a Carthusian calling was really only a fixture of my imagination.

I had entered the monastery in Spain with the personal baggage of a retiring disposition, partly phlegmatic and partly melancholy. I was introverted, disposed rather to withdraw from conflicts than confront them directly. In this I thought I shared a similarity with St. Bruno. Perhaps, like Bruno, I also had something of a distrust of authority. Whether or not like Bruno, I tended toward avoiding authority whenever I could. I presumed permissions, avoided asking, and asked for permissions only when I thought it was absolutely necessary.

Perhaps I should have been better prepared for my encounter with the enormous size of the Carthusian monastery. An established Carthusian monastery covers a great deal of ground owing to the monks' lifestyle, and the Charterhouse of Jerez was of a particularly large expanse. Some said it had the longest cloister in all Spain. All Charterhouses were built along the same basic principles: a grouping of hermitages, or "cells" as they are called, linked to one another by a covered walkway or "cloister," called the "great cloister."

The great cloister led to the communal places: the monastery church, refectory (dining hall). Connected to the church were several small chapels and the Chapter house. There was a lavatory in the common area in case a monk had to leave the church during Mass. In Jerez the community places were grouped around a beautiful inner courtyard with a fountain in the center. From this inner courtyard a door led to the "lesser" or smaller cloister, where the "obediences," or workshops of the Brothers, and their individual cells were located. Another door led to the Prior's rose garden and his cell. The Prior used the lower floor as an office. He had a skull on his desk to remind himself and us that the certainty of death made everything transitory. *Memento mori.*

Carthusian cells could be compared to two-story townhouses. Though the size and layout of the cell might vary from one charterhouse to another, I learned that they followed definite patterns that had developed over the centuries. All cells were entered from the common cloister to a kind of living room. Originally where the monks cooked their vegetables in the early years of the Order, the room was dedicated to the Blessed Virgin Mary, and known appropriately as the "Ave Maria."

On the lower level there would be a workshop area with the tools the monk might need for a workshop and a garden. A storage area would be for keeping firewood in colder climates.

In Jerez most cells had an extra room, which was sometimes completely empty. Some of the monks made this room into their sleeping area, especially if they were unable to climb the stairs to the upper rooms. Still others found it easier to sleep downstairs because it was cooler there in summer.

In addition, there was usually a covered or enclosed area for physical exercise in inclement weather. This opened onto a garden, where the monk could cultivate flowers, grow vegetables, or leave to the weeds. Some monks bragged about the abundance of wild vegetation. Some of the gardens were larger than others or laid out in a different order.

In some of the charterhouses there was a separate antechamber on each of the two floors of the cell. The bedroom and a bathroom were usually on the upper level. A bed with a straw mattress and straw pillow were sometimes in a separate alcove. One or two woolen blankets were there as needed. There was always a choir stall similar to the ones in the church, and a kneeler, either in a corner of the bedroom or in a separate alcove space known as the "oratory." A large crucifix or painting of a crucifix would be in the oratory. In my oratory was a reproduction of a painting by Velasquez: Jesus on the Cross.

Most cells are furnished in the same way with a table, chair, and bookcase. In the bookcase were a Spanish Bible, a copy of the *Statutes*, and a copy of the seventeenth century Prior General Dom Innocent LeMasson's *Directory for Novices*. I began to read and study the *Directory*. In Latin it began, *Vita hominis militia est super terram* (Man's life on earth is a struggle), a quote from the book of Job.

The *Directory* was intended to be a basic introduction to the Carthusian life for postulants and novices -- a kind of pep talk. Monastic life was a continuous warfare. To be victorious you had to keep your eyes focused on the goal, which was the heavenly reward that awaited you. You were advised to do everything with "alacrity," eagerness and zeal. As an example of this, Dom LeMasson expected you to start the day by jumping from your bed as if it were on fire.

Dom Gerardo supplied me with a few other pieces of reading and study material such as a Spanish history book and a brief Spanish language course. He gave me a few holy cards of Carthusian saints that I could put in my little oratory, and a picture of St. Benedict that I hung on the wall. I wasn't allowed to hang any other pictures on the walls.

There was nothing for heating the cell. In colder climates the cells had a stove and a small storage place for firewood near the stove. My cell in Jerez did not have a stove or any type of heating, although a portable electric heater was available if an older or infirm monk needed it. I could have used some heat in the cell during the cold and damp days of November and December, but I never asked for anything. I had already learned the motto, "Ask for nothing, refuse nothing."

The windows had glass panes; but there were no screens to keep out the bugs and mosquitoes. On the inside of the window were wooden shutters. The idea was to open the shutters at night to let in the cool air, and close them in the morning to keep the cooler air in and the warm air out. On many a summer night when I kept the windows open, I had to ward off swarms of mosquitoes. I finally gave up on the whole idea and kept the windows closed at night. Screens were installed in Jerez shortly after a monk had been seen walking on the roof outside the upper window. Another monk was accused of catching small owls and pigeons that perched on his window sill. The screens put a stop on all unauthorized and frowned-upon activities.

My "Guardian Angel," Dom Jose Maria, came to cell M during the first week to recite the hours of the Office with me. I was annoyed with the prospect of reciting my prayers with someone else in the cell. After all, I had entered the Charterhouse for a life of solitude and silence. I told myself that this situation would not last forever.

But the contact was good; and had its lighter moments. For example, one night when we were reciting a prayer with the words, "Bless the Lord, all you works of the Lord," a mosquito landed on his hand. At that point he surprised me by saying, "Not you, mosquito!" and squashed it against the wall! The whitewashed wall received many more red and black marks during the days to come.

Dom Jose Maria taught me the proper ceremonies when reciting the liturgical Office in cell. In the cell as well as in the church, I was to show as much reverence as possible when reciting the Office. I was to be aware of the majesty and divinity of Him Whom we addressed, and before Whom we stood, as He both watched over us and listened to us.

Dom Jose Maria was helping the Novice Master, whose principal task was to form the conduct of the postulant and novice, to direct him in his spiritual exercises, and to apply suitable remedies to his temptations. He had to be solicitous that the love of his charges for Christ and the Church grow daily. Like St. Bruno the ideal Novice Master was supposed to have "the tenderness of a mother together with the vigor of a father," so that the training of the novices might be both monastic and virile.

I felt very comfortable with Dom Gerardo. He was the ideal of the Carthusian Novice Master, outstanding in the community for his prudence, brotherly love, and regular observance. Among the other silent and solitary Carthusians, he was a notable cultivator of contemplative repose in the cell. He radiated love of the vocation, and later became Prior of the Jerez community. On several of his first visits with me, he advised me to concentrate on "being," rather than on "doing." He wanted to form the young active American into a quiet contemplative monk. Always discerning and encouraging, one of his favorite expressions was "animo!"

During my first few days and weeks in Jerez, Dom Gerardo came to visit me at unannounced times. Under his ever-watchful care I began to experience the solitary life in the cell with all its austerity. I felt that he visited me every so often to "take my pulse," so to speak. Sometimes I felt like a hospital patient under observation. Indeed, after a week in Cell M, I was feeling very uncomfortable with everything. It was a strange and unwelcome feeling. I would sit in the small upstairs oratory at 6:30 in the morning, trying to meditate before Mass, but all the while wondering what I was doing there. Something wasn't right.

One problem was that the size of the cell. There was just too much empty space. Then there was the cell's location in relation to the road that ran past the monastery. I was continuously annoyed by the noise. I was amazed at the amount of morning traffic, including cars and motor scooters, trucks and busses. At night I could hear the clapping of hands and music coming from a little bar down the road. I yearned for the peace and quiet of the hills and mountains

I had loved so much back home. I looked for a way to find interior peace in the midst of unwanted noise.

When I spoke to Dom Gerardo about this, he suggested that I might like one of the smaller, cozier, and newly renovated cells on the west side of the monastery. He didn't use those exact words, probably because that would have been contrary to the spirit of Carthusian austerity, but he did say it would be more quiet. On seeing it for the first time, I fell in love with cell L. This was my place! The rooms were smaller and brighter than those of cell M. The walls were whitewashed and the red clay tile floors were new. Most of all, it was definitely a quiet place. Very little noise came from the outside, and I could eliminate this by keeping closed the window that faced the road.

The cell had a large unfinished garden, with a balcony seat built into the wall. The balcony faced west so that I could look over the slow-moving Guadelete River, the "river of milk," visited by the Greeks and Romans, and named by the North African Moors. Beyond the river I looked toward the shimmering waters of the Bay of Cadiz and the Atlantic Ocean. Columbus had set out towards the Americas from this port less than twenty years after the monastery was built. As I looked toward the western horizon, I thought a lot about my family and friends who lived even further to the west in the new world. I began to miss them more than I had ever missed them. I should have passed more time with Mom and Mike and Marilyn.

As I think back on those days in the Charterhouse of Jerez, I am more aware than I ever was of how the days passed to weeks, and weeks became seasons and seasons became years. Each day passed without my being aware of the time. I felt that I never had enough of it. There was no time to be bored, or to look back on the past. There was a constant looking forward to the goal, which was union with God, and I focused on the way to achieve the goal -- constant prayer. Prayer was not an end in itself, but a means to attaining the goal. From the very beginning I knew that by continuing faithfully in my cell and letting myself be molded by it, I would gradually find that my life would become one continual prayer.

My monastic life was lived in silence, but not in a vacuum. I learned to do everything in a quiet, measured way. Under the Novice Master's direction, my life itself gradually became one continuous prayer. During my days and nights, like so many arrows toward the heart of God, I shot out short prayers of love and adoration. My prayer was not a prayer of petition -- the asking for favors; but rather a loving gazing on God -- a continuous conversation made of more of a silent watching than many words.

Solitude was a means toward remaining focused. Indeed, as the old monks said, solitude for the sake of solitude was only a vile sort of misanthropy and narcissism; it was isolation, and not prayer. Living alone in a controlled solitude eliminated outside distractions and facilitated continuous prayer.

Because I was not in the cell "to do" anything, the Novice Master taught me that my main duty was "to be there." "Being there" -- and fully aware -- was what I was called to do. I was a sentry or watchman on the wall, ever watching, ever vigilant. This made sense to me, although it took some of the romanticism out of the Carthusian mystique. Contemplative monks have been criticized for not doing anything. "Being there" might sound easy enough to those who have not experienced the solitude and silence of the cell; but let them try it before making a definitive judgment.

Constant prayer and continuous vigilance was a means to keep inner distractions under control. My days were filled with prayer in the true sense of the constant effort to raise my heart and mind to God. Prayer became a way of life, not just a plea in a case of emergency, as when as a child I asked God for help. I was an athlete, and prayer was my game. To make one's whole life a prayer takes practice, sometimes years of practice. I was at the beginning and had all the means, to which I did my best to remain faithful.

To further facilitate continuous prayer, the day was broken up into compartments by the specified times for liturgical prayer. Everything else fit into place around the times for our liturgical prayer. The liturgical celebrations, both in cell and in community, helped form my prayer life. Since the days when I visited the Benedictines at Mt. Savior, I had developed a keen interest in the liturgy as both personal and public prayer. In the Charterhouse my day revolved around the liturgy as a form of prayer that offered specific meaning to the rest of the day. Outside of the liturgical hours we differed in what we accomplished in the solitude of the cell. What we experienced as high points during the liturgy, however, had a profound influence over what was accomplished in the cell.

For those who might be unfamiliar with the term, "liturgy" referred to the public worship of God. In the Catholic Church, it was "performed" through the Sacraments, "the hours," and above all through the Eucharist, the Sacrifice of the Mass. The "liturgy of the hours," was also called the "Divine Office." It was the official prayer of the Church, and consisted of a group of meditations, chants, hymns, readings and prayers, all put together in such a way that made them relevant to a particular time of day or time of year.

Priests and religious, as official representatives of the Church were obligated to take part in the daily liturgical celebrations -- the public worship of God. The liturgy invited those who took part in it into the mystery of God, into the life, knowledge and love of God, and ultimately into a union with Him. As such, the liturgy was at once both the end to which the action of the Church tended and the source from which all her strength flowed.

When we accomplished the liturgy in any of its forms, but especially the Eucharistic celebration, we had access to the Father through His Son, the Word Incarnate, who suffered and was glorified, all through the outpouring of the Holy Spirit. Through the liturgy we achieved communion with the Most Holy Trinity. The participation of each and every member of the Church in the liturgy had positive ripple effects throughout the entire Church because of this communication with the Trinity. In the monastery, the "hours" referred to the times when the liturgy was celebrated. At certain times we focused our attention exclusively on God. It was as if we had an appointment to meet with God. It was not that we somehow failed to meet God in prayerful conversation at other times of the day; but we met with Him in a more exclusive and concentrated way at certain times of the day. Each hour was a celebration of life and love, whose intensity carried us to our next scheduled encounter. The total combination of the different hours was called the "Office." The name indicated both the responsibility and the honor given by the Church to her official representatives before the Lord God.

The liturgical hours were basically divided along the lines of the traditional ancient Roman day, a time before clocks and electricity. St. Benedict had set the guidelines. The first hour of the traditional Roman day was sunrise, about 6 a.m. by our measurement of time. The first liturgical hour was put here, and appropriately was called "Prime." Three hours later, at the third hour, "Tierce" was celebrated -- about 9 a.m. by our measurement of time. Three hours after that, the sixth hour of the day, "Sext" was celebrated. This would be, obviously, about 12 noon. "None" was celebrated at the ninth hour, or around 3 p.m. The evening hour called "Vespers" was celebrated in the late afternoon. Finally, the night prayers called "Compline" completed the day, as it were, just before bedtime.

Then there was "Matins," celebrated in the very early hours of the morning (or during the night), while the rest of the world slept. It consisted of the chanting of Psalms and a series of readings taken from the Bible and spiritual writers. During the shorter nights of the summer, Matins tended to be shorter in length. Following the original Benedictine tradition of celebrating Matins shortly after midnight, we rose from our beds to celebrate Matins, which we appropriately called the "Night Office." It took me a good six months to be able to get up during the night and keep my eyes open during the office.

The ancient hermit monks prayed all through the night. Towards dawn they celebrated "Lauds," a word coming from the Latin word for "praise." The monks sang praise to God at the beginning of the new day. When I entered the Order, Lauds was part of the night office. We celebrated it immediately after Matins, with no interval in between. We usually finished the night office around 2:30 or 3 a.m., when we stumbled back to our cells for more prayers and another period of rest.

On ordinary weekdays I was in the solitude of the cell all day, except for the night office, daily Mass and Vespers, when I went to the monastery church. At the end of those liturgical celebrations I returned immediately to the cell, as to "a safe refuge." St. Bruno and his first companions had put together a liturgy particularly adapted to their eremitical vocation and minimalist dimensions of their community life. Through the particular liturgy of the Order, we were able to express the deeper aspirations of the Spirit within our contemplative lifestyle. The individual monk's prayer, springing from the depths of the heart, acquired a new perfection when it found an echo in the sacred words of the Liturgy.

Our Carthusian liturgical celebration was characterized by its simplicity and sobriety in terms of external forms, and visible and sensible expressions. The liturgy was particularly suited to our semi-eremitical vocation and the smallness of our communities. It was directed primarily toward facilitating the union of the soul with God. Whether we celebrated the Divine Office in choir or in our cell, our lips were offering the prayer of the Church. Jesus prayed for us as our Priest, and in us as our Head.

Having left everything to seek God alone and to possess Him more fully, I was taught to carry out the liturgical functions with particular reverence. As soon as I heard the bell calling us to the church for those hours of the Divine Office that we sang together, I left all other occupations -- dropped whatever I was doing -- and hastened to the church. I tried to do this with "reverence and decorum." Sometimes this meant coming in from the garden, all sweaty from just being outside, washing my hands very quickly, and rushing out the cell door, arranging my robes along the way.

On entering the church I took holy water from the font and signed myself with the sign of the cross in the particular Carthusian way: joining the two first fingers of the right hand with the thumb, I touched my forehead, stomach and both shoulders, making a very large sign of the cross over my body. We were not ashamed of the sign of the cross! Before taking my place in choir I took my turn pulling on the church bell until the last monk had arrived and the Prior gave the signal to stop ringing the bell.

After making a profound bow to Jesus in the Blessed Sacrament, I went to my place in choir. We did not genuflect before the Blessed Sacrament, but made a deep bow instead. Whenever we passed in front of the Blessed Sacrament, we made the same profound bow at the sanctuary steps. Out of respect for the Divine Majesty, we tried to avoid all noise in church. Part of the "decorum" was to keep my black cape held closed at all times. With the Novice Master's help, I trained my eyes to be "guarded and discreet always and everywhere," but most of all in the church and the refectory.

Entering the church for periods of private prayer or adoration of the Blessed Sacrament before the bell called us was not permitted. On completion of the common prayers, the Prior left the church first, the rest of us following according to our seniority and ranking in the community. No one was permitted to remain in church after the office. We were required to return to the solitude of our cells. If for some special and highly unusual reason we were in the church outside of community activity, we were permitted to kneel for a short conversation with Jesus.

Nor were we permitted to leave the cell during the day for visits to the Blessed Sacrament. Adoration and Benediction were permitted only on Holy Thursday in honor and thanksgiving for the institution of the Eucharist. Jesus was present in the Carthusian community as a hermit monk, and should be left to His own solitude. Although we did not have the Blessed Sacrament in our cells, we conducted ourselves as if Jesus were present. The oratory was considered an extension of the church. I could adore Jesus in the Sacrament while in my cell oratory.

Upon entering the choir stalls in the church, we stood facing the altar with our hoods up, preparing ourselves in silence until the Prior gave the signal to begin the prayers. When the signal was given the community either knelt or bowed over leaning on the "mercy seat," according to the rank of the liturgical day. On ordinary days we knelt, while on feast days we bowed over. During the chanting of the Psalms we leaned against the back of the choir stall with our backside resting on the *misericord*, as the mercy seat was called.

The Carthusian liturgy included long periods of silence, the ban of all musical instruments, and a simplified form of Gregorian chant. Carthusian chant was slow and plaintive, since the duty of a good monk was "rather to lament than to sing." Although lamentation, and not the joy of singing, was supposed to be in our hearts, I did find joy and even a measure of consolation, in singing God's praises.

I found that the communal prayer really did carry over into my cell life. After the community celebrations in the church, I felt enabled to offer to God an intimate sacrifice of praise in the solitude of the cell. I gradually became enamored of silence and could forget all human cares. I was conscious of becoming a sharer in the fullness of the mystery by which Christ crucified, rising from the dead, returned to the bosom of the Father. What was signified by the entire liturgy became alive within myself. I could not explain how it happened other than I strove to be continuously united to the Lord in my thoughts and affections.

On Sundays and major feast days we celebrated all the hours of the liturgy in the church, with the exception of Prime and Compline. For a few years after the Vatican Council, Prime had still been sung in common, and was later eliminated. I didn't like going out of the cell for Prime so early in the morning, and was happy to see it eliminated. Compline was always prayed in the solitude of the cell just before retiring for the rest of the day.

All the hours revolved around the Mass, the Eucharistic celebration. This was the liturgical high point of each day for me, just as it was the center and summit of our Carthusian communal life. It was the visible sign of our unity as a monastic community. We choir monks gathered to celebrate the sacrifice of Our Lord, giving thanks for the gift of salvation brought about by His bloody sacrifice on the cross. The Eucharistic sacrifice was the efficacious sign of our unity, since it actually accomplished what it signified. It united us into a community of believers.

The daily Eucharistic celebration was at the center of my own monastic life. It provided me with the spiritual food I needed for my own journey through the solitary desert. Through it, I experienced a union with Jesus as He returned to God the Father. The presence and activity of Christ in this world became visible in the sacrifice of the Mass. At the same time, my participation in the Eucharistic sacrifice was at the source of my ability to live in the desert.

In many respects, the Carthusian day, my daily life in the desert, like the eternal day of the Lord, had neither beginning nor end. Like the faithful servant of the Gospels that I wanted to imitate, I was continuously watching for the return of the Master. I lay down to rest every evening a little before 8 p.m., after I recited Compline. At around 11:30 p.m., a junior monk, making the round of the cloister, rang the doorbell hanging near my ear to awaken me from sleep.

When I heard the sound of the bell, I reached for the walking stick that was near my bed and pounded on the tile floor once or twice with it to indicate that I was awake. On many nights I woke violently from a deep and sound sleep. On the few very rare occasions when I couldn't wake up, or if I couldn't find my walking stick fast enough, the junior monk entered my cell to find out if I was okay. On one occasion at the same time as the bell rang to wake me up, an earthquake began to rattle and shake my bed. I thought for a moment that the devil had entered my cell and was shaking my bed!

In the beginning of my Carthusian life I quite literally jumped up from my woolen sheets and bed of straw. After a while I took a few extra minutes to get up, especially when the cell was cold; but I never fell back to sleep. I quickly put on my holy robe, scapular, and belt, all the while trying to remember the prayers that were supposed to accompany the putting on of each article of clothing. They were the same prayers that the priest said as he vested for Mass.

I went to the bathroom and sometimes splashed a little cold water on my face. I was afraid that putting too much water on my face would influence the quality of my singing voice. Then I proceeded immediately to the oratory of the cell immediately to recite Matins and Lauds of the Office of the Blessed Virgin Mary. Following an ancient tradition, each hour of the Carthusian Office was either preceded or followed by the Office of Our Lady, the Virgin Mary.

When I finished those prayers, which took about a half hour, I put the black cape over my shoulders and stood by the door of my cell, ready to go to the church when the Sacristan rang the bell. At the sound of the bell I went into the cloister and followed the other monks as they silently emerged from their cells, hood raised and head down in concentration. We walked in measured pace through the cloister, single file, took our turn at ringing the church bell, and proceeded in silence to our place in choir.

To the postulant and rare visitor the night office would be very impressive. It lasted from two to three hours, depending on the celebration of the day or season of the liturgical year. A large portion of it was sung from memory, the church being in complete darkness except for the sanctuary lamps. The Psalms and chant melodies, since they were repeated day after day, year after year, stuck in your mind, so that there was no need for lights in choir.

The only light I would see was the reader's light, or the light of an old monk who kept the light on for the sake of an unwritten rule that there be at least one light on at all times. This was out of reverence for the Word of God. There could be no errors in reciting the Word of God. As a postulant and novice, I too was obligated to keep a light on during the chanting, even if I did not need it. This annoyed me since I was eager to show that I had already memorized many of the texts, and did not need the light.

When necessary, carefully shaded light was directed toward the large choir books, one book for every two or three monks. I felt uncomfortable about not having my own book to sing from. Because all solo parts were sung standing facing the altar, I had to slide the huge books forward when singing solos. If the book was not located in just the right place, I was in danger of performing my solo part poorly -- or at least this was the normal excuse that poorly prepared soloists used.

In the silent dark hours of the night, the psalmody nourished my interior devotion and enabled me to give myself to the "secret prayer of the heart." The psalmody was interspersed with periods of silence that allowed my personal prayer to be more deeply fused with the Word of God and with the public prayer of the Church. I learned to love this long office of the night, of alternating chants of psalms and readings of Holy Scripture or of Church Fathers, the times of silence and prayers of intercession. In union with my brothers and sisters throughout the world, I could enter into an intense and meaningful communion with God. It was one of the highlights of the liturgical day.

On returning to the cell on many a warm summer night, I ventured into my garden for a few minutes before going upstairs to the oratory. The smell of jasmine filled the air, I could hear the nightingales singing along the riverbank, and the stars seemed more bright and shiny than I ever could imagine. I never had seen so many stars in the sky. All this was sometimes as moving a spiritual experience as the night office. I looked forward to the time when I would leave this earth to fly up to those stars.

In the oratory I recited Prime of the Office of the Blessed Virgin with the *Missa sicca,* or "dry Mass," in honor of the Mother of God. Another leftover from the Middle Ages, it was called the dry mass because there was no offering of bread and wine, even though all the other parts of the Mass were recited as usual. I had already been exposed to it during my first retreat at the Sky Farm. Now I became so familiar with it that I recited it from memory.

After the required prayers, I returned to bed until around 6:00 a.m. The Statutes actually permitted the monk "to rest" after the night office. The word "sleep" was not used except in practical commentaries. It was beneath the austere and responsible dignity of the monk to sleep. He was expected to be vigilant -- awake and watching at all times. Sometimes it was very hard to fall sleep, especially so in the deep of a cold winter. At other times I was so tired that I fell asleep right away. I never knew if I would be able to sleep or not; but I wasn't much concerned about it. I wasn't going anywhere, nor was I expected to do anything in the morning beyond showing up for Mass. After some of the longer night offices, like the Easter Vigils, for example, I was so wound up emotionally that sleep came with difficulty. It was often in vain that I tried to "clear my mind" in an effort to relax.

With the woolen blanket, woolen sheets, and the woolen clothing I was required to sleep in both summer and winter, I was fortunate if I could sleep at all. I felt either too cold or too hot. The dampness of the cold straw mattress was an added complication. In the south of Spain it got cold in the winter months. Once or twice in my years in Spain, I observed a thin coating of ice on the pool in my garden. I didn't have a thermometer, so I had no idea of the exact temperature.

Some of the monks told me they had seen snow flurries on rare occasions; but the only snow I ever saw was on the peaks of the Sierra that I could see from my cell window. I could also see my breath in the air, even inside the unheated cell. In order to sleep in those conditions, one of the monks used to put his head entirely under the blanket with a breathing tube in his mouth for air. Out of desperation, I tried it too; but it didn't work for me.

Around 6 a.m. another junior monk went through the cloister ringing the wakeup bell. Making the sign of the cross, I would jump out of bed, splash some water on my face, rinse my mouth, put on my robe and scapular, and go right to my oratory for prayer. Kneeling in the oratory, I composed my mind and heart, offering myself with all my actions of the day to the Sacred Heart of Jesus. I was happy and felt secure in the knowledge that I was serving God in the place I knew I was supposed to be.

At the ringing of the church bell, I recited Prime, followed by Tierce of the Office of the Blessed Virgin. At 6:30 the *Angelus* bell sounded, at which I recited three 'Hail Mary's -- the Carthusian version of the *Angelus*. Out of habit I sometimes recited the devotional prayer: *The Angel of the Lord declared unto Mary,* as was the custom in the rest of the Church. On most days I remained at prayer and meditation, kneeling or sitting in the oratory.

At the beginning of my Carthusian life, the Jesuit-trained Dom Gerardo suggested that I use the meditation methods of St. Ignatius of Loyola. I was not used to anything like this and never got into it. It seemed too artificial. Rather, I learned to place myself simply in the Lord's presence as a child before his parent, loving, trusting, and expecting to be cared for. I would often think over the coming events of the day and picture how I wanted to react to them. Sometimes I read passages from the works of the Spanish mystic, St. John of the Cross, all the while concentrated on emptying myself and remaining silently in the presence of God.

At 7:00, I left my cell again to head toward the church for the community Mass. We were, like the Sacristan, slaves of the church bell. It ruled our entire life. The priest who celebrated the Mass had already gone to vest, so that when the community arrived everything was set to go. We sang the community Mass from big Missals. Each monk had one. Normally the Sacristan set them out on the forms beforehand, so that all you had to do was open them to the correct page. In the beginning I sometimes had to look at where my choir neighbor had opened his book.

The Carthusian Mass differed from the Roman Mass that I had been used to for the first twenty years of my life. It was the version of the Mass that was used in Grenoble, France, in the twelfth century, with accommodations dating from the time of the sixteenth century Council of Trent. There were no servers at this high Mass; rather a deacon, who wore the monastic cowl, attended the priest. For the Gospel reading the deacon put a stole over the cowl. A pre-appointed monk read the Epistle from the lectern in the middle of the choir.

One of the most impressive, and sometimes confusing ceremonies occurred after the consecration of the bread-host. During the consecration everyone knelt facing the altar with the head uncovered and the hands joined together. After the consecration we fell prostrate with our heads to the floor until after the consecration of the wine. Visitors and retreatants often didn't know if they were supposed to join the monks in this "prostration," as it was called. For the greater part of the Mass we either stood facing the altar in true solitary form with our hood covering the face, or we knelt leaning on the forms facing the opposite choir, again with the hood of our scapular over the face. Everyone present at the Mass was invited to receive communion.

Following the community Mass, the priests and servers went in silence to one of the small chapels for a private Mass. As a postulant and novice I recited Tierce of the Office of the Blessed Virgin with the priest before helping him vest. Serving the Carthusian Mass was easy. Basically, all I had to do was light the candles, answer the prayers, and remember when to serve the wine and water. I received Holy Communion at this Mass also. At the end of Mass, both the priest and the server prostrated on the floor of the chapel for a brief period of thanksgiving.

In every charterhouse it was the custom to have a Mass in honor of the Blessed Virgin Mary celebrated at the main altar following the Community Mass of the day. It was considered an honor to be assigned to serve at this Mass, and I looked forward to my turn. It was also a change from having to assist at the Novice Master's Mass. The postulants and novices who were not assigned to serve a private Mass went to the Novitiate chapel where the Novice Master celebrated his Mass.

At about 9:00 a.m. when the private Mass was over, I returned directly to my cell where I continued my thanksgiving in silent prayer. Once in a while I took the long way around the cloister for a little exercise. Once or twice I climbed to the top of the church bell tower for a view of the neighborhood. And almost every day before going upstairs to the oratory in my cell, I walked around my garden inspecting new growth and taking time to "smell the roses."

After a period of ten or fifteen minutes of thanksgiving in the oratory, I recited Tierce of the daily office. After that there was time for some light work in cell, like making the bed or watering the plants. For the rest of the morning I occupied myself with study and some manual work, cleaning the cell or working in the garden. The cool mornings passed rapidly in pleasant leisure.

The bell for the Angelus and Sext rang out around 12 noon. At the sound of the monastery church bell I again dropped whatever I was doing and went to the oratory for prayer. I sometimes felt guilty if I had to take a minute or two to wash up before prayer. According to St. Benedict, *Nothing was to be preferred to the work of God.*

Dinner was delivered to my food hatch a little after Sext. I often found myself listening for the sound of the food hatch opening and closing. Sometimes, if the Brother seemed a little late in coming with my dinner, I would peek out into the cloister to see if he was coming. The Brother always delivered the food in silence, and I rarely saw him. Any communication with the kitchen was by written notes.

After dinner there was about an hour and a half of free time or "recreation." Some of the monks fell asleep for a short siesta, even though this was strictly unauthorized. I sometimes sat outside in the garden with my back against the wall and fell asleep in the warm sun. Sometimes I amused myself by pitting two armies of ants, one black and the other red, against each other. Sometimes I fell asleep in the hot sun as I watched the clouds sail by. During the rainy months of April and November, I did odd jobs in the cell like cleaning the bathroom or sweeping the floor.

Free time was followed by None at about 2:00 by spiritual reading, or study, and another short work period. For reading and study I was given a carefully selected series of books for my spiritual and monastic formation. I studied the Spanish history books, and read and studied the Psalms in Latin. Most of my reading material was in Spanish, and I took abundant notes. In time I stopped translating the notes into English. My ability to read and write Spanish grew exponentially.

As for speaking Spanish, at first I attempted to mentally translate verbal conversations before speaking a word, thinking in English and then speaking in Spanish. Although occasions to converse in Spanish were limited, within two years I had become totally fluent in Spanish. I realized this when I heard the Prior say to someone that I was perfectly fluent in Spanish. Up until that time I hadn't even thought about it. And I was not only speaking and thinking in Spanish, but also dreaming in the language. I had arrived at mastery of the language! I have always given credit to the Holy Spirit for my progress in learning languages.

I loved being in the cell, and hated to leave my little house. And there was no need for me to leave the cell. For my work time I had all the tools I needed or wanted. I had a large wooden workbench equipped with carpentry tools in case I wanted to create a project. I had all the tools I needed for working in the garden too, including a shovel, hoe, rake, and watering can.

A certain amount of manual work was mandated by the rule, ostensibly to provide some relaxation from mental pursuits. I was told from the beginning that submitting of the body to the common lot of mankind also helped to conserve and nourish a sense of joy in spiritual things. I had no problem adapting to this mentality, and I suppose it accomplished its purposes without my dwelling much on the reasons.

Dom Gerardo brought me several potted plants, but most of them perished for lack of care and water. Only the hardy cactuses survived. One of the junior monks came by with a flat of perennials and helped me plant them. Strangely, I had problems with any other living thing, be it even a plant, occupying the cell space that was reserved exclusively for solitary converse with God. It was too much of a distraction.

One of my first carpentry projects was making a wooden stand that I put on the table to hold the book while I read from it. Another assignment was to make rosaries. I had to drill a hole through tiny acacia tree seeds and string the seeds together with wire to form a rosary. Many of the monks made rosaries. I wasn't too good at drilling the holes with a hand drill. I used one hand to hold the seed, and the other to work the drill. The drill kept sliding off the end of the seed, and I kept puncturing my fingers. When the Novice Master found out about this, he brought me beads that already had been drilled. All I had to do was string them together; and, after a few tries I was able to produce what at least remotely resembled a rosary.

I normally did at least an hour of manual labor in the garden, weeding or planting or watering the plants. I loved working in the garden. I had never used an adze, but found it to be my most useful tool for turning the soil and cultivating the ground. My particular garden was larger than most, so that there was a lot to cultivate. The garden was divided into two parts, a higher one, closer to the cell, and lower part, further from the cell. I planted a row of arborvitaes along the divide.

Several other trees were already in the lower part of the garden. One was an orange tree that gave me two or three large oranges a year. I ate them with my evening meal. The peach tree tried to produce peaches, but failed, probably from lack of sufficient water. But its leaves changed color in the fall, and I was pleased at this. It was the only tie to the autumn leaves I so fondly remembered back home in New York. In the center of the lower part was a pink oleander, which was more of a bush. They grew so readily that they were sometimes considered weeds.

The garden soil was not very good, being for the most part rubble from the reconstruction of the monastery. I used to dig up large pieces of rock that I then throw over the wall towards the river. Nightshades, a kind of poisonous weed, grew from the rubble. It was almost impossible to dig or pull out all of their extended roots. After a while, and with continuous digging with the adze, I was able to clear pathways through the weeds, and keep them open.

A water trough, or small concrete pool, was in every garden. I used mine for drawing water to irrigate the plants and for washing clothes. Some of the monks bathed in the little pool, while others said they used it for raising fish or turtles for the kitchen. I was never able to verify this. The water proved too cold for me to bathe, and it was obviously too small for swimming. The one and only time that I plunged into the water in an attempt to cool off, I came down with a severe case of diarrhea that lasted for three days.

I could ask the Prior or Novice Master for any plants or seeds that I wanted for my garden. Sometimes I received them, and sometimes I didn't. In the end I became totally detached from the whole process. I did receive and plant some annuals and a variety of perennial bulbs, including calla lilies, red and yellow cannas, and narcissus. I trained jasmine vines to climb the stone, stucco-covered walls. And there were three to four foot geraniums growing year round -- something that amazed me.

One year while I was still in the novitiate I planted melons and irrigated them with a homemade system of hollow bamboo poles and rubber tubes. Another year I decided to let the weeds grow in the lower part of the garden. To my delight, half the garden was filled with wild red poppies that spring. I let them prosper until I noticed that rats and snakes were beginning to use the underbrush for home.

Following the afternoon reading, study, and work, at around 4:30 the church bell rang for Vespers of the Office of the Blessed Virgin. At 5 p.m. I left the cell to sing Vespers in church, following which I returned to the cell for some spiritual reading until supper was delivered. From the 15th of September until Easter, there was no evening meal from the kitchen; but we were allowed to have some bread and wine for a brief supper, called a "collation." Finally, I took some recreation walking in the garden, did some spiritual reading, and made an examination of conscience in the oratory. Angelus and Compline officially finished the day. At about 7:30 I retired to bed.

On Sundays and holidays I followed a slightly different schedule, allowing for more community time and less time in cell. There was a lot of going back and forth from the cell to the Church on those days. When Prime was still sung in choir, it was followed with a sermon given by the Prior on major feast days or holidays. The Prior was the only member of the Carthusian community authorized to give sermons to the assembled community. It was always delivered in a simple and straightforward Latin, exhorting us to be faithful to some aspect of the Christian life or the monastic rule. We all listened intently and hoped it would be short. I saw some of the older monks nod off once in a while.

Once a month there was a "chapter of faults." The postulants and novices were excluded from this public acknowledgment of faults against the rule or common observance. Each professed monk was encouraged to kneel in his place and confess some particular transgression and receive a penance. When I began to attend the chapter of faults, I quickly learned what to say and what not to say. There were certain things you did not mention, in particular anything that might be material for confession.

I had the feeling that what had started out centuries before as something positive and worthwhile had lost its reason to be. One monk would confess that he had left a light on, a transgression of monastic poverty. Another of the brethren confessed that he had failed to get out of bed right away when called, a serious transgression against obedience. Once in a while someone confessed to breaking the rule of silence. The Prior kept a bundle of tree branches at his place, and for an infraction of the rule of silence you received two or three light whacks on the back.

While the professed members of the community were confessing their transgressions, the postulants and novices had retired to the chapels where we prepared the vestments and lit the candles in preparation for Mass. Following the Mass and thanksgiving I was happy to retire once more to my cell for a time of reading and meditation. The small chapels were unheated and sometimes very cold and damp, much colder than the cells. I learned that many monks developed rheumatism and arthritis from the exposure to the dampness and cold.

I have many unpleasant memories of the cold. The skin of my hands and fingers cracked leaving me with deep cuts -- chilblains -- sometimes on my feet and ankles too. Dom Gerardo provided me with a bottle of glycerin, which helped heal the cuts. One of the other novices told me that *the waters of May* would heal everything. During the first cold season I developed a case of sinusitis so severe that I thought I might have to leave the Charterhouse. It healed itself within a few weeks -- I think we were into the month of May.

On cold Sunday and holiday mornings I waited in my cell until the bell would call me again to the church. I sat in my oratory wrapped in a blanket meditating on God's Providence and how the "cold and chill," together with the sun and moon and all living creatures continued "to bless the Lord" (Dan 3:57-88). I united myself with all the elements of creation in a prayer of praise and thanksgiving to the living God. By nine o'clock, when we were finally summoned to the church for Tierce of the day and Mass, the air was beginning to warm.

The Sunday Mass was always sung with greater solemnity. After Mass and thanksgiving I returned to my cell for more reading, meditation and prayer. I wasn't supposed to do any work on those days. I was allowed to make up my bed and water the potted plants; but sweeping the floor or digging in the garden was not allowed. For relaxation I could walk in the garden. When I began to have classes, I was not allowed to study for them or for exams either. The day was dedicated totally to God. It was a day of total rest from normal weekday activity.

At around noon, I went to the church for Sext, following which we lincd up single file by seniority and walked into the refectory for the main meal of the day. Whenever we monks were marching to church, to chapter, to work, or to the refectory, always with the hood up, it was done in single file by seniority: the Prior, followed by the Vicar and the other choir monks down to the most recent postulant, and then the lay brothers.

Whenever we were out of the cell and walking in the cloister, we had our hoods up. If we happened to pass another monk going in the opposite direction, we bowed to each other and touched the border of our hood without removing the hood or exchanging any oral greeting. That was the way we greeted each other -- a kind of Carthusian military salute.

The strict formality of the rules generally guarded us against any familiarity, our solitude was maintained, and tranquility reigned. Everyone knew what was supposed to be done and was free from any anxiety of having to improvise. It gave me a lot of peace of mind. I always knew what was expected of me, and if I didn't, I went to the superior to ask questions.

During my first weeks in Jerez, I was a frequent visitor at the door of the Novice Master. I tried to do this just before Vespers or just after the morning Mass. When I went to the Superior's cell, or when he came to mine for some reason, we greeted each other with the words *Ave Maria Purissima,* to which was answered, *sin pecado concebida. (Hail Mary most pure, conceived without sin.)* This was in honor of the Immaculate Conception of the Virgin. Sometimes we said in Latin, *Laudetur Jesus Christus.* The response was *in aeternum. (Praised be Jesus Christ. Forever.)* After the greeting, we could each say what was on our mind, always in as few words as possible.

Before entering the refectory on Sundays, we took our turn washing our hands at the little water fountain at the entrance to the refectory. There was a little towel there to dry the hands. Inside I took my place in line in front of the long stone table, and with my fellow monks chanted the prayers before the meal. This was the official beginning of our dinner.

We then took our seats on the stone bench, and at a rap on the table by the Prior, the reader chanted a sentence or two from Scripture. Another rap on the table was the sign to unfold your napkin and begin eating the soup that had been set out by one of the brothers before the community entered the refectory. Everything was done at the rap of the Prior's hand on the table. I often wondered if the Prior's knuckles were sore from all that rapping on the hard surfaces!

Outside of the reader, no one was permitted to speak during community meals. We ate with our hood raised, and very quickly. As a postulant I did not eat with the community, but returned to my cell after Sext. After I received the habit, eating with my woolen robes and black cape on was another mortification that I endured. Eating in the refectory during the hot summer months was definitely a penance, and maybe contributed to the fast eating.

I normally ate slowly, and although I adapted in time to consuming my food faster, I did not enjoy eating with the community. There wasn't enough time to enjoy the food. The Novice Master informed me that we weren't supposed "to enjoy" the food anyway. Some of the monks preferred to eat very little in the refectory, and wait for the evening meal in the cell, which was more elaborate on Sunday.

There were lighter moments that helped me forget the penitential aspect of the refectory meal. One Sunday, for example, the Brother whose turn it was to cook had formed shoestring potatoes into what looked like a bird nest. He deep fried it, and served it with two hardboiled eggs inside. I remember seeing the Prior sitting in his place just contemplating the presentation when it was put before him. Such a presentation never appeared again, maybe because this particular Brother soon departed from the community.

And there was the time that the Superiors noticed that I held my fork in my left hand when I ate. They said it wasn't the thing to do and tried to correct me. I had been doing it for the past twenty years, but I tried holding the fork in my right hand for a while out of obedience. It didn't work too well for me. After a few weeks I just laughed to myself, and picked up the fork with my left hand as I had been doing in the cell. No one said anything further about it.

The first course of the meal was set out on the tables before the community entered the refectory. At each place were a pitcher of water and a pitcher of wine, along with several slices of bread and a plate of hard, sometimes slightly moldy, local cheese. When everyone had finished the first course, the Prior gave a rap on the table and several Brothers appeared to remove the empty plates and present the next course. I had the distinct feeling that the Brothers were simple servants.

If I hadn't yet finished the first course when the Prior gave the signal, I had to stop anyway. This happened frequently. After a while I resigned myself to being hungry on refectory days, and looked forward to eating a big supper in my cell that evening. Ironically, I was told to clean everything on the plate, and to wipe the plate with a piece of bread or with my fingers. The idea was that we were poor and were not to waste any food.

All the time we were eating, one of the monks read from the Bible, a biography of a saint, or a selection from Church history. We took turns reading each week. The reader ate his dinner after everyone else had finished and left the refectory. I looked forward to my turn at reading. If I had not read in a loud enough voice I was corrected afterwards. I read in both Latin and Spanish. I tried very hard to be understood, and was happy when I was told that my Spanish pronunciation was good. I had to pay special attention to the "r" and "rr." Eating afterwards at my own pace and with my hood down was an additional pleasure.

When the Prior decided that enough time had been spent in the refectory, he gave another rap on the table, at which time we took our place in front of the long stone tables to chant the prayers after the meal. We then filed out toward the church, chanting the *Miserere* -- Psalm 51: *Have mercy on me, Oh God, have mercy.* It was as if we were asking forgiveness for any unnecessary indulgence of the body.

In the church we recited a final prayers before filing out to our cell for an hour or so of solitude before being called to the church again for None. After None we gathered in a specially appointed place for a period of "recreation." We sat on hard wooden benches, smiling at one another, exchanging pleasantries and swapping stories. The novices and postulants had a recreation separate from the professed monks, and the converse brothers had one once a month.

Among my fellow postulants and novices at the time I entered was Dom Jose Maria, who was from Jerez. He had worked in the wine industry and knew English fairly well, since many of the Sherry wine producers were British companies. Dom Francisco de Paula had been a veterinary doctor before becoming a monk. He was from the south also, and was noted for the many rosaries he put together for shipment to the missions. Dom Bruno was a young priest from Santiago de Compostela in the northern Spanish province of Galicia. He struck me from the beginning as being very austere. He was to become Sacristan, and still later, Prior of a French Charterhouse.

There were three others who were not Spanish. Dom Andres Gomez y Gomez y Gomez was from Colombia. He seemed to have problems in Spain and talked about returning to Colombia, where he had plans to build his own monastery. His cell was adjacent to mine. About a year after my arrival,

Dom Andres became ill and was taken away by a couple of men in white coats. I didn't have the opportunity to say good-bye, nor was I ever told what had happened to him. Another young postulant from Colombia arrived in Jerez less than a year after I did. He stayed for a few months until he had to leave for health reasons. When anyone left the community, we rarely heard anything more about him.

Then there was young Jesuit priest whom I had met in New York before leaving for Spain. He arrived in Jerez a month or two after I did. But after a few months in Jerez, he decided against a Carthusian calling and returned to his native Philippines. After he had departed, the Novice Master brought me some of the materials he had left behind. One piece was a subway map with the words, "heaven on earth," referring presumably to a convent of Sisters. I mentioned something to the Novice Master about his having a "girlfriend" in New York, but heard nothing more about it.

During my time in the novitiate there were several retreatant candidates, two of whom stayed for a brief period of time. Dom Mariano had been a businessman in northern Spain and a personal friend of Dom Luis, the Prior. Because of his age he needed special permission from the Father General to enter the Order. Although he persevered through solemn vows and ordination to the priesthood, he had difficulties adapting to the austerity and was the butt of many jokes in the community.

Before I left the novitiate, a young monk was transferred from another Spanish monastery to Jerez. Dom Hugo and I were the same age and related well with each other. Although I related well with my fellow novices and postulants, I felt more comfortable with some more than with others. My relationship with Dom Hugo was the closest I ever got to a real mutual friendship in the Spanish charterhouse.

"Particular friendships," as they were called, were normally discouraged in religious communities, as somehow taking away from the common good. The Carthusian monastic community was no exception to this idea. Any candidate who showed a propensity for too much familiarity was simply and politely asked to leave.

We lived a solitary life, and love for our brothers was to show itself first of all in respect for their solitude. Outside of the ordinary occasions like the Sunday recreations and weekly hikes, we had to ask permission if we had to speak to another monk. I rarely had a need, but if I had permission to speak about some matter, I did so as briefly as possible.

At the recreations, the Novice Master often provided food for conversation in the form of current events he thought we should know about. It was mostly a question of relating facts. Spanish politics seemed to enter frequently. Sometimes we took turns reading short stories from some devotional book, or talked about the life of some saint. At other times the other Spanish monks taught me some typical Spanish jokes, tongue twisters, and puns. On a few rare occasions the Prior joined us as we sat along the bank of the river in the thick grass.

At the conclusion of the recreation, I returned to my cell, usually tired and sweaty from being in the sun. I had just enough time to recite Vespers of the Office of the Blessed Virgin. At the sound of the church bell I again left my cell for the church. Vespers was soon followed by supper in the cell, and consisted of some hearty vegetables, fruit or some favorite concoction made by the Brother cook or his assistant. I had a few minutes after supper for spiritual reading or a walk in the garden, and a brief examination of conscience. I thought over the events of the day and how I had reacted to them in thought, word, and deed.

Before I knew it, it was time for the last Office of the day -- Compline. The Psalms and brief reading was always the same: Psalms 4, 91, and 134, 1st Epistle of Peter, chapter 5, verses 8-9. Compline always ended with the *Canticle of Simeon* from St. Luke's Gospel (2:29-32): *Lord, now you let your servant go in peace.* The texts had been chosen centuries earlier to help each of us express in our own way our regret for any faults committed during the day, to help calm and purify the mind before sleep, and to ask for protection from evil during the hours of sleep.

My typical day was rarely filled with any sense of monotony. Particular holidays had their particular schedule, and I looked forward to the changing of the seasons of the liturgical year: Advent, Christmas, Lent, Easter, and Pentecost -- each one brought a welcome change to any hint of monotony.

114

Advent brought with it an anticipation of the birth of Jesus and a period of fasting and abstinence. Christmas day in the Charterhouse was a day of exceptional silence and solitude, so as to contemplate the birth of the Son of God in more depth. The Christmas night office was longer than usual, interrupted by a Midnight Mass, which normally began around midnight. We went to the church earlier, around 11 p.m., sang the twelve-lesson office, and assisted at the Mass. Following the Mass we sang Lauds and returned to the cell for a few hours of sleep, returning to the church again for Prime and Chapter at around 6:30 a.m.

On Christmas Day, as on all of those holy days that fell during the week, I followed the usual Sunday schedule, except that I had my dinner in the cell; nor was there an afternoon recreation. Each priest was allowed to celebrate more than one Mass. While a novice, I went to a chapel after Prime to serve two Masses, one following the other. The community Mass was followed by a third individual Mass in the small private chapel. It was a morning oriented entirely toward a celebration of the birth of the Christ Child.

There was no expectation of presents under the tree, no morning breakfast with the family. In fact, there were no presents, or Christmas trees, and or special decorations at all. In my first year, after telling the novices what we did at home for Christmas, one of them remarked: "They're all pagan customs. Here we decorate the houses with leaves and vines." It was as if this Spanish custom didn't have its roots in some long-forgotten pagan ritual! I felt as if I had been attacked; but I said nothing more. I silently concluded that I had come to the monastery precisely to be a humble religious, to leave my old ways behind, to dedicate my life entirely to God.

There was the usual Sunday schedule of Conventual Mass preceded by Tierce and followed by Sext. After that we returned to our cells to await the arrival of the noonday meal. I ate my Christmas dinner alone in the corner of the dining room. On Christmas day we received an extra portion of wine. That was more or less the extent of the human celebration of Christmas. One of the monks pointed out that in Europe the major celebrations were New Year's and the

Epiphany, or feast of the Magi. Christmas was lower on the list of important celebrations.

After dinner and a time for recreation in the cell, the bell summoned me to the church for None. There was no common recreation after None, so that I returned to my cell for an afternoon of complete solitude and silence. During the years I lived in Spain, on Christmas Day I would recite three rosaries while contemplating the Mysteries of the Incarnation and walking in my garden, do some spiritual reading, and sometimes take a nap.

I was forbidden by obedience to study for classes on solemn feast days like Christmas or Easter. On those days, I sometimes would sit at the balcony that was built into the wall of my garden, all the while contemplating the beauty of the Guadelete River and the Bay of Cadiz. The afternoons on those days usually passed quickly. I was in love with God and never felt alone, nor did I miss my family or friends back home. I felt that I was with them all, and all of them at once, as I grew closer to God. I was united to all of them through and because of my union with the Lord.

After Solemn Vespers in the Church, I had a supper and more "free time" until Compline and bed. Free time usually meant, as on other days, praying the rosary or doing light housework. In my first year the Novice Master visited me after Vespers and left a statue of the Christ Child in a small manger. He said I could keep it in my cell for the rest of the day and then pass it to my neighbor. It was customary to do this at Christmas: you welcomed the Baby Jesus into your cell and life. I was never very emotional about it. I never quite got the gist of this practice, which I felt was too emotionally oriented.

The schedule for Holy Week (the week before Easter) was very different from the other holiday feast days. The Office prayers for Thursday, Friday, and Saturday were simplified to leave more time for silent contemplation of the mystery of the Cross and Redemption. Holy Thursday was dedicated to contemplation of the Lord's Supper and the institution of the Eucharist. Good Friday was dedicated exclusively to the contemplation of the Passion and Death of Jesus. It was a day of complete fast and abstinence, bread and water for everyone. On Holy Saturday we contemplated Jesus in the tomb, awaiting the Resurrection. On this day the Sacristan, sometimes with the assistance of the novices, cleaned the church and prepared it for Easter.

There was a Midnight Mass at Easter, just as at Christmas; and just as at Christmas, I passed the day in the solitude and silence of the cell. The day following Easter -- Easter Monday -- was a day of community celebration. In fact, the entire week following Easter was one of community activity. Following the Carthusian custom of simplicity and poverty, there were no flowers or extra candles set out for the holidays. Looking at the high altar on those days you would see nothing that distinguished it from an ordinary Sunday.

The schedule for the day after Christmas, like the days after Easter and Pentecost, was like a Sunday. We had our meal in the refectory and gathered for a common recreation in the afternoon. Each of the eight days after Christmas, Easter, and Pentecost were celebrated according to the Sunday schedule. This meant little solitude and a lot of community life. Most of us were happy when the Order later did away with the Octaves, as the eight-day celebrations were called. They took us away from our principal calling to solitude and silence. But that was to come later on, and in the meantime, I endured still another disappointment coming from the institutionalized hermit life of the Charterhouse.

During the year, normally on the first free day of the week, we took a long hike of approximately four hours outside the monastery enclosure. It was known as the "*spaciamentum.*" We could speak freely with one another, walking two-by-two, changing every so often at the pleasure of the Novice Master, who kept a watchful ear on the conversations. Sext, lunch, and None were earlier and Vespers later so as to fit in the walk. I found the mornings to be a little rushed, and looked forward to the next day after the walk, which was one of greater leisure.

The hikes had for their goal the maintaining of "mutual affection and union of hearts," all the while assuring a healthy amount of physical exercise. Regardless of how dedicated I was to my cell, it was a welcome change to go out once a week. Our conversations were generally about the weather and minor community happenings. "What happened to Dom So-and So the other night when he didn't show for the night office?" "How is that plant growing in your garden?" We were discouraged from speaking about religious or spiritual matters, and in particular about our own individual prayer life. This was between you and the Lord -- a confidential affair between two lovers.

The Spanish monks were eager to explain to me their particular customs, just as they were interested in knowing our American ways. They gave me good-natured lessons in the Spanish language, and were interested in knowing the English word for anything that might come up. I preferred to speak in Spanish as much as possible. Generally I wasn't particularly enthusiastic over the conversations, since I had come to the monastery for conversation with no one but God. I didn't feel any need for exercising my tongue in what I considered idle and useless chitchat.

I always wore my heavy woolen robes while walking in the heat of the afternoon sun. We were quite a sight to passersby as we walked slowly along the roads with our wide-brimmed straw hats and walking sticks! We kept to more solitary locations like the open fields and dusty roads that were common in the largely agricultural area. Sometimes we walked to a nearby shallow lagoon, and sometimes we traced the course of the river. Often we would come across herds of sheep and goats, stirring up the yellow dust as they walked by. Before the death of General Franco, we often saw armed Civil Guards along the roads, looking for possible smugglers from Gibraltar or the mountains to the south and east.

As I walked along those dusty roads, I sometimes thought back with nostalgia to the long solitary walks I used to take in the hills of Newfield and Van Etten. During the summer months the weekly walk was an exhausting experience; but I did it without complaint. We were not allowed to carry water with us, but could stop at any open wells along the way to drink.

When I first started to walk with the novices, the Novice Master didn't want me to see the green color of the water that came from some of the open wells that we drank from. The same open wells served as watering places for pigs, cows, and donkeys, besides providing water for the owners and workers of the property! I became used to drinking the greenish water, and fortunately did not come down with any disease.

118

Everything in the life I led was ordained to solitude and prayer. Perhaps the only reason for prescribing the minimal community acts of prayer and the weekly walk was for the sake of the moderation and balance that were so characteristic of St. Bruno. United by love for the Lord, by prayer, and by a zeal for solitude, my fellow monks and I consciously tried to show ourselves true disciples of Christ in deed as well as in name. We were ever exhorted to the sometimes difficult task of being zealous for mutual love, living in harmony, forbearing one another, and forgiving each other the little real or imagined transgressions that occur in communal living.

Because we cloister monks retired to deserts remote from men and to cells removed from the noise of the world, we had to be careful to hold ourselves alien from all worldly news. I never saw a newspaper or magazine in all my years in Spain. Most "secular" reading matter was totally banned from the monastery, and I can't say that I missed reading the daily newspaper. Not to be totally isolated, however, the Prior did receive a weekly newspaper, which he rarely read. He did, however, pass to the Novice Master and the other monks whatever news he deemed would not disturb the individual monk's spirit.

The old monks used to tell us that a devout heart, a Bible, and *The Imitation of Christ* were the only things necessary to find God in the monastery. God tended to provide whatever might be lacking to those who truly were seeking Him with all their heart. It was a strange and unexpected feeling when I began to realize that my heart was not becoming more narrow as my intimacy with God grew. Rather, I began to experience what the older monks had experienced: an ability to embrace in God the hopes and difficulties of the world and the great causes of the Church.

There was wisdom in having at least some knowledge of what was happening in the world outside of the monastery. At the same time I knew that my concern for the welfare of men would best express itself, not by satisfying any curiosity, but by my remaining closely united to Christ. Each one of us was exhorted to listen to the Spirit within him, and determine what he could admit into his mind without harming his interior converse with God.

Even so, it was only by chance and highly unusual that I might come to know something of events in the world, like when Mom sent me some books wrapped in an old newspaper. We were advised to be careful not to pass any news on to others in the monastery. News of the world was to be left where it was heard. It was for the Prior to tell his monks those things, especially concerning the Church and her needs, which they ought to know.

From time to time I did receive bits of secular information. For example, on a cold and gray November afternoon in 1963, the Prior called me aside after Vespers and told me that President Kennedy had been killed. I don't remember being noticeably moved by the news. After all, I had voluntarily left not only the world in general, but even my particular world in the United States. While in Spain I ceased being an American. I was a Carthusian monk without any other country than heaven. I didn't pay taxes. I didn't vote. I didn't care about politics or politicians.

On another occasion Dom Gerardo related that "Luther" has been assassinated. He was referring to Martin Luther King. When I think over those years, some details come to the top of the memory pile, while others remain buried. In any case, I had left the world behind, and I wasn't moved by any secular news. Indeed, the major source of secular material for my mind was likely to originate in my imagination and memory. By applying myself to the ascetical life, and by avoiding as much as possible all outside distractions, sooner or later my memory and mind would be brought under control. As Dom Stephen had put it, "the newsreel would eventually run out."

For dealing with issues inside and outside of the monastery, I did not have what could be called a "spiritual director." There was no need for one, since the Statutes taught us all that was necessary for both our exterior and interior lives. If I followed the Statutes to the letter, my spiritual life -- my personal relationship with God -- would be all it was supposed to be. My exterior behavior would help and foster my interior life. With my exterior conduct in order, I had nothing else to concern myself with but to ardently seek God in the depths of my soul. Keeping to the letter of the Statutes as perfectly as I could would quickly lead me to find and to possess God in my soul. With the Lord's help, I might then attain to the perfection of love, which was the aim of the whole monastic life.

There was no need for any particular or specific instructions other than those corrections or admonitions given by my Superior, whether he was the Novice Master or the Prior. It was the Novice Master's primary job to instruct his novices in the observances of the Order. To this end, he took great care that I study the Statutes. On my part, I willingly studied them and asked questions if I had any.

We novices had a weekly conference, normally on Sunday after Vespers. In the conferences I learned about the Carthusian saints and liturgical celebrations that were coming up, whether they were ordinary days, or days when we remembered a specific saint. We also had our own particular chapter of faults. The Novice Master made accusations and a penance was handed out. Dom So-and-so did not sing loudly enough in choir. Another brother was heard working in his garden at unauthorized times. It seemed at times that I was back with the Recollects with the novitiate conference. Sometimes I longed for the days when I could be truly alone in the cell on Sunday afternoons.

The Novice Master's conferences were filled with references to the sources of all Christian life, the teaching of monastic tradition, and the original inspiration of the Order. Dom Gerardo fully explained the spirit of St. Bruno. Although Carthusians did not normally write for publication, later on he published a book about St. Bruno, *Father of Monks*. He taught us the authentic traditions that had been observed from the beginning of the Order, how those traditions had evolved, and how they were to be practiced in our time. Always interested in history, and wanting to be a perfect Carthusian, I was especially fond of this part of the conferences.

Dom Gerardo taught us that all Christian spirituality was derived from the Spirit of Jesus sent to dwell among believers in Christ. The workings of the Holy Spirit were wonderfully varied. The gifts that He continuously bestowed -- and bestows -- upon the faithful were called "charisms." They were usually appropriate for a particular historical time, and sometimes to a particular place. There was a definite Carthusian charism, but there never has been in a "school" of Carthusian spirituality as there has been with the Carmelites or Franciscans, for example. If there were a Carthusian school, its expression would be the Statutes.

The Statutes were a real work of monastic spirituality; and for the Carthusian monk they are "the transmission of a voice of prayer." Their faithful observance truly would lead to contemplation -- "the savoring knowledge of God." To attain this, the monk had to labor faithfully and carefully in the regular observance that was handed down by those Statutes. I imbibed all that I could of the Statutes, striving all the while to make the rules part of my automatic response to life around me, from my relationship with others both inside and outside the monastery, to my interior prayer life with God and the saints.

Since my teen years I had a great and strong devotion to the Virgin Mary -- the Madonna. In this I was no different from all Carthusians, who have expressed great devotion to Mary, Mother of God, through the centuries. Every monk nourished a deep practical devotion to her. Carthusians felt that Mary guided them through their solitary lives each day. As one older monk used to say, "A Carthusian life unaided by Mary is unthinkable." She is the principal Patron of the Order. All Carthusian monasteries are dedicated in the first place to the Blessed Mary ever Virgin, along with St. John the Baptist, one of the first desert hermits.

The Spanish priests and religious seemed to be extremely devoted to Mary, and sometimes to my mind, in an excessively emotional way. Besides reciting the *Angelus* four times a day in honor of the Annunciation to the Blessed Virgin and the Incarnation of Jesus, it was customary in Jerez, at the Prior's instigation, to recite an *Ave Maria* at the top of every hour. Because this was not officially sanctioned throughout the whole Order, I resisted doing this at first, but later gave in to the practice. My greatest desire was to become a true Carthusian in the most authentic and purest form possible.

As was customary in the Order, I added "Mary" to my religious name, not only to honor the Mother of God, but also to proclaim that I was choosing her as my special patron and mother. I was known as Dom Benito Maria. As a rule we also used our family names, even when writing to our family or close friends. Only the Father General signed documents using his first name without last name. I found this a little strange and awkward at first; but like everything else, I accepted things as they were and became accustomed to doing them in that way.

Religious life and the accompanying spiritual life, goes through stages similar to those of a marital relationship. There is a meeting, a period of becoming acquainted, and a courtship. In the spiritual life they involve making choices, which the writers call a "purification." There is an engagement period, which continues and confirms the purification. You let go of some things for the sake of something else. Then there is the marriage, the definitive commitment, prelude to the union and fulfillment. Beyond this there is the constant and continuous work of striving to keep the relationship alive and well, while at the same time attempting to keep your own identity intact.

Within six months of living in a monastery a young man sometimes felt that he was losing his identity with nothing to show for it. This was quite a normal human feeling. Having taken the step to enter the monastery, you were well into what was referred to as the "purgative way." You were getting the body and all its lusts under control, purging them, as it were. You learned to walk with your eyes cast down, and with your hands stuck neatly inside your black cape, and you didn't let your mind wander. You spoke only when absolutely neccssary or when spoken to. You followed the Novice Master's directives in every detail.

I remember experiencing all of these things, but I don't remember ever experiencing any loss of human dignity. I felt that my true identity as a Carthusian and a true son of God (in the spiritual sense) was emerging, as from a cocoon. I knew that God had called me to the monastic life in the Charterhouse, and I was willing to surrender to all that the calling entailed. As I surrendered myself more and more completely, I began to feel a great freedom of spirit. This was the true monastic spirit!

I never counted the costs; in fact, I was willing to surrender my life in love to my God. I wanted to lose myself in Him forever. I was willing to undergo any trial and tribulation, should it be necessary. They said that if you did not have a calling, the cell would "vomit you out." You didn't have to worry about leaving of your own accord; you would have to leave, or otherwise lose your physical and mental health -- if you had any left.

It has been suggested that this type of existence came close to being a cult, that we were brainwashed, or held prisoner. With all the emphasis on strict obedience, silence and separation from influences outside the monastery, deprivation of sleep and food, we were still free to leave if we so desired. We were not prisoners, except by choice, in what I came to think of as a "prison of love." My mission in life -- my calling -- was to be there.

The Novice Master and the Prior could visit me in the cell if they so wished; but after a few months I began to dislike and even resent any such intrusions. I counted the hours and days when I spoke to no one and saw no one. They were the happiest and most joyous times. Although I could leave the cell during the day to seek out the Prior or the Novice Master, I made less and less use of this privilege after my first few weeks in the monastery.

I was encouraged to go to confession frequently, at least once a week, and even as much as every day. We were taught that, God, the Father of mercies, through the Paschal Mystery of His Son, reconciled us in the Spirit with Himself, with the Church, and with ourselves in the Sacrament of Penance. Through that same Sacrament of Penance, conversion of the heart, which was the primary aim of the monk, became enrooted in the mystery of the death and resurrection of Christ.

The solitary, silent Carthusian hermit monk did not have much occasion for committing sins of word or deed. Sins of thought and omission were more possible. There was an ever-present feeling of unworthiness and sinfulness that tended to develop from the recitation of Psalm 51, as many as ten times a day in the Office. Regardless of actual personal sins, I felt that by my frequently receiving the grace of the Sacrament, I was doing penance and gaining grace for the whole human race -- for each and every individual, living or dead. I was atoning for the sins of others and gaining them the grace of forgiveness, flooding the world, as it were, with forgiveness.

The Prior had appointed several of the more discreet monks to hear the confessions of the others. Even so, any member of the Order could go to confession to any priest who had legitimate faculties to hear confessions. I never made use of this option, and I know of only one monk who went into town to go to confession there; but it was definitely an option. Even with the inviolable secrecy of the confessional, it could be advisable to go outside the community for confession if you had something to confess that you didn't want anybody at all in the community to know about. It was not that you were concerned with the express publication of your confession; but rather you would be conscious of the human implications of telling intimate secrets to someone you lived with in an enclosed environment.

In the beginning of my career in Spain, I went to confession at least once a week with the Prior. He had suggested this unusual arrangement because he knew English and he knew that my Spanish might not be sufficient to relate my thoughts clearly. It was an unusual arrangement because the Church's law did not permit Superiors to hear the confession of their subjects. I had no problem with this arrangement and did it for the first few months, until I became comfortable enough to recite my peccadilloes in Spanish with the Vicar, who was the ordinary confessor for the community.

Before being admitted to the novitiate I had to prove to the community that I could sing. I didn't have to be a trained opera singer; and as I was later to find, many monks were notably handicapped when it came to carrying a tune. As was customary, I had classes in the Carthusian chant in preparation for my receiving the habit and beginning the novitiate.

Always nervous of performing "in public," I wanted to be as technically well prepared as possible. To chant our prayers was the main job of a monk, and I wanted to do the job as perfectly as possible. I practiced almost every day for a half hour in the free time following the noon meal. The Novice Master provided me with a round pitch pipe and a leather-bound, eighteenth century edition of one of the choir books used at Mass so that I could practice the chants in my cell.

I had to learn the various "inflections," as they were called, that were used in chanting the Latin readings at the night office of Matins. After some of the Latin words in the reading were markings that indicated how to inflect your voice when chanting the last syllable of that word. The readings were called "lessons," because they were meant to give instruction, and were sung from a lectern in the center space between the two choirs.

One of the older monks, usually the Vicar, followed the reading from his place in choir, and informed you if you made a mistake by rapping on the wooden stand. At the dreaded sound, you had to repeat the word or inflection correctly, and then kneel and kiss the floor in acknowledgment of your mistake. It was a small humiliation, but done out of reverence for the word of God.

The lessons were in groups of four, with a sung response following each of them. After your reading you returned to your place in choir, and at the completion of the next reading you had to stand facing the altar and intone the "responsorial" by singing the first few words of the piece, which the community then picked up and continued. You sang your solo part and the community again took up the rest of the responsorial. The monk who was to sing the fourth lesson sang the solo verse of the response following the first lesson. The responsorial verses had their own tunes and were eight in number. Some were easier to sing than others.

When it seemed likely that I was close to being acceptable for beginning my novitiate training, the community had to vote on whether I would be admitted. Several times during the first few weeks and months I had asked Dom Gerardo how long my postulancy period would last. I was impatient to begin the novitiate. Then, on a day in late November, he told me that the community would meet to discuss my admission, and that if all went well, I would become a novice on December 8th, the Feast of the Immaculate Conception. I was elated at the news! The Feast of Immaculate Conception would be my anniversary day during my Carthusian career. I had always been devoted to the Mother of God and considered it a great favor to receive the habit on her feast day.

A few days after this, I went to the Prior's cell with the Novice Master, where I was given an oral exam to show that I knew Latin. I was asked to translate a few passages from the *Directory of Novices,* and from the Latin Bible. I passed the test with flying colors after being coached beforehand by the

Novice master, who may have been anxious about my Latin to Spanish translations. Because I had been forewarned of the passages I would have to translate, I hesitated a bit in several places, and tried to make a few small errors. Dom Gerardo understood and after the test told the Prior what had happened.

Before receiving the habit and officially becoming a novice, I had to chant a lesson and sing a responsorial verse in the choir. My knees shook and my voice quivered as I chanted the lesson with the proper inflections. I managed to get through it without hearing any rapping on the wooden forms. I took my place in choir and after the next lesson stood to be ready to sing my response. The head chanter intoned the first few notes, as was customary. When the community had sung their part, the chanter again gave me a note to begin my response verse. Though my voice quivered and I was slightly off key, I managed to do the job to the satisfaction of the community. I had proven to the community that I could "sing," or at least carry a tune.

On another appointed day, which I think was a Sunday, lying prostrate before the community assembled in Chapter, I asked for "mercy." Whenever a Carthusian formally requested anything in the presence of the community, "mercy" was the first request; and then he proposed whatever else he wanted, preferably according to an established formula. The Prior told me to rise, and in a strong and unquivering voice, I recited my formula: "I ask for the love of God, to be received for probation in the monastic habit, as the most humble servant of all, if this should be pleasing to you, Father, and to the community."

The Prior asked the questions the Church's law required as a formality before entering any religious community: Had I made profession in another Religious Institute? Was I free from the bonds of marriage? Did I have any incurable disease? Was I in a position to advance to Holy Orders? Had I paid all my debts? The Prior reminded me that I could be expelled from the Order, even after profession, if I concealed anything.

After answering the questions, the Prior then presented to me the manner of life I desired to follow. He told me in the presence of the whole community what I was getting into, as if I didn't already know! I replied, again according to the formula I had memorized, "Relying solely on the goodness of God and the prayers of my brothers, I will fulfill these obligations insofar as the divine goodness allowed."

The Prior reminded me that I would be free to leave at any time before profession, and that the community had the power and liberty to send me away if they found that I was not suited to the Carthusian life. Having given my oral assent to this also, I was then instructed to return to my cell while the community deliberated and voted.

A short time later, a smiling and obviously happy Dom Gerardo came to my cell to inform me that I had received a favorable vote from the community. I felt a great sense of relief at the news, as if a burden had been lifted from my shoulders. I was full of joy at the good news. I would finally be receiving the Carthusian habit I had waited to receive for several long years; and I would receive it on the day dedicated to the Immaculate Conception of Mary. I had begun my postulancy on her day, and I would begin my novitiate on her day too!

During the postulancy, the whole purpose of the monk's life had been put before me on many occasions, perhaps to discourage me, or to shake out any idealistic idea I had of the Carthusian life. The hard and austere things to come were presented, so that every aspect of the life I wished to embrace was, as far as possible, exposed to my view. And the glory that the monks hoped would be given to God by their particular sharing in the work of redemption was also set before me.

In the face of all this I had remained firm and promised myself that, relying on the promises of the Lord, I would walk this difficult path, desiring to die with Christ so that I might live with Him. The hard and austere things never daunted me, nor did I think much of the difficulties that might possibly lie before me. I remained undaunted as I experienced for myself how good and joyous it was to leave all things and strive to hold fast to Jesus. In the end, I did what I knew I had to do without regret or counting the cost.

On a warm and sunny December afternoon, one of the Brothers came by my cell to measure me for the habit and the monastic shoes. I put most of the clothes I had brought with me in a suitcase. I wouldn't be allowed to wear the new and comfortable shoes I had brought with me. Instead, the monastery's Brother shoemaker made me a special pair. Being homemade, they never felt exactly right on my feet; but I wore them the whole time I was in Spain, even on the weekly walks.

On still another day I was told to go to the community barbershop, which was located in the Brothers' section. One of the Brothers was to shave my face and head with a straight razor. After he had soaped my face, he took the razor in his hand and blessed himself with the sign of the cross before starting. I thought he was joking, and I blessed myself also. He may have thought I was making fun of him, so I think he tried a little harder than usual to cut me. When he had finished, all by hair was gone except for an inch-wide band of hair around the back and sides of my head: the Carthusian tonsure.

The head shaving was to be a monthly procedure. A note placed on the community bulletin board announced the monthly "haircut." The same Brother who had first shaved me, on other occasions took pieces of skin with the hair. After having my head and face scraped with the straight razor, I went to a sink and wash off the soap and blood with cold water. In colder weather the Brothers who did the shaving graciously and gratefully provided a pitcher of warm water. It was a small, but welcome, consolation.

The weekly shave of the beard was still another separate story. Since we had neither mirrors nor shaving equipment in our cells, once a week we were at the mercy of the Brother barber for a required shave. My facial hair grew quickly and was thick since my teen years. While in the world I had often to shave twice a day. In Jerez I often returned to the cell from the barbershop with bloody cuts on my neck and ears. It's a wonder I didn't lose an ear! I was much happier when the Order finally permitted us to have a small mirror and a razor in cell so that we could do our own weekly facial clean-up.

I actually put on the Carthusian habit on December 7, 1962, before first Vespers of the feast. Dom Gerardo came to my cell with the robes and helped me put everything on. After Vespers the community led me in procession to the cell I had been living in for the past three months. The monks had their hoods up as they sang the Psalm verses: "How lovely is your dwelling place, Oh Lord. Oh Lord, remember me, do not desert me. Have mercy on me, Oh Lord, have mercy." The Prior led the way, followed by me, a monk who carried holy water, and the rest of the community in order of seniority.

On arriving at the cell door, the Prior sprinkled it with holy water, saying "Peace be to this house." Then, in a moving part of the ceremony, the Prior took me by the hand, and led me into the cell to the oratory where I knelt and prayed. I had diligently cleaned the cell that morning and put a vase of fresh flowers from my garden before the image of the Blessed Virgin in my oratory. The Prior advised me to keep faithfully to the cell and to all other practices and observances of the Order: "May you cling to God alone in silence and solitude, in constant prayer and ready penance." He then commended me to the care of the Novice Master.

On beginning the novitiate, I entrusted the little money and few other possessions I had brought with me to the Prior. The Prior was to take care of them, as if on deposit. I had now left all things to follow Christ. He instructed me to leave the suitcase in my cell "for the time being." Later on, after final vows, I gave the suitcase to the Prior. The clothes inside were stained with mildew. I was told that they were cleaned and donated to the poor.

Though he very rarely came to my cell, the Prior was generally solicitous for my welfare. If I had occasion to go to his cell, I always felt well received, and he always gave a willing hearing to me. The monks -- especially those suffering trials -- could have recourse to him, as to a loving father. He was a stabilizing presence both in the community and in my life. Together with his monks, he strove to listen to the Spirit in a common seeking of the will of God. He had received a special mandate for the interpretation of the Lord's will for each of his brothers.

During my first year of novitiate, I had some lingering doubts about my choice of Charterhouses. Perhaps I should have gone to England or to France, where some of the other American candidates had gone. I was still having problems with the culture, language, food, and with some of the monks, who themselves did not relate to the American spirit. It had finally sunk into my consciousness that I was an American living abroad in a foreign culture.

I confided all this to the Prior, who suggested that I would most likely be returning to the United States when the Charterhouse was completed there. He told me that it wouldn't look good "on my record" if I changed Charterhouses at this point of time. It might be seen as a form of instability. I accepted his judgment, and had no further thoughts about transferring to another Charterhouse. Looking back on the incident, I know it was the right one. My years in Spain were to form me into a model Carthusian monk. They provided me with a unique experience that very few men could even imagine.

The novitiate was a two-year period of training and probation. I was warned to avoid being worn down by the temptations which were wont to beset the followers of Christ in the desert. I was to put my trust not in my own strength, but in the Lord, who had called me, and who would bring to perfection the work He had begun. If I persevered, at the end of the novitiate I would make temporary vows that would last for three years. Solemn or permanent vows would be made at the end of those three years, at which time I would give myself to the Carthusian life before God and the Church forever.

There weren't any big changes in my life after I became a novice. I had already been living the full Carthusian life in the cell for four months. The biggest change was wearing the heavy woolen monastic robes, "the habit." The mandatory clothing in those days consisted of woolen undergarments (shirt and shorts), woolen stockings reaching to the knees, and the twelfth-century woolen foot coverings that we called "pedulios."

I had been wearing the woolen stockings since the beginning of my postulancy and was used to them. The woolen shirt and woolen shorts were scratchy and uncomfortable in warm weather. In time I got used to them too. I wore all this clothing twenty-four hours a day, since it was obligatory to sleep in our "underwear." It was sometimes difficult to sleep on those summer evenings when the sun was still shining and I was wrapped in all that wool, lying on woolen sheets with a woolen blanket over me. Using the blanket was not

131

obligatory, but the sheets were. Though no one came to the cell to see if I was doing it as prescribed, I knew God was watching.

I also wore the infamous "hair shirt," that so many people are curious about. I was curious about it too; and I was disappointed to find out that it wasn't really a "shirt" after all, but rather a six inch square scapular made of woven horsehair. It fit over my shoulders and was fastened and tied around the waist with a rope. Wearing it was intended to remind me that I was to keep my bodily impulses under control.

When I wore the hair shirt, I couldn't help being reminded that I had a body. Whenever I moved I felt it, because it was extremely itchy, especially since I already had hair on my chest. I wore it for about a year, but it caused such a severe rash that I was given permission to wear it only on Fridays. Wearing the hair shirt later became optional, but you still had to have the Prior's approval to take it off.

Over the medieval underwear, I wore a monastic robe made of the same white wool as the underwear. The robe had two very large pockets into which many and varied objects from a handkerchief to a penknife to a pocket calendar could be stuffed. I had two robes, one for everyday use, and another of heavier wool for Sunday and holiday wear. A cinture, or leather belt, kept the robe gathered at the waist. From the belt hung a white Carthusian six-decade rosary. Wearing the rosary became optional, and later the younger monks no longer received it.

Over the robe we novices wore a short woolen scapular with an attached hood. The scapular reached to the knees. The professed monks wore a longer scapular joined in the peculiar Carthusian way by two bands of cloth at the sides. This outfit was patterned after the common twelfth century clothing that was worn by the shepherds who lived in the region of the Alps where St. Bruno and his companions had settled. The side bands kept the scapular from blowing in the wind.

Although I always wore the robe with the cinture, when working in the cell I wore a modified scapular that reached only to the waist. It had an attached hood and was fastened around the waist with cloth ties. As for footwear, while in my cell I often went barefoot. Sometimes I wore a pair of Spanish *"alpargatas,"* a kind of slipper with hempen soles that the local poor people wore.

When in community exercises, I wore the same black cape I had worn as a postulant. In cold weather I had a woolen jacket that I could wear under the robe and over the woolen shirt. We were not allowed to wear the jacket on the outside over the robe. Because the whole outfit was rather bulky, I seldom wore it. In fact, I remember wearing it only once on a cold Christmas morning.

I worked in my garden and shop, studied and went to class, went on the weekly walk and to the Sunday recreations in my heavy woolen habit. Some monks even slept in their full habit, something I tried only once or twice in the coldest part of the year. When I went out of the monastery for a dentist or doctor appointment, I wore a black woolen cape over the white woolen habit. It was supposed to show that I was dead to the world. None of us had regular physical check-ups, but we were permitted to go out to see a doctor if necessary.

Soon after arriving in Jerez, in fact, I felt some discomfort in my mouth, and had to go to see the dentist in Jerez. The Father Procurator suggested to the Novice Master that one of the Brothers accompany me to town. But the Novice Master replied, "No, he's from Brooklyn." That was that! No more was ever said about my getting around outside of the monastery. Apparently anyone from Brooklyn could take care of himself without help from anyone else.

I took the bus that passed by every hour into town and found the dentist's office with no trouble. After a cursory examination and questioning, he told me that I had a severe abscess under one of the teeth. The tooth had to be pulled. I don't remember if any x-ray was taken, and I had no choice but to submit to his determination. He pulled the tooth and stuffed cotton wads into my mouth, advising me to rinse my mouth with peroxide several times a day for the next few days to prevent an infection.

With a headache and my mouth full of bloody cotton, I didn't want to wait for the next bus back to the monastery. I managed to walk the distance on the pleasant warm afternoon. I went to the Novice Master's cell and told him what had happened. He notified the Procurator that I needed a bottle of peroxide. That night I woke up to the sound of what seemed like a million mosquitoes buzzing around my face and mouth, drawn by the blood.

There were other trips to the same dentist during my first years in Jerez. I lost two more teeth over the course of my time in Spain. I wasn't at all happy about this, and I continue to wonder if it was necessary. I must have mentioned to the Prior my perception of the dentist's penchant for pulling teeth, because on one of the visits for what turned out to be a routine filling, the dentist told me that he had to pull more teeth. I thought he was serious and refused to open my mouth. He was joking.

In addition to tooth problems, I had eye problems, due in part to the strong sunlight, and in part to a vitamin deficiency. When I went to Spain I had eyeglasses, but rarely wore them. After a year or two of reading by the light of a twenty-five watt bulb in my cell, and the meager light of the Church choir at night, my eyesight deteriorated to the point that I needed to wear the glasses through the day. At one point I asked for sunshades for use on the weekly walk, and eventually I received them. But the Prior continued to think that I should have suffered through the bright sunlight without them.

I lost a lot of weight during my first few years in Spain, probably as much as thirty pounds. Though there were no scales or mirrors in the cell or monastery, I could see my reflection in the glass of the door that led to the open porch of my cell. I was getting more and more slender. I became so thin that the Prior had a blood test done, but nothing was found. One of the Brothers, who had been a nurse in the world, gave me a series of vitamin B shots. I don't know if they helped, but eventually my weight leveled.

Otherwise, my health seemed to be good. I did not feel ill. I came down with one or two colds and had a bout with the flu one day in March. I had taken a shower in the morning and changed my shirt. The next day I became seriously ill with the flu. I really thought I was going to die. I was ready. I prayed to St. Therese who had died young. It was just before Pentecost Sunday, and I knew I wouldn't be able to attend the community prayers. The Prior had to call in a doctor, who assured me that I was going to recover. He also assured me that the Holy Spirit would come to me even if I missed the night office! After that experience I only showered and changed my shirt in the warmer months.

I experienced a loss of my eyesight on one occasion. It was a very strange and frightening experience. The pupils dilated and would not close. I saw only bright light and nothing else. One of my fellow novices suggested that that was what heaven would be like. But after a few days, the condition resolved itself and my eyesight returned to normal. No one ever found out what had caused the problem. The most plausible explanation was that some chemical in the air, perhaps a chemical fertilizer could have caused it. There was a large farm with olive and pear trees on the other side of the river from the monastery, and the orchard was sprayed from the air once or twice a year. It had been sprayed a few days before by problem developed.

As for the sicknesses and unavoidable infirmities of growing older, I learned that they invite us to a new act of trusting confidence in our heavenly Father. By means of infirmities, He conforms us ever more perfectly to His Son Jesus. Indeed, even through the minor experiences I had, I felt united in a very special manner with the great work of redemption, and ever more intimately united with the entire suffering Mystical Body of Christ.

Those who suffered from some nervous or mental problem, which in solitude can be especially oppressive, were encouraged to give glory to God through their infirmity. I had heard of some who suffered from mental problems in the Charterhouse, and there were times that I thought I might be losing my mind. When I mentioned this to the Prior, he listened to me, but didn't think there was anything unusual in what I told him. He encouraged me to be forgetful of self, and to offer myself whole-heartedly to the loving designs of Him Who is my Father. With many examples from Holy Scripture in mind, I began to think of God as my Father in a very real and personal way. I strove to put my trust in Him as a loving and docile son would.

For my relaxation, and to give me more needed exercise, the Novice Master presented me with a little book that introduced me to Christian yoga. They were mostly stretching and breathing exercises, and why the word "Christian" was added was a mystery to me. Using the techniques -- which were totally new to me -- every day for a half hour at a time I stretched, stood on my head, and lay flat on the tile floor of my cell. I practiced breath control while on the weekly walks. I did all this for more than a year, finding the exercises kept my body and soul in a state of clam anticipation as a preparation for prayer. I had to let up on the exercises after one day falling from a headstand and landing on the hard tile floor with a knee. The knee was sore for several days, and the pain would come back to haunt me years later.

Ever eager to know all that I could about our monastic tradition and the original inspiration of the Order, I read as many works of Carthusian writers that I could during those first years of my Carthusian life. Some Carthusians had been effusive writers, perhaps because they had nothing else to occupy themselves with in cell. I heard of monks whose cells were filled with manuscripts when they died. Most such writings were burned. Only serious scholars have heard of the Carthusian authors who lived during the Middle Ages, whose works were published by the Order for devotional or historical purposes. Many of the readings served simply to introduce me to the curiosities of Carthusian history.

I struggled through the Medieval Latin *Life of Christ* by Ludolf of Saxony, who died around 1340. I read some of the short works of Henry Kalkar, who died around 1408. He was credited with converting Gerhard Groot, who was involved in the same spiritual movement as the author of *The Imitation of Christ*. The works of Denys the Carthusian, who died in 1471, comprised forty-five volumes. I read through some of the volumes out of curiosity. Denys was called the "Ecstatic Doctor" for the great insight he had into spiritual things, though I can't say that his spiritual insights made much sense to me.

I read some of the works of Lanspergius, who died in 1539, and of Dom Innocent Le Masson, Prior of the Grand Chartreuse, who died in 1703. I was already familiar with his *Directory of Novices*, which I continued to use as a reference manual. I found the short anecdotes about monks and monasteries in the multi-volumed *Annals* of the Order interesting and insightful. Dom Le Couteulx, who died in 1709, was considered the official historian of the Order.

In the second year of my Novitiate I started my studies toward the priesthood. The studies were ordered toward a formation that was supposed to be both monastic and priestly, according to the directives of the official *Program of Studies* in effect in the Order. I studied a complete seminary course that would lead to the equivalent of a Bachelor's Degree in Philosophy. More emphasis was placed on materials and subject matter that would be useful in the monastery. We delved lightly into subjects and issues that were more suited to a ministerial priesthood.

Among the courses was a very thorough introductory History of Philosophy. I studied Logic, never quite mastering the putting together of all those A, B, Cs, and Ds. Epistemology was the study of scientific method, which pointed out the principles of analysis and synthesis. This I understood. I particularly liked the Cosmology course -- the philosophic consideration of the physical world. It gave me a lot of food for thought. Was what we saw with our eyes actually there? And how was it there? And I was always interested in Psychology. This course was a study of the inner workings of the human mind from the philosophic point of view. What was the basis of our thought?

I particularly liked Metaphysics, which dealt with the nature of reality, and Ontology -- the study of being in general. Both of these philosophical courses were an introduction to the Theology courses yet to come. They afforded a good basis for the study of the Supreme Being. My mind was filled with many questions: What is the nature of being? What does it mean when we say that something exists? Serious philosophical questions entered my mind: Who made me? What is the First Cause? Why am I here?

The philosophy courses followed the thinking St. Thomas Aquinas, who in turn followed closely on Aristotilian philosophy. It was not until the professor asked in class, "Do you think all this is true?" that the remote possibility that all this was a cleverly concocted intellectualization, ever entered my mind. Whether of not all the questions were answered, and whether or not the answers were true, it didn't really matter. The courses gave my mind a yardstick or a gage that I could use to measure ideas against. It was a firm foundation.

In addition to Philosophy, I studied Greek to the point of being able to enjoy the New Testament Scriptures in their original. I was able to read the Greek poets and historians. As a concession to the times we were living in, I had a course on the Church's social teachings. This course was in Spanish, and I had to find new Spanish words to express myself in class. Since many of the official documents of the Order were in French, I also learned to read French.

I completed four years of college seminary material in two years' time. At the end of my philosophical studies I wrote a well-received thesis in Latin on "the nature of beauty." I drew from St. Thomas and Aristotle, as well as from St. Augustine and Plato. I concluded that beauty consisted of the shining of the "form" on the material object. Beauty was something tangible and real, and not only a figment of imagination "in the eye of the beholder." The Prior had it professionally bound and placed in the monastery library.

The studies, including texts, classes, and oral exams, were in Latin. During my first year I was the only student; later we had one or two other students. For an hour, twice a week, I went to the cell of the appointed professor for a class, which was more like a tutorial session. At the end of each semester I had an oral exam in the presence of both the Prior and the Novice Master. I found that the best way to remember the material and to cope with the oral nature of the program was to memorize the text. I memorized pages and pages of Latin text that I would later spew out in class and in the Prior's office.

As a student I was allowed an hour in the morning and an hour or two in the afternoon for study. Many an afternoon, in the heat of the summer, I found myself dozing off at my study table, reciting verses of the Psalms I had memorized while praying the Office. It was forbidden to study outside of the appointed times, and especially during meals. My novitiate schedule was set out in great detail, and I had to apply for an exception with the Novice Master if I needed extra time for study or work.

I applied myself diligently to my studies and to my other occupations in the cell. It was all very helpful for maintaining physical and mental equilibrium. I knew, however, that it was not enough for me merely to be occupied in my cell and to persevere there in a commendable manner until death. A spirit of prayer was required. That was the essence of my calling. If a life with Jesus Christ and intimate union of my soul with God were lacking, faithfulness to schedules, ceremonies and regular observance would be of little profit. My life could justly be compared to a body without a soul -- a total and complete waste of time.

Towards the end of the second year of my novitiate, I was presented to the community again. This time they would vote on my admission to vows. On my part, I would have to affirm to the members of the community that I wanted to bind myself freely to the Carthusian Order.

Though this was a first and temporary profession of vows that would bind me for three years, the profession of vows had to be a free, personal commitment. It would be expressed in the public reading of the Formula of Profession. I would be totally dedicated to God in a firm and stable pact. I would make Him the exclusive center of my life.

On the day before I was to make my simple vows, I lay prostrate in the Chapter in the presence of the whole community and asked for "mercy." At the Prior's bidding, I stood and asked to be received for profession as "the most humble servant of all." The Prior then gave a sermon, during which I remained standing. I think the Prior had mercy on me and gave a short sermon, but I don't remember anything of what he said.

Being under scrutiny for admission to any organization is always stressful. The professed monks who voted on my admission made their judgment on what they had observed of me during community exercises, and also from what the Novice Master had related concerning my life in solitude and the novitiate community.

The Novice Master later told me that someone had asked whether I would be going to the Charterhouse in Vermont after profession. The house where you made your first profession is considered your house for your entire Carthusian career, even if you were sent elsewhere. You always had the right to return to the house of your profession, regardless of whatever else might happen to you.

I was approved for profession, and in the early morning hours of December 8, 1964, I made my first profession of vows as a Carthusian monk. At the end of the next three years, it would be for the Prior, with the favorable vote of the community, to admit me to solemn profession -- to permanent membership in the Carthusian brotherhood. But I was very happy to have come this far in my monastic journey. I had made it through the novitiate. I was a Carthusian at last! But the old monks used to say that it took at least ten years to become a true Carthusian; and so I was still in training, still under the general direction of the Novice Master.

On the day of my profession, some relics of the saints were placed on the altar. During the Conventual Mass the Novice Master put my new scapular of the professed monk on the choir stand in front of me. After the Gospel reading, I took the scapular and went to the sanctuary steps, where the Prior then blessed it and sprinkled it with holy water.

I knelt before the Prior and recited verses from Psalm 16: *Protect me, Oh God. I trust in you. You, Lord, are all I have.* The Prior took the black cape and the short novice scapular from me, saying: "May the Lord put off your old self with its past deeds." As he covered me with the long scapular of the professed, he continued: "and may He clothe you with the new man, created in God's image, whose justice and holiness are born of truth."

I read the formula of Profession that I had written a few days before in Latin:

> *I, Brother Benedict Mary, promise for three years stability, obedience, and conversion of my life, before God, His saints, and the relics belonging to this hermitage, which was built in honor of God, the Blessed Mary ever Virgin, and Saint John the Baptist, in the presence of Dom Luis de Arteche, Prior.*

I had a bright red pen in my cell and had used it for writing the first word, **"EGO"** (Latin for "I"). Both the Prior and Novice Master questioned me about this, apparently thinking I had written the letters in my blood! They knew that I was not above such an act. The certificate of my profession, signed by the Prior and me, would be kept in the archives of the monastery.

After I pronounced the vows, I gave the document to the Prior, and continued reciting the Psalm, ending with the "Glory to the Father ... Amen." I was so moved by the words of the Psalm -- that I had chosen the Lord for my inheritance, that I belonged entirely to Him -- that I had sobbed when I read the words, *You are all I have, and you give me all I need; my future is in your hands.* I returned to my place in choir, and the Mass continued. There was no clapping or any other sign of congratulations.

Vows are not in style today. They are easily broken, and people question why they were ever made in the first place. Why should I have had to -- or even wanted to -- make the vows? Already dead to sin and consecrated to God by my baptism, by profession I would be still more totally dedicated to the Father and set free from the world. By so doing I would be able to strive more directly and easily towards perfect love, which was the whole purpose of my life. Linked with the Lord in firm and stable pact, and sharing in the mystery of the Church's indissoluble union with Christ, I wanted to bear witness to the world of that new life won for us by Christ's redemption.

According to ancient monastic tradition, I did not make the traditional three vows of poverty, chastity, and obedience, nor did I have a vow of silence. The Carthusian formula promised stability, obedience, and the conversion of customs. I vowed to change my lifestyle in a radical way, which included the embracing of poverty and chastity. As for silence, there was really no need for a vow. The hermit monk had no one to talk to. Except in emergency situations, or other occasions allowed for by the Statutes, we refrained from speaking.

My surrender to God would not have been perfect unless I had the intention of faithfully persevering each and every day for the rest of my life. Before making such surrender, I had to consider whether I really wanted to yield myself to God forever. Before I entered the monastery I might have dreamed of a "contemplative life" marked by mystical raptures and heavenly consolations; but I soon learned that the everyday struggle was more common. By the vow of stability I was incorporated into a family chosen for me by God, in which I promised to settle down in mind and body. Totally dedicated to God, I resolved not only continue in that state, but also to strive to do so with ever greater perfection.

Stability also included keeping my body in one place, for I learned that it was not possible to keep my mind firmly fixed on God if I did not perseveringly keep my body in one place. If my mind was to draw near to Him in whom there was neither change nor shadow of alteration, it had to persevere unshakably to its undertaking. In my youthful enthusiasm, this idea of stability posed no problem. I understood the consequences of my actions and choices. I was willing to accept all the consequences. It was my calling.

From time to time I heard quiet rumors that all the Americans being trained in Europe would return to the United States soon. Dom Stephen had told me this as a fact when I made my retreats in Vermont, so that it was no real surprise. Because of the implications associated with the vow of stability, however, such rumors were kept very quiet.

While I was preparing to pronounce the vow of stability, certain scruples presented themselves. I was aware that I could be sent to the new American Charterhouse. But how could I vow to stay in the same place when I knew that I could not fulfill the vow? I took the problem to my confessor, who advised me that I should not worry about it. After all, he explained, my going to the United States was not yet a done deal; it was but a possibility. He pointed out that if I were sent to Vermont, it would be under obedience to the General Chapter, the supreme authority of the Order. Obedience took precedence over everything else.

In my heart I did indeed harbor hopes of returning to Vermont, to the greater silence and solitude of the mountains; but when the weeks and months turned into years, my expectations began to dim. The prospect of remaining in Spain for the rest of my life seemed like a distinct possibility. Through all the problems and doubts, I had been intensely happy in my Spanish Charterhouse during the first two or three years, to the point that one of the monks called me *felicito Benito* -- happy little Benedict. The intensity of the happiness diminished with the passing of time, and I had become resigned to remaining in Spain for the rest of my life.

The more sublime the path of life set before the monk, the more easily he could fall away from it, not only by obvious transgressions, but also by the drag of ordinary routine. I was now clothed with the cowl of the professed, which symbolized my complete conversion of life and total consecration to God. But as the saying goes, "The habit does not make the monk." I knew that to persevere would require constant recourse to Him to remain steadfast in the combat. I knew too that God gives His grace to the humble; and to further remind myself of this, I was ready to make a solemn promise to keep my nose to the grindstone of my new life as a professed Carthusian.

In reality, the continuing quality of the Carthusian way of life depended more on the fidelity of each individual to the life's demands, rather than on the multiplication of laws, or the updating of customs, or even the zeal of Priors. It was not enough to obey the commands of superiors and observe faithfully the letter of the Statutes, unless, led by the Spirit, I savored the things of the Spirit. I had been placed in solitude from the very beginning of my new life, though under the careful eye of the Novice Master. Now I would be left more to my own counsel and had to be responsible in this undertaking.

I was no longer a child in the Carthusian monastery. I could not let myself be tossed to and fro and carried about with every new wind or novelty that might come by. Rather I would be expected to seek out what would please God, and do it of my own free will, all the while enjoying that liberty of God's children. I would in the end have to render an account of my life before God.

As for poverty, and the more important spirit of poverty, the vow of conversion of customs reminded me not to model myself on the behavior of the world, especially concerning material things. Living under the spirit of poverty meant sometimes doing without what I thought I absolutely needed. It also meant doing with what was available or provided, even if those necessities were not perfect. It meant adaptation and accommodation. I was trained that too eagerly to seek, and too readily to accept, the comforts of modern life was altogether opposed to the monastic lifestyle. Monks have ever believed that novelty always called for more novelty; and so all novelty and passing fads were avoided as totally alien to the monastic life.

In the desert, where men are tried and their faith purified, the Father was leading me on a path of dis-possession which questioned all logic of "having" -- of being successful, of finding fleeting happiness in material things. I had received a clear calling to the religious life, and it was my goal to respond to it. I did not decide this all by myself; it was a gift I received. Nor was it ever a simple personal choice that I made. It was a true love story, a story of two. It was out of love that Jesus invited certain men to follow Him in solitude, in order for them to live with Him and contemplate the splendor of His face. I had received that invitation and was captivated by it.

Since the disciple, if he wished to follow Christ, was called to renounce all things, before I made my profession I had to part with everything I possessed, or might possibly possess in the future. If I so desired, I could have carried this to the extreme of making a binding will. Not having any tangible property to dispose of, and not expecting any future windfalls, I saw no need to have a will. The monastic community cared for all my needs. The prospect of being poor and promising to remain poor did not affect me in any great way. Since my days at home on the hill, I had learned to appreciate the little things in life, and felt a certain pride in being able to reject the possessions many people seemed to need to be happy. I had no use for wealth and riches.

When I received a small income tax refund the first year I was in Spain, I duly handed it over to the Prior. And when Aunt Mae passed away in 1966, she left me a few hundred dollars in her will. To receive the inheritance I had to go to the U.S. Consulate in Seville to have the proper papers notarized. Though grateful for Aunt Mae's remembering me, I felt that the whole thing of collecting the inheritance was a nuisance. I also surrendered this money to the Prior who put it into a special trust account for me.

The Carthusian Order has always held that the resources granted by Divine Providence were not given so that the individual monks might seek the good things of life. As every Carthusian knew, it was by getting rid of burdens, and not by loading ourselves with them, that we more easily traveled toward God. Like the monks who had gone before me, I wanted to free myself from all possessions. Having given up everything, I might then hope to share in the way of life of the first Carthusian Fathers.

Among the resources granted by Divine Providence for the financial security of the Carthusian Order, are a number of liqueurs appropriately called *Chartreuse*. These liqueurs are made only by the monks and are based on a manuscript recipe given the monks in the seventeenth century. The manuscript was titled "An Elixir of Long Life," and by 1737, an exhaustive study of the manuscript had unraveled the complexities of the recipe. The *Chartreuse Elixir* was born. This *Elixir Vegetal de la Grande Chartreuse* is still made by the monks following the ancient recipe, using all natural plants, herbs, and other botanicals, suspended in a wine alcohol base.

In the early years of the twentieth century, when the Carthusian monks were expelled from France as part of the secular government's policy of confiscating all religious property, the Brothers in charge of making the liqueurs were sent to Spain to set up a distillery there. When the Carthusians were allowed to return to France, a distillery was reopened in the south of France to operate during the summer months. The one in Spain was in use during the winter months for many years.

According to the Carthusian lore that I learned in Spain, the monks of the Grand Chartreuse community collected some of the hundred and thirty herbs, plants, and flowers from which the *Chartreuse* was made. They were crushed and blended and eventually taken to the distillery to be mixed under the direction of only three monks, who supervised the process, from mixing and distillation, through the ageing process. The most commonly known *Chartreuse* is green in color, from which originated the color we call "chartreuse." There is also a yellow *Chartreuse*, which is milder in flavor than the green.

A large portion of the proceeds from the sale of the *Chartreuse* was devoted to various works of charity in France and all over the world. The proceeds also assisted in paying for the maintenance of various Charterhouses and the building of new ones. The profits had no influence at all on the secluded, poor, and austere life of the monks of the Grande Chartreuse, or of any of the other Charterhouses. But the sale of the *Chartreuse* liqueurs allowed the Order the funds necessary to survive in the commercial world, besides affording the monks the ability to dedicate their lives free of worry to prayer and meditation.

By embracing a life of voluntary poverty with the freedom of God's sons, by accepting the hardships and anxieties of this life, and by renouncing my own will, I promised to follow in the steps of Jesus along with my fellow Carthusians. In accordance with monastic tradition I followed Christ in His fast in the desert, treating my body hard and making it obey me, so that my mind might burn with longing for God. Mortification of the flesh and the desires of the flesh was part of my profession of poverty and of obedience.

With my fellow Carthusians, and following the practice of the ancient hermits and monks, I practiced mortification of the flesh primarily to be freed from the tendencies of the lower nature. I knew that I would be able to follow the Lord more readily and cheerfully by doing penance for my own sins and the sins of everyone else in the world. I had a humble and small part in the saving work of Christ, who redeemed the human race from the oppressive bondage of sin by offering Himself to the Father in sacrifice.

The desert fathers saw the satisfaction of sexual desires, the "demon of fornication," as leading to the social entanglements of marriage, family, work, and other responsibilities in this world. Sexuality had to be renounced because it led back to the social world of commitments, attachments, and distractions from which the hermits had escaped. Besides, sexuality was for procreation, which was good in itself, since it was -- as the word suggests -- a helping to create, a participation in God's work. The emphasis was on creation. It was a calling in itself.

Neither before my entering the monastery, nor after my entrance, did I feel called to procreate; nor did I have any desire to experience sexual relations. I consciously and intentionally left my physical sexuality lie dormant. In a singular way it was the most suitable means by which I could dedicate myself with undivided heart to the service of

God and the works of the apostolate, however hidden that apostolate might be.

I valued the chastity that I professed for the sake of the kingdom of heaven as a gift of unsurpassing worth. Chastity and celibacy freed my heart in a particular way, enabling me to cling more easily to God with undivided love. It called to mind the hidden nuptial union by which the Church has Christ as her only Spouse.

Living under chastity meant more than merely abstaining from sexual relations. I still had to deal with my sexuality. We hardly ever talked about it, nor did I feel any urge to talk about it, unless under the seal of confession. For the most part we were left to our own resources to come to terms with our sexuality. I was a man, and related to the world outside myself as a male. Through my theological and philosophical studies I learned to live my sexuality on a higher plane than the physical.

Without having the need for sexual relations, I truly began to feel that I was father to a multitude of souls, most of whom I might never meet in the course of my life. I felt this very deeply. As a true father who loved his children, I sensed that I had many individual souls under my care. It was true that the chastity that I professed freed my heart in a unique fashion so that it became inflamed with love for God and for all souls.

I was consciously fulfilling my role in the People of God by being a living sacrifice acceptable to God. I knew that I could not do this if I allowed any relaxation of life to creep in, or if I entertained distractions of mind and useless conversation. I couldn't give myself to vain cares and trivial occupations. I had heard that if he were not careful and watchful, a monk in cell might become captive to some miserable anxiety arising from love of self; and most anxieties arose from an inordinate love of self, an excessive concern for one's self. Any of those things could separate me from the Son of God -- from Him Who is life itself and the Supreme Sacrifice.

Striving to be faithful to what I had promised, I strained onward, putting my faith in the words of the Lord, and trusting in God's help rather than presuming on my own strength. I trusted in Mary, who by her humility and her virginity merited to become the Mother of God. I practiced mortification and custody of the senses on walk days or trips outside of the monastic enclosure. Women could not be admitted within the cloister. On our weekly walks the Novice Master avoided going through places where females might be present. When we spoke with women, we observed a monastic modesty.

Once in a while I saw glimpses of heavily clothed women working in the fields on the hill above the monastery. Sometimes when I served Mass in the chapel adjacent to the guesthouse females would attend. When riding on a bus or train I would sometimes find myself staring in detached awe at what were to me strange and novel female creatures. But there was no desire to take the matter any further, and I left the images at the monastery gate, or at the entrance to my cell.

As a monk dedicated to God, I refused to be influenced by those doctrines that scorned celibacy, perfect continence, and mortification of the senses, as being impossible, or harmful to human development. With my brother monks I was reminded by the Statutes and our Superiors that chastity was guarded more securely when true brotherly love flourished in the common life of the community. Together we trusted in Mary, the Mother of God and our mother.

I was forbidden to indulge in any penitential practices over and above those prescribed by the Statutes without the Prior's knowledge and approval. No unauthorized fasting, no flagellations, no wearing pointed objects next to your flesh. The Prior would probably not have allowed such things; and in reality I was never fond of those additions either. But if the Prior wished me to have some additional food or sleep, or anything else, I had no right to refuse or resist. By resisting the Prior, I would be resisting God, whose place he held towards me.

None of the monastic observances, in fact, would profit me without the blessing of obedience. Without the blessing of the superiors, my life might have no value in God's eyes. Indeed, by the vow of obedience, I retained no power over anything at all. This meant not only my activity, which was secondary in a contemplative community, but everything to do with myself, without the permission of the Prior. In a very real way I was relinquishing my personality for the greater good of the People of God.

I knew that all who wished to live according to a religious rule had to observe obedience with great zeal. In the measure that our Carthusian way of life was more exacting and more austere than other ways, I had to observe obedience all the more ardently and carefully. If the blessing of obedience were lacking, my labors might well go unrewarded. Obedience was better than any sacrifice. Being the very serious person that I am, I could admit no exceptions. I felt that every detail of my life made a difference if offered under the blessing of obedience.

St. Benedict called the monastery a "school of the Lord's service." The lessons I learned in the monastery were designed to lead me to God; and the greatest of these was that a person comes to God through obedience. I learned that the greatest of all the virtues was to do the will of another rather than your own. Obedience was the act of faith, hope, and love that joined man to God.

Any act contrary to obedience might separate me from God, just as Adam's disobedience separated all of us from God's favor. It was through the supreme act of obedience of Jesus on the cross that man again regained God's grace. It was up to the individual to unite himself to God's will, to know Him, and love Him, and be loved in return.

I knew from the very beginning of my Carthusian life, and even from those all-too-brief days spent in Vermont, that obedience would be hard for me. I was used to doing what I wanted to do, when and how I wanted to do it. I did not look forward to having somebody constantly telling me what to do, how to do it, and when to do it. Perhaps there was a touch of anarchy in my blood; or perhaps I was jealously guarding my own will, as most men do. Obedience was for children and animals, not for grown men.

Through it all I never thought of running away. The thought of telling the Superiors what they could do with the monastery and the Carthusian life never even entered my mind. I followed the Statutes, and did what I knew I was supposed to do. I did what the Superiors asked me to do, not in an attempt to please men, but trying always to follow the example of Jesus. He came to do the will of His Father, and learned obedience through what He suffered. Following His example, I subjected myself by profession to the Prior, as God's representative.

I became so much a stranger to the things of this world that I had no power over anything -- not even myself -- without the permission of either the Prior or the Novice Master. It gave me great peace of mind. I submitted with a joyful heart. I didn't have to plan anything or make any important decisions. All I had to do was to consult the Novice Master or the Prior if I had a question or doubt. I sometimes passed long periods of time waiting to see the Superior to consult with him on small details.

Now a Carthusian monk under vows, I continued, nevertheless, to be under the general direction of the Master of Novices for the next three years. My life in the cell remained virtually unchanged, and any changes that did occur related mostly to the communal aspect of my Carthusian existence. Perhaps the greatest of those changes, and the one that would have the most far-reaching consequences in my life as a Carthusian, was my being asked to assume the role of Chanter -- a kind of choirmaster.

The Carthusian chant underwent a sort of restoration in the mid 1960s after Vatican II. The musical experts of the Order drew up a *Method of Chant*. Copies were distributed to the various houses of the Order, and everyone was expected to make an effort to conform. As a novice I was instructed in the updated "method of chant," and encouraged not to neglect this study when I left the novitiate.

I especially loved singing the psalms. For a long time, as a postulant and novice, I carried a little piece of paper to choir on which I wrote a few words to remind me of the general meaning of each psalm. I looked at it when we were bowed over singing the "Glory be" after each psalm. Later on I concentrated on key words like *misericordia* (mercy), or *auxilium* (help), or *Domine* (Lord).

Gregorian chant was an integral part of the liturgy in choir. We were exhorted to take part in the Divine Office "with vigor and purity," so as to stand before the Lord with reverence and a ready will, not lazily nor half asleep, not sparing our voices nor clipping our words, but with virility, letting the Holy Spirit inspire both heart and voice as we sang. We were exhorted to observe the proper manner of chanting, singing in the sight of the most Holy Trinity and the holy angels, penetrated with fear of God, and aflame with a deep desire for Him.

"Simplicity and measure" were to so regulate the chant that its hallmark would be "a gravity that would encourage the spirit of devotion." We were to sing and praise the Lord with both mind and voice, entering into the sentiments with which the psalms and canticles were written. In the lessons, the psalms, and the chant in general, the accentuation and the interrelationship of the words were not to be neglected. The correct phrasing of the words was of the greatest help for grasping and relishing the meaning of the text.

The ideal way of singing the psalmody was to avoid making the verses either too long or drawn out, or too quick and shortened. There was a happy medium. It was to be rendered with a voice that was "full, lively and clear," so that everyone could sing with devotion and attention, without any shouting. The idea and ideal was to combine depth of feeling with diligence in execution.

We were to make a "substantial pause" in the middle of the psalm verse. At the beginning, the middle and the end of the verse we were to start and finish together. No one was to presume to start before the others or to sing faster than the others. While we sang together and paused together, we were always listening to the voices of the others.

Conforming to the new method was difficult for some of the older monks, and there was some resistance among the older monks in Jerez. Younger and more docile monks were named chanters in some of the houses, and Jerez was no exception. A monk who had been a musician in the world, and who was an expert in interpreting the new method of chant, was sent from another Spanish charterhouse to help reform the chant in Jerez. The Prior asked both Dom Hugh and myself to be chanters, under the general direction of the new chant expert. Dom Hugh was wise enough to respectfully decline; because I had always been interested in praising God through song, I accepted the responsibility, only to regret it later.

The typical community, like ours in Jerez, was divided into two choirs. Each monk had his place in the choir according to length of time or status in the community. The Prior always had the first place in the right choir; the most ancient monk was first in the left choir, etc. The two choirs faced each other on opposite sides of the church and sang verses of the psalms back and forth in alternation.

In his own choir, the chanter raised or lowered the pitch of the chant, as seemed expedient, so that all could sing without strain. He could also slow the chant, or speed it up, if he thought it was necessary. Both chanters normally accommodated to each other's corrections, and when they were present, no one else was to correct the choir except the Prior.

After a few weeks, I realized that being chanter was not as pleasant an experience as I had thought it might be. It was my first introduction to politics in the monastic community as well, since I later found out that the chanter whom I replaced was not well thought of by the Prior. The Prior thought of him as lazy and un-cooperative. My taking his place was the Prior's way of telling him that "enough was enough," but I didn't know that at the time. The community accepted me in the role of chanter for a while, until I began to make corrections.

The chanter had the sometimes-difficult task of gently and tactfully correcting those individual monks who sang either too slowly or too quickly, or otherwise than was laid down by the *Method*. This was preferably done outside the choir. Still under temporary vows, I did not have full and easy communication with the permanent members of the community. I was not able to "gently and tactfully" give corrections in private outside of the choir. I didn't have the opportunity to ask some of the professed if they knew they were constantly singing off key, or more slowly, or too loudly.

All the corrections I made had to be made in public in the choir. I did not like being in that position, and told the Prior that I would like to be removed from the position; but he would not hear of it. Being corrected without knowing why obviously did not sit well with some of the older monks. I began to experience resistance. Some of the monks gave up singing or sang in a hardly audible voice. This placed greater pressure on me to keep singing and to sing louder. I began to experience sharp and continuous headaches from the efforts I constantly made in choir to carry the chant sometimes by myself.

I was trying too hard, and there was a growing tension in the community. Although the Prior had full confidence in me and gave me the necessary authority, some of the monks wanted things to return to where they had been. In the meantime, my prayer life was suffering from my putting too much attention on the technicalities of the chant. I was losing sight of the prayerful contemplation that was supposed to be aided by the chant.

The songs we sang were designed to raise our minds to the contemplation of the eternal realities as our voices blended into one cry of jubilation before God our Creator. I was quickly losing sight of the prayerful ideal. I was concentrating too much on the technique to my own detriment and the community was becoming tense. After a few months of experimentation the Prior relieved me of the duties of chanter. But the headaches would continue for many years to come.

The Carthusian Order was and is totally dedicated to contemplation. My principal duty as a Carthusian monk was to maintain a strict separation from the world so as to dedicate myself completely to God without any distraction. This separation was a seemingly negative thing, but it was guarded in a very positive way. Nothing else mattered. As part of my separation, I could never leave the monastery to visit my family. There was no going to funerals or weddings. There were no vacations.

For all its poverty, austerity, and physical restrictions, it was a life of great freedom. I often felt that I was on a perpetual vacation. I didn't have "to go out to work." My job was being there, and this meant that for most of the day I could be alone and work alone in my cell. I could be alone with God. I was not interested in visits or visiting. I wanted to be left alone as much as possible.

I wanted every word that I uttered and each one of my smallest actions to give testimony that I lived, breathed and thought God to the exclusion of everything else. I did not want to be a fanatic, but I became obsessed with God's presence. The thought of God dominated me, and I related all of my actions back to Him with a logical rationality. I tried consciously to keep my emotions in check, even when talking about the marvels and wonders of God's creation and providence.

As the weeks turn into months, and the months turn into years, any feelings of missing my family and relatives began to fade and disappear. As it was for most Carthusians, from the very beginning of my life in the monastery it was my express and conscious intention to be dead to everything and everyone in the past -- just as those things and persons were dead to me. When I passed through the gates of the monastery, I had passed into another life. I didn't look for any contact either by letter or in person.

Soon after I began my monastic life, Nana passed away of a heart attack. She had had a heart attack a few years earlier, and had never fully recovered. Uncle Charlie went to live with Mom on the hill until he passed away. Aunt Mae passed away in 1966. I don't remember any strong feelings about any of their passings. I don't remember wanting to attend their funerals. I knew I didn't have to be there physically. I knew God was in full control. All things happened for the good. I didn't see any reason to ask why things happened. God wanted it so, and that was that. I had left everything in His hands when I entered the Charterhouse.

As a general rule I could write to my family three or four times a year. The Prior or Novice Master read all incoming and outgoing mail. The only letter writing I did was to my immediate family in Newfield. After two or maybe three letters the first year, I found that there really was not a whole lot to relate. I lived in silence and almost complete solitude. There wasn't much happening in my environment. In my letters I mentioned a few Spanish words relating to things we knew at home, I told of my garden and of my health. I did not have the need to talk of many things. I sent picture postcards with my letters: an aerial view of the monastery, and a picture of the Charterhouse Patroness, *Nuestra Senora de la Defension.*

While guests were rare at the Carthusian monastery, I was permitted to receive visitors if any presented themselves and had a reason for visiting me. I did not seek to have visitors, and the only visitors I would have wanted would have been immediate family members. On one occasion, however, the Prior came to my cell with two American priests who were on vacation in Spain. I was surprised to see them. I showed them my garden, and how I worked in it; but I had the impression that they were not too interested. They stayed for a few minutes.

On another day the Prior brought a group of naval officers from the nearby naval base of Rota who had come for a visit. They told me things weren't too good back home in the States at that time, without going into any details. They thought I was much better off in a Spanish monastery than back home on the streets. I think I was more of a curiosity than anything else to the Americans who visited the Charterhouse. I was an American living in a Spanish Carthusian monastery -- a rare thing.

One summer afternoon Dr. Davidson and his wife visited Jerez. They wanted to see the Spanish Charterhouse, and visited with the Prior for a time. But I think they were also interested in looking over those monks who might be living on their property in Vermont. I was taken by complete surprise when the Prior came to my cell and told me that we had guests from Vermont. We had a very pleasant visit, and I think I passed the test. I was especially impressed by the graciousness of Mrs. Davidson.

As part of our total separation from the outside world, I was exempt by the Church from all pastoral ministries. To explain this exemption, *The Statutes* appealed to the Gospel image of Martha and Mary, the sisters of Lazarus:

Let Martha have her active ministry, praiseworthy indeed, but not without worry and anxiety; however, let her put up with her sister as she follows in the steps of Christ in stillness, knowing that He is God; she purifies her spirit, prays in the depths of her soul, seeks to hear what God may speak within her; and tastes and sees -- in the measure possible, as in a dark mirror -- how good the Lord is.

She pours forth prayer both for Martha and for all who, like her, labor actively in the service of the Lord. In this Mary has not only a most just judge but also a very faithful advocate -- the Lord Himself -- who deigned not only to defend, but even to praise her way of life, saying, "Mary has chosen the best part, which shall not be taken from her." With these words He excused her from involving herself in the solicitude and agitation of Martha, however pious and excellent they might be.

I had already begun to experience a little of "the benefit and divine delight" that solitude and the silence of the hermitage could bring to those who loved them. But it was not solely my own advantage that I had in mind by embracing a hidden life. I did not intend to abandon mankind; on the contrary, by devoting myself exclusively to God, I knew that I was exercising a special function in the Church, where things seen were ordered to things unseen, where all exterior activity ultimately sprang from, and led to, the contemplation of God. I would have found life in the Charterhouse too difficult if I had intended or experienced anything different.

If I truly lived in union with God, my mind and heart would necessarily open up to embrace the whole universe and the mystery of Christ that saves it. Apart from all, to all I felt united. I experienced this union at least once while I was kneeling in my oratory after Vespers. I saw myself engulfed in flames -- flames all around me -- and people screaming for help. Was this a vision of hell or of purgatory? Had I somehow been transported to a war zone? Were they calling to me for help? The experience lasted only several minutes, and I never knew what had happened, nor did I mention it to anyone. In my heart I felt that this was in some way a confirmation of the effectiveness of my hidden vocation.

I always knew that I could not attain any measure of peace and happiness in the monastery except at the cost of a stern battle. I could reach it only by living austerely in fidelity to the law of the cross, and by willingly accepting the tribulations by which God would try me "as gold in the furnace." I knew I would have to be cleansed in "the night of patience." Through my journey through the desert I was consoled and sustained by meditation on the Scriptures.

Through the Scriptures, the Holy Spirit was leading me into the depths of my soul, where I would be ready not only to serve God, but also to cleave to Him in love and forgetfulness of self. As a beginner, I looked for consolations in my prayer life. I concentrated on achieving certain experiences and raising certain emotions in my life of prayer; but with time I learned that these experiences and emotions were ephemeral and meant little. Dedication to prayer was what mattered most, and after that I stopped looking for consolations in my prayer life.

Love became my obsession. I read and re-read and memorized St. Paul's description of love to the Corinthians (I, 13: 4-7):

> *Though I speak the languages of men and of angels, if I have no love, my speech is no more than a noisy gong or a clanging bell. Love is patient and kind; it is not jealous or conceited or proud; love is not ill mannered or selfish or irritable; love does not keep a record of wrongs; love is not happy with evil, but is happy with the truth.*

Growing in love was what the vow of conversion of customs was all about. Some monks were prone to intellectualize this thing of brotherly love, without really advancing in it. I did not want to fall into such a trap. I realized that brotherly fellowship between men could never be perfect unless it was based on mutual esteem. If I lived in the house of God, and wanted to remain in God's house, I had to bear witness to the love that came from God. I made a sincere effort to hold my brothers in high regard.

In December of 1968, I had to decide whether or not the Carthusian monastery would be my place for the rest of my life. I sat for hours watching the dark purple and gray sky as the sun set over the Bay of Cadiz, all the while pondering to myself, "Did I really want to do this? Should I remain in the Charterhouse?" My mind hashed and rehashed the pros and cons in computer-like fashion. The pros won out in the end.

I decided that I did indeed love God so much as to give my life to Him in a definitive and exclusive way. I felt that He had chosen me in His love for me. He had called me and I had accepted beforehand the sacrifice I had to make. But in the end, neither God nor man could force me to make my solemn, permanent vows. I did it of my own free will.

As was customary, I went on retreat in preparation for my vows. During my first few months in the Charterhouse I had been surprised when I learned that Carthusians had an annual retreat! But a Carthusian's whole life was a retreat! What need was there for a separate or additional retreat? I learned that a retreat meant not attending recreations with the community. It meant taking a breather from the ordinary occupations in cell like studies and normal reading activity. I was to devote myself with greater zeal to the quiet of cell and recollection. I had more time for prayerful reflection. Each year for eight days I was to do this, preferably on the anniversary of my first profession.

The Novice Master gave me a little book composed by a Carthusian that could be used specifically for retreats. I remember some of the phrases: "The Carthusian vocation is to live to die, and to die to live eternally. The cell is a tomb in which you prepare for death." In all actuality the entire life of a Carthusian monk was a preparation for death, for that perfect union with God that the monk so desperately and wholeheartedly sought. I had to consider these things carefully, because the commitment I was about to make was a permanent, lifetime commitment.

If I remained in the Charterhouse I would never be canonized as a saint; but the thought of canonization really never entered my mind anyway. Carthusians had never paid much attention to the apparent sanctity of their members. We knew it more important to be saints than to be called saints. *Sanctos facere, non patefacere.* "To make saints, not to publicize them" -- was one of the sayings developed over the centuries.

The Carthusian Order has never taken steps to procure the canonization of their saints. To be canonized by the Church would mean that the Church would set up the solitary and silent Carthusian as an example of life for the average Catholic to imitate. There was, however, nothing "average or common" about the Carthusian life and the calling!

When a monk of exceptional virtue died, the highest public honor he received in the Order was the comment, *"laudabiliter vixit."* (He lived in a praiseworthy manner. He did a good job.) This was the equivalent of a Carthusian canonization. And even with the "laudibiliter vixit," someone who had lived with the deceased monk would perhaps have pointed out some character flaw or little slipup.

As a Carthusian I knew that I would not have the personal distinction of a grave marked with my own name. I would be laid away in the cemetery under a plain unmarked cross, and vanish into anonymity. One old monk put it very aptly when he said, "A Carthusian is supposed to appear on the scene of life and disappear without leaving any trace of his existence."

My body would be buried in the cemetery in the central cloister. Clothed in the habit with the hood over the face, it would be lowered into the ground on a wooden plank without the benefit of a coffin. When all the burial sites in the cemetery were filled, they would start over from the beginning, digging a new hole and perhaps placing the bones of the previously interred monk reverently alongside my body.

I loved the Carthusian life. I had proven to myself and the other monks that I was able to live the solitary life. The cell did not "vomit me out," as it had a tendency to do to those who were not chosen. Few were called and fewer still were chosen. I lived this solitude not for it's own sake, but as a privileged means of attaining intimacy with God. There was a great sense of joy in my heart and soul. I was at peace. I had a sense of eager anticipation, and at the same time felt the jitters that most couples must feel when they are nearing the time of their marriage.

The community voted to admit me to full and permanent membership in the Order. I wrote my vows again, inserting the Latin words *"in perpetuum."*

I, Brother Benedict Mary, promise in perpetuity stability, obedience, and conversion of my life, before God, his saints, and the relics belonging to this hermitage, which was built in honor of God, the Blessed Mary ever Virgin, and Saint John the Baptist, in the presence of Dom Luis, Prior.

The vows would be "solemn vows," which meant that they would bind me for the rest of my life. Only the Pope could free me from their obligations. The profession ceremony took place during the community Mass. After the Gospel reading, I went to the center of the sanctuary steps, and sang the verse: "Sustain me, Lord, as you have promised, that I may live; disappoint me not in my hope." I sang the verse three times, each time in a higher tone of voice. The community replied in the same way and on the same tones.

Then the members of the community prayed for me in silence, while I went down both the right choir and the left choir, kneeling before each monk, saying, "Pray for me, Father." After this I stood before the altar, read the Formula of Profession, kissed the altar, and placed the profession document on it as an offering. I then knelt before the Prior, who gave me a blessing and sprinkled me with holy water to end the ceremony.

All this passed in a blur for me. My solemn, permanent vows were a logical conclusion and final culmination of the simple, temporary vows I had made three years earlier. I was now a full and permanent member of the Carthusian family. I felt complete, secure in the knowledge that this was where I was supposed to be. I belonged to God exclusively and forever as a Carthusian monk. I was happy.

On that December morning I put on the scapular of the solemn professed. In my daily routine I was no longer under the direction of the Novice Master. I was on my own, having to answer only to God and the Prior, who was His visible representative. I went to the community recreations on Sundays and holidays, and took the weekly walks with the solemnly professed. Several of them had preceded me to solemn vows during the past six years. Others I came to know and to talk freely with for the first time since I had come to Jerez.

Through our conversations at the weekly Sunday recreations, I learned a great deal about the Spanish Civil War (1936-39). It was the topic that invariably came up in our conversations, more than any other. I was fascinated by some of the stories, listening attentively as the men I had lived with for the past seven or eight years revealed some of their almost unbelievable experiences.

Many of the older monks had fought in the war on the side of General Franco's Nationalist forces. They told many interesting and exciting stories. Several, including the Prior, had been in prison; several had had personal communication with Franco. I was told that one of the Brothers had been in the "Blue Division" that had been sent by Franco to Russia to fight on the side of the Nazis against the Communists. All had been pro-Franco nationalists and in favor of the monarchy and decidedly against the atheists and Communist legions.

Except for having no further formal contact with the Novice Master, my daily life changed little. If anything, it became more solitary. But I did not feel lonely, for I had God to converse with, and my brothers were only a door or two away. From the community library I chose my own reading material. If I needed anything, I went directly to the Procurator or the Prior. The Prior continued to keep a kindly and careful watch over my life in cell and the state of my soul, all from a respectful distance.

The next step in my Carthusian career would be ordination to the priesthood. I could not be ordained before making solemn vows and completing the course of studies. I had already begun theological studies with Dom Gerardo, who was also the Prefect of Studies. I followed a program of studies established by the Carthusian Order and approved by the authorities in Rome. The local Bishop also had to be informed of the course of studies.

The program of studies included all aspects of morality and Church law, delving more deeply into some subject matter more than others according to its usefulness for the solitary monastic life. It was a six-year course, leading to the equivalent of a Bachelor's and Master's Degree in Theological Studies. I had a particular interest in Church Law and Moral Theology, and was fortunate to have Dom Gerardo, the former Jesuit, as a Professor.

After solemn profession, some monks received a job or "office" within the community. It might be Sacristan, Novice Master, Procurator, Cantor, or something else determined by the Prior. Most Carthusians were unwilling of themselves to exercise, or much less actively seek, an office, and I was certainly no exception. But I think because I was ultimately destined to be one of the "Founding Fathers" of the American Charterhouse, the Prior determined that I should not only be well formed as a Carthusian, but also be experienced in some of the more useful jobs in the community.

I had no desire to be the Sacristan, who had charge of the monastery church and chapels. He saw that everything concerned with the divine worship was properly prepared and carried out. It was he who rang the bell summoning

161

the others to prayer. In a way he was a slave not only to the liturgy, but also to the clock. The Sacristan was the only monk who had permission to carry a pocket watch. The rest of us followed the chimes of the church clock and the ringing of the bell.

The Procurator was in charge of the Brothers and material aspects of the monastery. He celebrated Mass for the Brothers every morning and distributed their work for the day. If a choir monk needed anything, he went to the Procurator, who would, as the title suggests, "procure" the requested item. He might also consult with the Prior and deny the request. It was the duty of the Procurator to look after guests, to meet them on their arrival, and to briefly visit with them.

There was a very fine Procurator in Jerez, and he had one of the Brothers for an assistant. Consequently, I had nothing to do with this office. Besides, for various reasons, the Prior was advised not to appoint the younger monks to this office. This was also true of the office of Vicar, who was the Prior's right hand man and substitute when the Prior was not in attendance at community functions. He was the normal Father Confessor for the monks.

Soon after solemn profession, however, I was appointed Librarian. I was happy with this appointment. I had always liked books, and had some experience with library work with the Legion of Mary in Brooklyn. I set into my work with eagerness and energy, dusting and rearranging the books on the library shelves. I placed some of the more obscure and unread books in a less conspicuous location, and began to prepare a card catalogue of the entire collection.

I had to leave my cell, usually in the afternoon, sometimes after dinner. I was not entirely pleased with this, and tried to be as solitary as possible while out of the cell. I was able to catalogue the entire library collection in a period of about three months. All during this time I kept the library clean and neat. After completing the card catalogue, I stopped at the library after Vespers on most days to see that everything was in good order.

The monastery library was well stocked with the works of theological and spiritual writers, as "the continual food of our souls." Some of the books were old and valuable. I kept careful track of them. The Prior chose new books and additions to the collection. If an individual monk wanted to read a certain book that was not available in the monastery library, he could present his request to the Prior, who would either obtain the book, or deny the request.

Throughout the Middle Ages the Carthusians were famous for copying books and manuscripts with great diligence, with the intention of preaching the Word of God by the work of their hands, since they could not do so with their mouths. With the invention of the printing press, there was no need for this work. However, when I entered the Order, one of the occupations helpful for the community was the placing of musical notations into the choir books, so as to adapt them to the *Method of Chant.*

When the choir books were originally printed, there were no Gregorian musical notations, such as, for example, dots after notes indicating the note had to be doubled. There were no lines over certain notes to indicate that the sound should be prolonged. Many vertical bars that had indicated pauses had to be crossed out. This re-doing of the choir book musical notations required a great deal of work. It was extremely helpful to the community members for all of the books to be notated in the same way. It prevented us from making a scene by not pausing where everyone else in the choir did, or not prolonging a note where the note should have been prolonged.

After solemn profession I continued to be involved with the chant, and was moved from one side of the choir to the other as the Prior directed. I was sometimes in the position of head chanter; sometimes I was assistant chanter. Sometimes I annoyed even the Prior by insisting on raising or lowering the tone, or by attempting to make other corrections in the chant.

The Prior once remarked that I was more interested in the chant than in the prayer that was supposed to be assisted by the chant. This gave me a great deal to think about; and from then on, I concentrated more on praying rather than on the technique of chanting the prayer. I attempted to create more of a continuous balance, keeping in mind the saying attributed to Saint Augustine: *He who sings well prays twice.*

In addition to working in the garden and the daily chant practice in my cell, I taught myself to bind books the old-fashioned way. While working in the library, I sometimes came across books that were in need of repair. Instead of sending them out to be repaired, I asked the Prior about doing it myself. He obtained a pamphlet and a few basic bookbinding tools, including a sewing frame, an edge trimmer, and a press. In a short time I had taught myself the basics of sewing, binding and covering books. Several of the Fathers gave me books to practice on, and perhaps to test my ability. After some primitive first efforts, I became pretty good at it.

As for the weekly walks, because there were no novices, for a time Dom Gerardo graciously offered to walk with Dom Hugo and me on longer walks than those taken by the older or less athletic monks. But after a time our long walks became too much for him too, and Dom Gerardo excused himself from further walks with us. Dom Hugo and I, with the Prior's permission, continued to take longer walks together without any leader. We were both pleased at this, because we both needed more exercise than some of the others.

In the meantime, I continued my studies for the priesthood and was ordained to the sub-deaconate in the summer of 1969. This was one of the most joyous days of my life. I cannot explain why, but it was. Six months later, when I was ordained a deacon, I did not feel the intense joy that I had when I received the sub-deaconate. But I knew that "feeling" was not important in the spiritual life. I was advancing toward the priesthood and toward the sacrifice of myself.

According to an ancient custom, I wanted to have Mom's wedding dress made into a vestment for my ordination and first Mass. I wrote to Mom, and a package arrived a few weeks later. The dress was now thirty years old, and was full of tears and moth holes. The sister of a recently ordained monk offered to cut and sew the dress into a chasuble just as she had done for her brother. She was able to salvage enough material; in addition, she provided red cloth for a lining and sewed a single red stripe down the front and back. Needles to say, I was very pleased with the outcome!

At that time we avoided being photographed as part of our Carthusian anonymity. Without my knowing it, someone took a picture of me when I was at the guesthouse seeing about the sewing of the vestment. It was the first picture ever taken of me in my Carthusian habit; and I was amazed at how I actually looked -- how much I had changed from the time I entered the monastery. I eventually sent the picture to Mom.

I was informed that I was to be ordained to the priesthood on July 1st. The Prior certified to the Auxiliary Bishop of Seville that I had completed the required course of studies, and that I was a person of good character in the Carthusian order. I asked the Prior if he could arrange for Mom to be present for my ordination, since I didn't think she could afford the travel expenses. The Prior took my request to the Father General, and added that my sister had to come too, because my mother couldn't travel by herself. I was pleased when the Reverend Father approved the request and directed Dom Stephen, who was still in Vermont, to provide Mom with the funds for the trip.

Dom Luis, who had been my Prior from the beginning, had to go to another house of the Order for a Visitation at the time of my ordination. He was one of the principal Visitors of the Order. When he asked if the Visitation could be postponed so that he could be present at my ordination, the Reverend Father refused. Perhaps he judged the event not important enough. I was very disappointed and felt very hurt by this, even though Dom Luis assured me he had pleaded the case. He missed the ordination and the visit from my family.

One of our friends, Don Roberto, a one-time aspirant to the Carthusian life, met Mom and my sister in Madrid. Don Roberto was a highly intelligent and cultured Colombian. He accompanied Mom and Marilyn from Madrid to Jerez, where he found them a hotel. In Jerez we arranged for Jim and his Spanish wife, Carmen, to entertain my visitors when I was not available to visit with them.

I had met Jim on one of our weekly walks several years before. The Novice Master thought he was an American and encouraged me to say a few words to him in English. He had retired from the navy and married a Spanish woman. They owned a small piece of land on a hill overlooking the monastery. From that first encounter, we saw Jim from time to time if we happened to pass by his farm.

Finally, after almost eight years, I saw Mom and Marilyn! Mom had gained weight and seemed a lot older than the image that I had kept in my mind. And Marilyn had grown up, graduated from high school, and intended to enlist in the Air Force in the fall. Both were happy to see me. I was overcome with emotion -- my heart beat rapidly and my hands began to sweat. It must have been an emotional experience for them too, but they didn't show it.

Mom told me all about Don Roberto and their first experiences with Spanish culture. Don Roberto had met them at the airport and taken them to an expensive restaurant. He took them to a bullfight in Seville, and Marilyn became sick at the cruelty of the presentation and the profuse bloodletting. Marilyn was always an animal lover. Always full of life and surprises, Mom had learned a few Spanish phrases for the trip.

After a few hours with them, I returned to my cell. I was so overcome with emotion that I began to sob loudly. The encounter with the past - with my family - had been a shock for my system. I had not anticipated it, and even if I had, I would not have thought it so severe! I don't think I slept much that night. I was so "worked up" from the visit combined with my ordination the next day.

On the morning of July 1st, 1970, the Feast of the Precious Blood of Jesus, I was ordained to the priesthood in the Catholic Church. I wore the chasuble made from Mom's wedding dress. The Procurator drove me to the Bishop's residence in Jerez where we met Mom, Marilyn, and Jim and Carmen. I was so nervous with anticipation that day that I remember very few of the details of what happened.

During his Mass the Auxiliary Bishop of Seville, following the age-old rite approved by the Church, anointed my hands and forehead with holy oil, and placed his hands on my head as a symbol of transferring to me the authority to carry out my priestly functions. I was a priest forever "according to the Order of Melchisedek." I was the only one ordained that day.

According to the Fathers of the Church, a man's ordination to the priesthood completed the union between Christ and man, between Jesus and the Church, making the priest "another Christ." When I offered the Holy Sacrifice of the

Mass, I consciously and explicitly intended to reenact the sacrifice of Jesus on the cross; and even to sacrifice myself along with Jesus, thus completing and perfecting my calling within the Christian community.

It was an old Carthusian custom that every cloister monk was called to the sacred ministry of the altar. In this the Order saw the harmony that existed between the priestly and monastic consecrations. After the example of Christ, I became both a priest and a sacrifice whose fragrance was (hopefully) pleasing to God. Through my association with the Lord's sacrifice, I hoped to share in the unsearchable riches of His Heart. My being ordained on the Feast of the Precious Blood added special significance to my consecration.

I have always believed that my personal and individual calling was first and foremost to the monastic, eremitical life in imitation of the early desert hermits. It was not specifically to the priesthood. The mandatory and obligatory making of Carthusian choir monks into priests came about during the Middle Ages, largely in keeping with the Church's legal requirements having to do with financial obligations and prayer stipends. A certain number of ordained monks were needed to use up the stipends or trusts for guaranteed prayer.

The Desert Fathers for the most part had tried to avoid both contacts with Bishops and ordination to the priesthood. They realized that Bishops would give them an official assignment within the Church community after ordaining them. When a man was ordained, he was "called" by the Bishop. Priests were trustworthy "elders" who assisted the Bishop in his territorial ministry. Any kind of assigned ministry would have taken the hermit monk away from his primary calling to a life of constant prayer.

My assigned ministry as a Carthusian priest-monk was one of continuous prayer and intercession. The Church recognized that monks tied to contemplation acted as intercessors. On a daily basis, at all the liturgical offices, and especially during the Eucharistic celebration of the Mass, we prayed for the living and the dead. Sometimes this was explicit, sometimes implicit. Even though we abstained from exterior activity, we believed that we exercised an apostolate of a very high order, since we were sincerely striving to follow Christ in the inmost heart of His saving task.

Following the ordination ceremony, we all returned to the monastery, where I spent several hours with Mom and Marilyn. She took pictures and presented me with the gifts she had brought. Jim and Carmen presented me with a beautiful rosary. I gave Marilyn a little book containing her school pictures from the past twelve years that I had prepared and bound. After a while Jim suggested that I might want to be alone for the rest of the day. Before I could say anything like, "I'd like you to stay longer," they all left, promising to return the next day.

Mom and Marilyn passed the rest of my ordination day with Jim and Carmen. The next day they returned for morning Mass, which I celebrated in the little guesthouse chapel. Dom Bruno, who had been a fellow novice, served the Mass. He made certain that I performed all the ceremonies correctly. I remember being very nervous and self-conscious, even though I had practiced saying Mass in my cell for several weeks before ordination.

Mom stayed in Jerez another day or two. Then Jim and Carmen accompanied her and my sister to Seville, from where they started their journey back to the States. Later she sent me photos, which I showed to my brethren at our community recreation. Those days passed by in a flash before my eyes. I had lived in silence and almost complete solitude for so many years. The events of those few days disturbed my life of tranquility and balance! It took several more weeks for me to become fully aware of what had happened. The course of my life had passed another milestone of the journey.

Monastery
Spain

Monastery Entrance
Spain

Walk Day
Spain

In Choir
Spain

Monastery
Vermont

The Church
Vermont

The Cross
Vermont

In the Cell
Vermont

Vermont

While Moses was still in Midian, the Lord said to him, "Go back to Egypt." **(Ex 4:19)**

Having been ordained to the priesthood, and after visiting with Mom and Marilyn, I felt a strong desire to return to the States. The Charterhouse in Vermont was finished in the summer of 1970, and the monks began to occupy the cells in August of that year. Most of those Americans who had been sent to Europe for training were gathered together from England and France, and sent to Vermont. When I heard the news, I knew my turn would come soon. I waited to be called.

Dom Stephen remained the Superior in Vermont until the General Chapter or the Father General could appoint a Prior. To my surprise, the Reverend Father asked my opinion of who should be the Prior, without mentioning anything about my returning to the States. Perhaps he presumed that I could figure it out for myself; or perhaps he had the vow of stability in mind. I didn't know anyone but Dom Stephen and Dom Raphael; and I hadn't had much contact with Dom Raphael. I told the Reverend Father that I thought Dom Stephen would be the best choice.

Since there were not enough professed Americans in the Order to form the necessary quorum for a community, several monks who knew English were sent to the new monastery. Among them was a New Zealander, Dom Boniface, who had been stationed at the wagon shed for a year or two before being sent back to Parkminster in England. Dom Philip, a hardy Norwegian, who spoke English very well, was sent from one of the French Charterhouses.

Dom Louis, an American, was sent from France, and became the first Procurator, having charge over the several American Converse Brothers who had returned from Europe. Besides me, at least three other Americans priests remained in Europe. One who had entered the Order in 1952, wanted to remain in Italy where he spent much of the day painting floral engagements. Dom Bruno remained in Switzerland for a time, requested a leave of absence, and eventually returned to his Charterhouse in Switzerland.

Dom Denis remained for the time being in the only Charterhouse in what was then Yugoslavia. He had initially been sent from France to oversee the building of the American monastery, the Charterhouse of the Transfiguration. Dom Denis was replaced by Dom Raphael in the mid-1960s. It was he who completed the arrangements for the Charterhouse and was appointed its first Prior in 1971.

Dom Raphael had been born into a Jewish family, but raised as a Christian Scientist. Highly talented, he was both artistically and intellectually gifted. As a graduate student in philosophy at Fordham University under Dietrich von Hildebrand, he was searching for the truth, trying to find meaning in his existence. His teacher was instrumental in bringing him into the Catholic Church, and he was baptized in 1948.

It seemed that God had important plans for him, because soon after his baptism he realized that he had a vocation to the religious life. He responded to God's calling in a radical way by entering the Grande Chartreuse in 1952. He stayed in France for several years, and was sent to England by the General Chapter, where he exercised several offices. He was in Vermont during the early 1960s, where I met him for the first time. Later he returned to England for a short time, finally being sent to Vermont, where he arranged for the building of the new monastery.

Supreme authority in the Carthusian Order belonged to the General Chapter, which met every two years at the Grande Chartreuse, "Mother and Font" of the Order. Its ordinances had the force of law in matters relating to individual persons and to the individual houses. The General Chapter gave strength to the bond of perpetual charity that existed between the houses and between all the members of the Order who were striving to advance together along God's path.

The first General Chapter of the Carthusian Order had been called at the Grand Chartreuse in the year 1140, with the express purpose of keeping and maintaining the Carthusian ideal in unchanging vigor. The first Priors submitted their houses to this Chapter with a view to correction and preservation. To it they promised obedience both for themselves and for their communities in perpetuity. Between the General Chapters, the Prior of the Grande Chartreuse had the task of preserving the unity and peace of the Order. He was the "Reverend Father."

The Priors gathered for the General Chapter of 1971 decided that I should be transferred to the Charterhouse in Vermont. Dom Luis returned from the Chapter with the welcome news that I had been hoping for. He brought a handwritten note from Dom Raphael, who at that time had been appointed Prior. He expressed his pleasure over the Chapter's decision, and included a few dollars for my trip. I felt a sense of relief that I was finally returning to the United States.

Ironically, I also had some mixed feelings and apprehension over the news. During the ten years I had lived in Spain, I had overcome difficulties of language, climate, and culture. I had come to like where I was, and I liked (most of) the members of the community. I liked my cell and the garden I had cultivated for the past nine years. I experienced a reluctance to leave it. I truly was at peace in my heart and soul.

It was customary for the General Chapter to send an official copy of the minutes and decrees to each monastery after the Priors had departed from the Grand Chartreuse to return to their individual communities. No decrees or determinations took effect until the official papers were received and officially publicized. I think everyone in the community knew that I was being transferred before the official news was announced. In a silent and solitary community of hermit monks news seemed to travel with extraordinary rapidity sometimes.

Normally the reading of the decrees and ordinances of the General Chapter were read to the Fathers on the Sunday after the papers arrived in the mail. This year the Prior decided to read the decrees to the entire community of Fathers and Brothers together; and for this purpose he proposed a rare Sunday afternoon "common recreation."

When the decrees naming individual persons were being read, my heart was beating so fast that I thought it would jump out of my chest! Everyone congratulated me with effusive sincerity that I was returning to my country. Almost everyone, even the most serious and dour of the brethren, felt happy and lighthearted. I had a chance to speak freely with the Brothers, and some expressed their sorrow at my leaving. Finally -- and to the delight and surprise of all -- wine, coffee and pastries were brought out. It was the first and only time I had tasted coffee since my arrival in Spain.

A few days later, I spoke to Dom Luis about what I was to wear on my trip to Vermont. He said in a matter-of-fact way, "The habit, of course." He wasn't going to buy a black suit just for this one trip! I suggested I might wear the one I wore when I arrived, but he told me that it had been given away. Although I had bought it new just to travel to Spain, it was probably out of style by this time anyway, and probably would not have fit either. I knew that Dom Luis was right, and I just said, "Okay."

Dom Luis made arrangements for the journey. I packed the old white cardboard suitcase I still had with my good Sunday habit, a set of woolen underwear and stockings, and a few books. The Prior gave me a paper bag full of Sherry wine for the community in Vermont, and told me that he would send the chasuble from my ordination sometime in the future.

After the noonday meal, on a bright and sunny June afternoon, I bade farewell to the cell I had lived in through my novitiate and profession. I wished the plants in my garden well and said good-bye to the choir books I had accumulated for chant practice. I had finally come to a deep peace and contentment, and it was with a sense of sadness that I closed the door of that cell for the last time.

I went to the Prior's cell, as was customary, for a final blessing before setting out. One of the monastery workmen drove me to the train station in Jerez and bought me a ticket for Seville, from where I would begin my journey the next day. The family of one of the Jerez monks met me in Seville and took me to their apartment for a meal and a bed for the night. They were very kind to me, but I still felt uncomfortable and anxious about the trip. The monk's family treated me with supper, asked many questions, and wanted to entertain me further; but I excused myself from their company.

For the first time in almost ten years I was outside of the monastery for the night. I didn't think I was good company at dinner, especially since I wasn't accustomed to eating in anyone's presence. So much visiting and the general excitement of the day had tired me. After trying as best I could to pray the office, I finally gave in to fatigue and tried to sleep. It was the first night I had slept in a bed with a real mattress, and I slept very little that night. I kept hearing someone walking on the floor above. Any little noise woke me. I was like a fish out of water.

I survived the night and the following morning I was driven to the airport. I was going from Seville to Madrid to New York City to Albany, New York, wearing my white woolen habit, the same black shoes that were made for me when I received the habit, and the black woolen traveling cape. While I was excited about going to Vermont, I was not excited about making the trip. If I could have wished to be there in an instant, I would have preferred it. In Madrid I had a few hours to spend before boarding my flight for New York. The Prior had told me that I would be able to have Mass at the airport; and sure enough, I was able to celebrate a Carthusian Mass in the airport chapel while waiting for my flight to New York.

Once on the plane I listened to classical music for a long time. Later I watched a movie - my first in ten years -- *Goodbye, Mr. Chips*, starring Peter O'Toole with Petulia Clark. I immediately fell in love with Petulia Clark! I hadn't seen many females during my years of enclosure in the monastery. As I was getting closer to the States I began to think about Mom, Marilyn, Mike. Wouldn't they be surprised that I was coming home from Spain!

I had suggested to Dom Luis that Mom might meet me at the airport in New York and drive me to Vermont; but the Reverend Father Dom Andre denied the request. My family didn't even know that I would be returning, since the Reverend Father prohibited me from telling them beforehand. He felt that it would be out of keeping with the true Carthusian spirit of solitude and detachment. Perhaps he felt that I would not go to Vermont at all, but rather to Newfield with my family. One of the young American monks recently had gone AWOL when he was sent back from France.

I had no intention of doing this; but there was no possibility of appealing the decision.

As the plane made its descent to Kennedy Airport, I mused to myself that somewhere down there were my uncles, aunts, cousins, and friends. Were they still there? Were they still alive? Would I be able to contact them? Would they remember me? I prayed for them and left the rest to God. When I entered the Charterhouse I had renounced my former life, my friends, my family, and even my country.

Now it seemed that the Lord was prompting me to renew contact with them. It was a little confusing to me until I began to understand that was the way God did things. He asked for a sacrifice, and I made the sacrifice with a joyful heart. Then, after He was satisfied with the sacrifice, He was returning what I had sacrificed, perhaps in greater measure than it had been before.

I had been out of the country since August, 1962, and many changes had taken place in society, although I knew nothing about them when I landed in New York. At the airport my very first impression was how free and easy everyone seemed. There was more informality and less courteousness in the air. The shuttle bus driver yelled at his passengers in a friendly and joking way. It seemed to me that a generation of free spirits had arisen, unaccustomed to the respect for authority I had known in the 1950s and early '60s.

I had spoken nothing but Spanish for so long a time, and felt more comfortable asking for information and directions from the Spanish courtesy desk. I perceived that the young woman at the information booth became nervous when I approached -- I with my shaven head, religious habit and black cape. I felt like an alien in the country of my birth! I felt a special welcome when I presented my passport and the officer said, "Welcome home!" He probably said that to everyone, but it was truly meaningful to me. I took some time to look around and try to get my bearings.

One of my first priorities was to telephone Mom in Newfield. I knew her telephone number, but did not know that area codes had come into existence since I had been gone. The operator found the new telephone number for me. That Mom was surprised to hear from me on the phone was an understatement! At first she didn't believe that I was in New York. I explained the whole story to her, how I wasn't permitted to tell her about it beforehand and all that. We spoke for a while and agreed that she should make arrangements to drive up to Vermont once I was settled.

I had plenty of time before my flight to Albany. Now that I had received a crash course in using the new telephone system, I tried to call Aunt Shirley and Uncle Jack, not knowing if they were still in the area. But I was able to reach them, and they too were very surprised to hear from me. They knew I had gone to Spain, but hadn't heard anything more about me. They lived near the airport, and drove right over to see me. We had a pleasant visit and they too promised to visit me in Vermont. After they left, I sat in the airport, watching a world go by that was very new to me.

The plane to Albany left around 6 p.m. When I arrived in Albany and entered the waiting room in my robes and black cape, a distinct "hush" of silence came over the room for about fifteen seconds. I had a feeling that time had stopped, almost as if I had entered a "twilight zone." Then everyone resumed his or her business as if nothing had happened. I looked around, expecting someone to be there to meet me. Seeing no one, I wandered around for a few minutes, looking at different people in the hope that they were the ones. I think I scared some of them. I think others thought I was looking for a handout!

Finally, after about a half hour, I used my newly acquired telephone skills to call Vermont to find out what was happening and what I should do. I asked for Fr. Stephen, still unaware that Dom Raphael had been appointed Prior. Dom Stephen suggested that I try to catch the bus that passed by the gate of the monastery. But I wasn't sure how to find the bus or the bus station; and I don't think I had any money left to pay for a ticket. I had spent the few dollars I had brought with me on telephone calls. Dom Raphael, who had picked up his phone extension in the meantime, told me to wait at the airport for a car that would be sent.

The monastery employed several secular persons to do some of the work that the monks were unable to do. They kept the property in good order, and they did some shopping and other odd jobs like meeting people at the airport. The monastery property included the Mount Equinox Skyline

Drive, "the longest privately owned paved toll road in the U.S.", slightly more than five miles long. Restrooms were located at the tollhouse and the first parking area, and there were six other picnic and parking areas. The road was open from 9 a.m. to dusk, May 1st through October 31st, weather permitting.

I learned that the seven thousand acre monastery property in Vermont had a general manager, with whom the Prior had daily contact. A layman handled the shopping and mail pickup and delivery for the community. On occasion he would drive one of the monks to town for a doctor or dentist visit. A few seasonal workers lived off the property. Ed and Ella had charge of the tollhouse on the main highway at the foot of Mt. Equinox. An elderly couple, they lived at the tollhouse during the season. They acted as a first reception point for visitors and deliveries for the monastery. I had met them ten years earlier when I visited Mt. Equinox for the first time.

The workmen had to regulate the hydroelectric power stations that provided electricity to monastery and all the other facilities on the Mountain. In 1957, the construction of two lakes, Lake Madeleine (named after Mrs. Davidson), and a smaller one named after Mr. Davidson's faithful dog, Barbo, were undertaken as a flood control, soil conservation, and water storage project. The water from the two lakes was used to run two gravity-fed hydroelectric stations. The water that would have flooded the lower valley was dammed up in the two lakes.

In order to have someone on hand twenty-four hours in case of an emergency, one of the workmen lived with his family on the monastery property. He had an apartment in an upstairs wing of the home that Dr. and Mrs. Davidson had built in 1939 in the gap known as "Southeast Corners," on the south side of Mt. Equinox. The house served them until the Davidsons built a modern sprawling ranch further up the mountain on the northeast side overlooking the Rt. 7 valley.

The monks had turned the main part of the house into a guesthouse for their families during their visits. The house had four bedrooms, three baths, a large living room with a fireplace, and a large kitchen where the guests could prepare meals if they wished. The monks supplied food staples like milk, butter, and bread. One wing of the guesthouse was dedicated to a garage and office area.

Above this was the apartment where the workers' supervisor lived with his family. He was the one who was asked to drive the fifty miles to the Albany airport that night to pick me up. When he finally arrived at the airport around 9 p.m., he had no trouble recognizing me in my Carthusian robes and shaved head. I felt more than a little sense of relief when he found me. I was nearing the end of my long journey from Spain to the Carthusian Foundation in Vermont. As we drove into Vermont my driver told me most of the Mt. Equinox story.

It was dark as we drove into southern Vermont. I had all but forgotten about the picturesque villages with their town greens, old clapboard houses, and white church spires. We drove up Rt. 7, and passed the antique shops and ice cream parlors located in renovated barns. All the businesses were closed except for a tavern here and there. Most of the motels along the road showed "No Vacancy" signs.

The driver, whose name I have since forgotten, mentioned that the mosquitoes were "fierce" that night. He had to stop several times to wipe the windshield of his older model station wagon. The early June air felt cold and damp. Having been in warm, sunny Spain less than twenty-four hours earlier, everything seemed cold and bleak to me.

Sometime around 11 p.m. we reached the Skyline Drive Tollhouse, located in the little settlement of Sunderland between Manchester and Arlington. We climbed about two and a half miles up the toll road that I had first driven up many years before, and turned off toward the guesthouse. Past the guesthouse the road descended toward the old wagon shed that had also been familiar to me. I noticed that a locked gate had been placed at the beginning of the access road to discourage the curious.

I felt a great sense of relief when I arrived at the door to the Charterhouse enclosure at around 11:30. The bell was just ringing to wake the monks for preparation for the night office. Dom Raphael was waiting at the door to greet me warmly and lead me to my cell. As I entered the building and walked down the steps that led to the Fathers' cloister, I felt physically cold, and there was an odor of damp concrete everywhere.

The design of this monastery was a distinct architectural challenge. The architect, Victor Christ-Janier of New Canaan, Connecticut, used large slabs of unfinished Vermont granite, each of which measured approximately three feet wide by eight feet high. They were eighteen inches thick. These blocks were stood on end and concrete was poured between them. A flat crushed-stone covered roof was added to form an enclosed cloister walkway. All this gave the monastery a feeling of simplicity, permanence, and austere beauty. It was built to last a thousand years.

When the monastery was finished in 1970, one architectural critic called attention to the ingenuity of Christ-Janier's design, but lamented that few people would ever have the opportunity to see his architectural triumph. The Charterhouse, the critic wrote, is "a private dialogue in stone and does not encourage eavesdropping." But for us Carthusians inside those thick granite walls, the quiet conversation with God was of primary importance.

The stark design, and the massive stones that surrounded us reminded me of a tomb. As Dom Raphael led me through the cloister to the cell that had been prepared for me, it was as if I were entering the monastery for a second time. A fully trained Carthusian monk-priest, I was reminded again that when I entered the monastery, I had come to stay. When I entered the Carthusian order, I left the old world behind me forever. I cherished no worldly ambitions inside the Charterhouse walls. Only God would know how I spent my days in the cell.

I was reminded again that I would have virtually no contact with the outside world, that I truly would be alone with God. When I died I would lie buried on these monastery grounds, in a grave marked by a simple cross. I knew all this when I entered the monastery in Spain; and now on that night when I arrived from Spain, a fully trained Carthusian monk-priest, I was reminded of this again.

Dom Raphael excused me from the night office, giving me permission "to sleep in" when morning came. I was feeling exhausted from the long day of travel, so tired that I didn't take the time to explore the cell that night, but fell fast asleep on the hard straw bed. In the morning, I awoke to the sound of rain. It was damp and misty. I would have liked to have started a fire in the stove, but decided to wait until someone showed me the intricacies involved. I soon learned that foggy mornings in the mountains were very frequent. All this was again in severe contrast to the dry, sunny, and usually warm June mornings in Spain.

Dom Stephen, who occupied the adjacent cell, escorted me to the church for Mass that first day in Vermont. There was no doorbell ringing, or stamping the floor with canes, for wakeup calls. A buzzer system was in place by which the Vicar could ring into your cell from his cell to wake you. In answer you could press a button above your bed. However, for several years we used alarm clocks and the ringing of the church bell instead of the buzzer. A separate buzzer system was attached to a button located outside the cell door -- a doorbell, or in this case, a "door buzzer." When someone wanted to visit me, or when a Brother brought my food, he pressed the buzzer button.

After Mass on that first full day in Vermont, I found my way back to my cell with little trouble. Just as I had done in Spain, I took time to explore my new habitation. According to the usual Carthusian layout, the entire cell was a small two-story unit, but much smaller than the cells in Jerez. The general design corresponded to the classic model common in the French Charterhouses.

On the first floor were a workshop and a wood storage area. A door opened out onto my private, enclosed garden. The lower level had that damp smell of concrete that had not yet completely cured. It also had the strong smell of raw wood from the logs that had been pushed into the cell, ready for me to split and cut into smaller pieces. I saw a sawhorse and a small ripsaw, and a workbench too. Pieces of tape here and there showed where the flat, exposed part of the roof had been leaking. Except for the noise made by someone chopping wood in one of the cells, the place was very silent, much more silent than Jerez had been.

Upstairs was a small anteroom called the *Ave Maria*. There was an iconic image of the Mother of God with a kneeler before it. We Carthusians had the custom of kneeling to pray a "Hail Mary" before the image every time we entered

183

our cells from the cloister. In Jerez, the *Ave Maria* was the first room I entered into from the cloister -- I used to call it my "living room."

In Vermont, as in most of the European Charterhouses, the *Ave Maria* was the antechamber of a larger room called the *cubiculum* -- the cell proper. Two wooden doors separated the two rooms with a space of about twelve inches between the two doors. The two doors were for insulation purposes. Whenever I had a visitor in the *cubiculum*, I left the outer or first door open with the inner door closed. In warm weather I left both doors open.

The cell contained a simple wood frame bed with a straw mattress, a desk built into a wall, a chair, and a set of bookshelves over the desk. A corner of the room was dedicated to the oratory. The *cubiculum* was no more than twelve by twelve; but there was nothing dark or stuffy about it. The walls were of natural knotty pine panels, while the floors were of polished hard wood. A very large window overlooked my garden. At a small table in front of this window I ate my meals while I admired the beauty of the hills and sky. The table folded down when not in use. Next to the folding table was a small cupboard where I could store any leftovers from my single meal of the day.

I was very pleased with the cell, and especially with the knotty pine paneling. It gave the cell a somewhat rustic look and an odor of pine. It was what I had dreamed of when I first felt the call to the hermit life as a teenager. I liked the hardwood floor too, and was always careful to remove my shoes whenever I entered the *cubiculum*. I did not want to soil or scratch the polished floor. I asked for a dust mop so that I could mop and polish the floor every day during my morning work period.

Unlike the cell I had occupied in Spain, this one had a source of heat: a small, specially made wood-burning *Franklin* stove. Although it could also burn coal, we always used wood from the abundance surrounding the monastery. A metal stovepipe rose up through the ceiling. Often the pipe would get so hot that it would glow. A sheet of steel behind the stove and the pipe prevented the wooden wall from catching fire.

A small closet would hold my wardrobe, which eventually consisted of two white cotton shirts, two pair of white briefs, and two pair of white socks. In keeping with monastic tradition, our wardrobe was "neither elegant nor superfluous, nor otherwise offensive to poverty and simplicity." Our Fathers had aimed simply at covering themselves and protecting themselves from the cold. They believed that it was fitting for Carthusians that our clothes and everything else we used should be well worn. While inspired by this ideal, I had been trained, nevertheless, to take care of my clothing and to see that my cell was well kept and clean.

When I arrived in Vermont I received a new set of underwear. I was taken aback by the prospect of giving up the usual Carthusian underwear, and complained that I didn't think it was "Carthusian enough" to wear anything else that was not white and woolen. But Dom Raphael explained that it was less expensive, and therefore more in keeping with the spirit of poverty, to buy shirts and underwear, shoes and socks, rather than to make them in the monastery from expensive woolen cloth. Besides, the monastery received donations and gifts of clothing and shoes from benefactors that the Brother tailor put into a common storeroom. If any of the monks needed something, he had but to ask for it.

In my first week in Vermont I was given a pair of shoes from the storeroom, while keeping my ill-fitting monastery-made shoes for working in the garden. Eventually I adapted completely to the American Carthusian way. I not only gave up my woolen underwear -- in fact, I stopped wearing any underwear at all. With the Prior's permission I stopped wearing the hair shirt, as many of us had already done. I wore socks sometimes, usually only at community activities because of the coldness of the church and common buildings. I always thought that socks were an invention of the textile industry.

Brother Charles made a new habit of lightweight wool for everyday wear; and when in my cell I wore a hooded pullover robe of white cotton denim that Mom had specially made for me. In one of her first visits, she also brought some long underwear, heavy socks, and even a pair of slippers. According to our custom, I handed everything over to the

Prior, who returned some of it and give the rest to someone else.

Something else I did not think was "Carthusian enough" were the white cotton sheets on my bed. Some of the other monks didn't feel that they were in conformity with monastic austerity either, so they slept without any sheets at all. I eventually became accustomed to the sheets. For covering I used an old "army blanket" or two. Otherwise, the bed was in conformity with "monastic austerity." Since I didn't have the woolen underwear to wear at night, I wore a store-bought nightshirt to bed. And sometimes I just stripped naked and crawled under the blankets.

A separate bathroom area off the *cubiculum* had a sink and a toilet. Above the sink was a medicine cabinet with a large mirror. A drain opening in the tile floor allowed me to take a sponge bath if I wished. But since the water was cold in both summer and winter, I rarely used it. Instead, I made good use of a unique feature of this Charterhouse: a common shower room, complete with tub and hot water. Normally I did not leave my cell to shower, except on walk days.

Beside the door that led into the cloister was a passage in the wall: the customary "food hatch" into which a Brother placed the daily meal. Without any conversation, a Brother brought the dinner to the cell in the usual Carthusian way, inside a wooden box that kept it warm. Just as in Spain, we never ate meat. The Fathers never had breakfast, and we fasted on bread and water every Friday. Brother Hilary baked excellent whole wheat bread, and I tried it for a while, but had to give it up for health reasons.

As in Spain, our single meal was deliberately simple, consisting of soup or cereal, a vegetable dish, and some form of eggs or fish. Compared with what I had been served in Spain, I thought the food was very good. I had no problem digesting it, as I had in Spain; nor did I have any other stomach problems. Dom Raphael remarked once that everything came from a can, while in Europe mostly everything was fresh; but I didn't think either part of the statement was totally true.

After the Brothers had established their big kitchen-side garden, we enjoyed a variety of fresh vegetables and fruit. For a beverage, instead of wine or beer, we drank apple juice from apples that were pressed locally. Orange juice was also available, and sometimes I had both with my meal. I had only to ask for either or both. Anyone who wanted milk with the meal had but to request it. Hot beverages like coffee and tea were never available. Most of the time we gratefully took what the kitchen gave us.

During the first few months I was in Vermont I was cold and hungry all the time. I put messages in my food box for the cook to give me larger portions, but my requests went unanswered. Finally, one day in desperation, I went to the Prior's cell and asked, "What do I have to do to get more food around here?" Dom Raphael was obliging to my request and immediately called Brother Anthony on the intercom, instructing him to have larger portions delivered to my cell. This worked, and on some days I received portions so large that I couldn't consume all of it. I gained about thirty pounds in a period of two months. Then I stopped eating so much, asked for normal portions, and my weight began to level off.

It helped to have a garden for regular daily exercise. The cell gardens in Vermont were completely un-worked because no one had as yet lived in most of the cells. Nothing was growing -- only weeds. But the soil was rich due to the fact that before the granite perimeter walls were set in place to close off the gardens, truckloads of rich topsoil had been brought in from the valley and dumped on the existing rocky soil.

I liked the idea of creating a garden from scratch. I had always liked working outside with my hands, ever since growing up on Long Island, when Mom and Dad would pay me for doing lawn and garden work. I had a lot of gardening practice in Newfield and even in Kansas with the Recollects. In the monastery, the work offered some necessary physical activity and a break from reading and formal prayer. Some of the gardens in time would furnish food for the community.

There were slabs of shale and slate under the newly placed topsoil, and I used some of the rocks to outline plots that I could fill in with plants. Several pear trees had already been planted close to the granite wall, and Dom Raphael provided me with a flowering plum tree to add to them. At the same time, he advised me not to put too much work into the garden.

Since we were a new community, it was likely that some of us would be moving to other cells later on. It was, in fact, about a month later that I moved to another cell.

At one end of the garden was a hatch, or passage, built into the wall through which one of the Brothers would slide rough-cut logs taken from the surrounding woods. In the workshop area I learned to split those logs, and cut them down to the appropriate size for the wood stove in my *cubiculum*. The process of cutting and splitting wood provided useful exercise in addition to logs for warding off the long bitter winter cold on the mountain. Another side effect for some of us was the release of tension. One of the Fathers told me that when he was upset with one of the brethren, he pictured that poor soul's head on the block of wood he was chopping!

During my years in Vermont, I sometimes fired up my wood stove to an eighty-degree temperature in order to stay warm enough. I never got used to the cold. Apart from all the other common austerities of the Carthusian life, it was perhaps the physical coldness that caused me the most suffering. Even with my woolen robes, there always seemed to be a chill coming from somewhere. In Spain I had no choice but to endure it, while in Vermont I could sit in front of my little stove for hours at a time.

There has always been a movement in certain parts of the Church to seek after suffering for its own sake, perhaps in a misguided attempt to imitate Jesus in what He is presumed to have done. Carthusians have at times been accused of being either too strict, or not strict enough. I could understand how easy it would be to fall into one or another distorted view of life. My own view of life in the Charterhouse was to "let it happen."

You had to try your best to follow God's will in your life -- "to conform," as we used to say. Anything that might hinder following His will would simply have to be killed, put to death, mortified. The Carthusian Statutes, along with the Superior's guidance and his interpretation of the Statutes to your particular case, were clearly the expression of God's will. Solitude and silence and the officially sanctioned Carthusian lifestyle were mortification enough for any man. I didn't have to look for more.

Soon after I arrived in Vermont, Dom Raphael took me on a tour of the Charterhouse complex. As was customary for Charterhouses, the entire complex was made up of a series of cells, or individual hermitages, that opened onto a central cloister, which in turn connected with the church, private chapels, refectory, and library. Not as large or as beautiful as the Charterhouse of Jerez, this one was impressive in its own right. It imbibed to a great extent the Carthusian trait of rusticity with its bare granite and concrete walls, its hardwood floors, and its wood paneling. Everything was very simple and austere.

The church was small and simple, about a fifth the size of the church at Jerez. The walls were formed from two levels of granite blocks, one block placed on top of the other. Into the flat roof were built skylights that let copious amounts of light fall directly onto the large choir books. Several narrow windows between the granite blocks in the sanctuary area were covered with crudely made burlap curtains. The floor of the church was paved with gray and orange granite from Colorado.

In the center of the sanctuary at the front of the church was an altar, a solid block of black granite. In one corner of the sanctuary, looking over the nave of the church, was a thirteenth-century statue of the Blessed Virgin; and against the back wall of the sanctuary was a simple crucifix above a box-like tabernacle that held the Blessed Sacrament, the dwelling for the hermit monk Jesus.

The choir stalls facing each other on opposite sides of the church were of solid cherry wood. The individual stalls were much smaller and closer together than the ones I was used to in Jerez. Being in closer proximity to my neighbor didn't always allow me to lose myself in silent and solitary prayer as easily as I would have desired. The electric lighting was more than sufficient and much better than the lighting in Jerez.

The Fathers' section of the choir was separated from the Brothers' section by a break in the book stands, which also served as an entryway to the stalls. Following Carthusian tradition, the Brothers attended office in the back stalls. Later they were given the option of participating with the Fathers in singing the office. Brother Anthony took advantage of the general permission, read a lesson at the night office, and even sang a solo response from time to time.

A unique feature of the church was the hot water radiator system running under the floor where the monks rested their feet while leaning on the choir stall seats. Unfortunately, it was never turned on because it needed oil to run it. In especially cold weather, I used to wear several pair of heavy woolen socks to the night office, and my feet were still cold. I kept my hands well inside the sleeves of my robe. For most of the office we had our hoods up, and this kept my hairless, shaven head warm.

Brother Michael had converted a large fifty-gallon oil drum into a wood-burner in the back of the church to serve to warm the church in the coldest part of the year. It wasn't much help during the night office though. By the time I started to feel a little warmth, the office was over, and it was time to return to the cell. It was so cold in the church that some of the older fathers wore fingerless gloves to keep their hands warm.

Across from the church entrance was the community bulletin board. It was outside the entrance to the chapter room. The Sacristan prepared the board every day before Vespers. It told which priest would be scheduled to celebrate Mass in which chapel, who would be the server, who would perform the readings during the office, who would be the principal chanter for the week, etc. Everything pertaining to the celebration of the liturgy was listed on the board. If there was a special event requiring a schedule change, that too was listed on the board.

The chapter house, or chapter room, was a simple, unadorned and bare room with a wood floor and small granite altar at one end. The altar had a simple wooden crucifix on it, along with the customary set of candles. The Sacristan did not normally assign a priest to have Mass in the chapter room. It was used primarily for those same community exercises and meetings, as were all chapter houses in all Charterhouses.

We individual priests celebrated our private Mass in one of the small chapels that were off a corridor that opened to the church and to the large cloister. The chapels were totally bare of ornamentation and unheated. On the cold concrete floor of each chapel was a mat made of woven palm leaves. Each chapel was known by the name posted on the door. I celebrated Mass most often in the chapel dedicated to St. Therese. Others were dedicated to the Holy Trinity, the Holy Spirit, St. Bruno, and the North American Martyrs.

Adjacent to the chapter room was the refectory, another cold and bare room with long wood tables and wooden benches. The floor was of ceramic tile, and it had a door that led to the kitchen area. The refectory was used only on Sundays and holy days. Even though there was never any food there, no one was permitted to enter outside of those times.

Next to the refectory was the community library. It was well stocked with Church documents and theological works, current theological and spiritual periodicals, and several diocesan newspapers. Newly received books were placed on a special stand for all to see. Each monk could sign out as many books as he wished and was expected to return them within a reasonable period of time; but books sometimes remained in the cells for months at a time. If you needed one of these books you could ask the librarian or speak to the Prior. The library was available to the Brothers also.

Beyond the community places was the Brothers' wing with the various "obediences," or work areas, where each Brother exercised his particular function in obedience to the Procurator and the Prior. First and foremost of all work areas was the kitchen, with a pantry and a bakery attached. In the center of the Brothers' cloister, with a door opening from the kitchen, was a large vegetable garden.

There was an electrical shop, a carpentry shop, a laundry, a tailor shop, and a garage area. The individual Brother's cell was basically the same as the Father's *cubiculum*, with a small antechamber. These cells had no individual gardens and were of one story. Normally the Fathers did not venture into the Brothers' area of the monastery complex. The Brothers could not enter the obediences of other Brothers. When not in their obediences, or otherwise occupied, the Brothers kept to the silence and solitude of their cells.

Brother Anthony was the principal cook, a distinction that made him the head Brother. It was his job to prepare the main meal of the day and to generally supervise the kitchen and pantry area. He was very proud of having been a student at St. Vincent's College in Latrobe, PA, and spoke of his days there frequently. Brother Anthony was also the *infirmarian*, or community nurse. If his cooking made you ill, he provided a remedy from the medicine room.

A man of many talents, Brother Anthony was also the community barber, exercising this duty in the barbershop adjacent to the shower room. In Vermont, the monthly haircut was quite different from what I had experienced in Spain. All barbering was done with electric clippers, so that I didn't have to worry about my scalp being scraped and cut. After my haircut -- or more precisely, after the hair on my head was shaved down to a quarter of an inch -- there was no need to wash off the soap and blood as in Spain.

Brother Charles was an excellent tailor. He also did the laundry and performed other functions, wherever he was needed most. Brother Conrad was an excellent carpenter and electrician. He could do just about anything with his hands. Both he and Brother Charles had been Trappists before transferring to the Carthusians. Brother Michael was a Donate Brother. He repaired the monastery vehicles and was in charge of logging. He provided the rest of us with firewood, cutting the trees, splitting the logs and dragging them to the cells.

Other Brothers came and went during my time in Vermont. Brother Nicholas had been trained in England like most of the Brothers; but soon after his arrival in Vermont, he decided he would rather be a professional baseball player and left the community. Brother Hilary had been a Franciscan and was an excellent baker; after a few years he returned to the Franciscans. Several Brothers came from Trappist monasteries, some to stay, and others to find the Carthusian lifestyle too different from what they were used to.

Back in my cell, I noticed that it rained almost every day. That June was a particularly wet one. This was a new experience for me, since in Jerez I normally saw no rain for the entire summer from May to September. I thought back on my days in Spain. During the months of March and November the rain fell heavily in the south, and it was not unusual to see flooding there during the 1960s. Much of the area from Seville south beyond Jerez was a swampy flood plain formed by the Guadalete and Guadalquivir Rivers.

At one time the Guadalete rose almost twenty feet above its banks to lap against my garden wall. We had no electricity for a week, and had to use the typical Carthusian oil lanterns and candles for the night office. During the day I sat close to the window to read. In Vermont, there was little possibility of being without electricity. Our problem was using as little as possible out of respect for our voluntary poverty.

I was becoming accustomed to living in my cell in Vermont gradually. I worked in the garden and cut wood for the winter season. I began to gather a few spiritual books from the library overflow. I noticed new things in the cell every day. However, I continued to feel physically cold all the time, and also felt depressed from the changes. During my first week or two in Vermont, Dom Raphael suggested that I go to the shower room during the day, thinking that this might help me adapt. I left the cell reluctantly, and found that the hot showers did help raise my spirits.

Dom Stephen was aware of my situation and encouraged me: "You'll gradually accumulate things in your cell and feel more at home." He was right, and I often think about his great wisdom. He used to say that when he entered the Order he felt like a caged lion, and would pace the floor for hours. He never doubted for a moment the validity of his calling, just as I had no doubts about mine. I relied on the strength that came from the Lord Jesus and His Mother for my perseverance in this new situation, just as I had when I arrived in Spain. I tried to live in the present moment, striving consciously to be like a leaf blown in the wind of the Holy Spirit.

Because the walls of the hermitage shielded me from all outside distractions, most of the struggles I experienced originated in my imagination. Although I had lived in the Charterhouse for ten years, my daily battle was the same daily battle that every Carthusian was familiar with: the daily struggle to achieve what the older monks called a "serene equilibrium" of the interior life. At times I wondered if "the newsreel" of my imagination would ever run out. It was a constant and demanding battle, one for strong men who did not lie on the floor of their cell sobbing over their plight.

Long ago I had realized how little control I sometimes had over my emotions. If I was disturbed at something or someone, I tried to wait a few hours, or sometimes a day, before I complained to the Novice Master or the Prior about it. I gradually learned that if I remained docile to the Holy Spirit, I would be all the more certain of "doing the truth in love." I would be at peace. I would be suspicious of no one. I learned that it was often better to keep silence altogether, rather than dwell on matters that were frivolous, or on defects that were already being corrected.

Many times the "problem" either solved itself or I got over it. I knew from experience that the daily quest to master one's impulses most often involved simple matters, such as the struggle to remain alert at prayer, or to cope with any of the minor details of communal life. The life of solitude and the limited community life did not afford many opportunities for conflicts between personalities; but when it did, the overexcitement of the cell and the lack of opportunity to "talk it over" could magnify petty issues out of all proportion. Petty issues most often originated in community exercises, and especially in the choir.

Soon after I had begun living in the cell, I noticed that two white doves were making a nest on top of the granite garden wall. Was this some sort of sign of the Holy Spirit? Dom Raphael disabused me of this idea, relating that the two doves from Fatima, Portugal, had been given to the monastery a few months earlier. They had gotten free of their cage and had been roaming free.

Now they decided to join me in cell G. Maybe it was a special welcoming from God or the Blessed Mother. Stranger things had happened to me. In any case, I knew that I could not keep pets in my cell. It was against the rule. A cat or two might be allowed to roam through the Brothers' section, sniffing around the kitchen area, but there were no dogs or other "pets" as we knew them. Dom Raphael suggested that I leave the birds to their own resources.

Aside from the major and minor personal adaptations, the fundamental patterns of my Carthusian life did not change in Vermont. I gathered in the monastery church with my brothers for the daily community Mass and the chanting of the canonical hours. I lived in as complete a solitude as I had in Spain. On Sundays and holy days I participated in the community activities.

On some Sundays we concelebrated at the community Mass. According to our rules, the Eucharist could only be concelebrated on days where the Carthusian life showed its communal character, namely on Sundays and significant holy days. When concelebration was later permitted, the Vermont community decided to have it only on Sundays. Later, when everyone saw that it worked well, we had it on more occasions.

When I entered the Order, concelebration -- the celebration of the Mass by several priests acting simultaneously -- did not exist. One priest celebrated the community Mass with his back to the congregation, reciting the Eucharistic prayers in a very low voice. The rest of the community took part in this liturgy by singing parts in the Gregorian chant, by silent and internal prayers, and by receiving communion. That was the way it was still done on most holy days, and ordinary days during the week.

Only one priest celebrated the Mass for the community. I would be in the choir stall with my hood pulled so far over my head that I couldn't see my neighbor standing in front of me. It was a prayerful experience, allowing me to unite myself with the sacrifice of the Mass without any distraction. Through all this, we certainly were far removed from the pop liturgists who tried to tell us that we had to be holding hands and having intimate eye contact to really be participating in the liturgy!

On Sundays we gathered in the refectory for a common meal, during which one of us read from Scripture and the Church Fathers. We took dinner together on Sundays and holidays, so that we might taste something of the joy of "family life." Sharing a meal with my brothers in the refectory brought to mind the Last Supper -- the meal made holy by Our Lord Jesus Christ.

In Vermont, after the priest who had celebrated the community Mass blessed the tables, instead of having the Brothers serve each course separately, the entire meal was on the table before each of us from the very beginning. The metal containers were in front of us, while a pitcher of water and another pitcher of apple juice were on either side of the containers. Just as in Spain, when the Prior gave the signal, we began to eat, and the reader began with a passage from the Bible. While we were taking nourishment for the body, we were at the same time spiritually nourished by the readings.

After the meal and the prayers in the church I was happy to retire to my cell. Sometimes I would rest by lying on the floor, basking in the abundant sunlight. At other times I washed a shirt or cut some flowers in my garden. For a time the Prior gave some lessons in chant to the community during the last fifteen minutes before None.

Just as in Spain, on Sundays and holidays we got together for conversation for recreational purposes after None. There were only a few of us and there wasn't too much to talk about. It was up to Dom Raphael and the Vicar, Dom Stephen, to keep the conversations going. Never did I hear uncharitable words, much less arguments of any kind. The Prior quickly cut off any subject that might be leading to open disagreement.

While none of us separated ourselves from the main body for private conversations, I experienced a sense of guardedness, almost secrecy, permeating our common recreational periods. There were things we just did not talk about in public, such as our personal prayer life, or certain things that took place in our community activities. At first I found all this very stiff and lacking in honesty; but as with everything else, with time I learned to accept it and recognize it was the wisest course to follow.

The biggest difference between Spain and Vermont was where the recreations were held. In Spain, we had always sat outside, either in the open cloister or in the fields surrounding the monastery. In Vermont, because of the cold, we sat in a specially designated recreation room, our hard wooden chairs placed in a circle so that no one was left out of the conversation.

In warmer weather we sometimes walked toward Lake Madeline, where we sat for a time under the trees on the shore. And at other times we gathered outside at the benches near the huge concrete cross at the entrance to the monastery enclosure. From there we sometimes watched the cars climbing the mountain on the toll road to enjoy the New England scenery.

In the fall the tourists could look down across the valley to see the full palette of nature's colors on display. Never did they realize that we monks, who had shut ourselves off from the world to worship God in solitude and silence, were watching them. Most of them did not realize that once they passed the tollgate, they are on the property of a Carthusian monastery. Those who did realize this stopped along the toll road at a place called "the saddle," where from a distance they could look down on the monastery.

Monday was usually the walk day. In Vermont we walked together along the roads and forest paths of the extensive monastery property. St. Bruno had observed that, *when wearied by our quite austere rule and application to spiritual things, our rather delicate natures could often be refreshed and renewed by the charms and beauties of woods and countryside.* His words, spoken more than eight hundred years before, were totally relevant to our weekly walks in Vermont. We Fathers had an all-afternoon walk every week of the year with the exception of Holy Week -- the week before Easter.

Before we had novices in the community, all of us Fathers walked together, taking the same route, each one in turn talking with the others. Since there were only five of us in the beginning, we walked together for part of the time, and then split up into two or three groups, according to who wanted to have a longer or shorter walk. The older and more infirm Fathers would walk a certain distance and then leave the younger and more energetic monks like Dom Philip and me to continue our walk, while they returned slowly to the monastery. All of us were back at the monastery in time for Vespers.

During the week I had occasional conversations with the Prior or the Sacristan, usually after Vespers and at the entrance to the church. It was always at their bidding, and at first I did not appreciate these short exchanges. I wanted to return immediately to the silence of the cell. After a while, however, I began to look forward to them, glancing in the

Prior's direction when I saw him standing at the entrance to the chapter room.

Otherwise, the norm at all times was silence. We were taught not to seek conversation with those visitors who sometimes came to our house, unless there was a real need. Making or receiving visits without good cause was of no advantage to the monk who was firmly attached to solitude and silence, and thirsted for contemplative repose. The keeping of silence and solitude was God's will.

After the evening Angelus was rung, there was a period of "great silence." No one was to go to the Prior's cell unless summoned during that time of silence. If I was in the Prior's office, he sometimes asked me to remain for a few minutes to wrap up our conversation; but even then I felt a nudge from my conscience reminding me of the rule. If I was with guests in the guesthouse, I left them for the rest of the evening and retired to my cell.

Once I was established in Vermont, Mom visited with Marilyn and Mike, who also brought his wife. Our parents and other relations were allowed to visit each year for two days twice a year. We all knew that this concession of the rule was primarily for the benefit of our family rather than ours. Because I had been in Spain for such a long time, during that first year in Vermont I was permitted to have more visits from my family than normally allowed. Dom Raphael bent the rules in favor of my family; but when my Aunt Shirley and Uncle Jack started to visit me too frequently, the Prior asked me to remind them that they would be welcome no more than once a year.

In Vermont there were really two "guesthouses." The larger one was where the visitors slept and prepared their own meals. The other guesthouse was what we called the "guest parlor." It was located in a small building just outside the main entrance to the monastery. In this building were two parlors, a bathroom, and a chapel. When I was not with them, my visitors were free to roam the monastery property or stay at the large guesthouse. I was not permitted to share meals with the guests and had to leave them when the bell rang for office.

I was always glad to see my family and spend some time with them. I celebrated Mass for them in the morning at the small guest chapel and met with them in the guest parlor during the day. Apart from parents and other relations, we avoided visits from friends and conversations with seculars, unless some rare and inescapable necessity was imposed on us by the love of Christ. As in everything else, we knew that God was worthy of this sacrifice, and that the sacrifice would be of greater profit to them than our words could be.

Sometimes I felt a "let-down" when my visiting guests left. All of us felt this human twinge from time to time, and some of us obviously felt it more than others. Someone even claimed that he wished for no more visits because he could not bear the pain he felt when they left. In a real sense, your carefully regulated life was interrupted when you had a visitor. Even after a few hours of visiting with relatives, it was difficult to resume my cell life. After visiting with me, one visitor observed to Mom that I "didn't seem happy." When I had problems of this sort, I thought to myself, "It will pass."

Soon after arriving in Vermont I informed the Prior that I didn't want to be named Chanter. I told him of the problems I had suffered through in Spain. But Dom Raphael, who was a good musician, told me that he hadn't decided on anything yet. Since we were a small community, I might be called upon to exercise the office. And despite my pleadings to the contrary, he later appointed me Chanter. I had little choice but to obey. I did the best I could to try to avoid the mistakes I had made in the past; but eventually the position began to cause problems.

My years as Chanter in Spain had indeed prepared me for the position. I was still nervous about singing solo pieces. But year after year I had come across the same pieces, so that I could now sing many of them without looking at the choir books. Intoning the psalms was never a problem, but upholding the pitch and setting the pace were sometimes difficult. In any case, I found that being Chanter in Vermont was not as terrifying as I thought it would be. Most of my apprehension came from the Mass pieces and some of the night office responsorial pieces, mainly because my voice was not always sufficiently warmed up at those times.

Then, quite unexpectedly, the Prior also appointed me to the position of Assistant Novice Master. In addition to being totally surprised, I was not entirely pleased by this either. I had entered the monastery to be *hidden* from the world (which, incidentally, was not the same as *hiding* from the world), and I did not relish the idea of having responsibilities that might put me in contact with the world that I had abandoned.

Going over the pros and cons as they related to each member of the community, Dom Raphael convinced me that I was the only one qualified for the job. I was young, an American, and well formed as a Carthusian. Again, I had no choice but to accept the position out of obedience. For a long time, however, I felt very insecure about it. Being Assistant Novice Master would mean that I was an "officer" and a "superior." I did not feel up to the task or the responsibilities.

As Assistant Novice Master, I was really expected to do most of the work of Novice Master, but without the title. In reality, the title of Assistant Novice Master did not exist. In most houses of the Order, the job and the responsibilities of assisting the Novice Master were given to a senior novice. It was not always easy to remove a superior from office once he had been appointed or elected. In other words, it was always easier to test someone by having him do the work without the title, than it was to give the title, see the individual fail and then have to remove him from the position.

At the same time that he appointed me to the office of Assistant Novice Master, the Prior granted me permission -- *faculties* -- to hear confessions and administer the Sacrament of Penance. I was enabled to hear the confessions, not only of the members of the community, but also of any retreatants or postulants who might come to test their vocation with us. But again, even though I had completed most of my theological studies, I did not feel up to the responsibility of hearing confessions or of giving spiritual counsel. I felt slightly overwhelmed by the responsibility.

The Prior did not have many individuals to work with when he assigned offices; but even so, I felt that he had confidence in my abilities. I also felt he did everything he could to support me in my responsibilities, and it was a way for him to contribute to my "continuing formation." That was one of the buzz terms that emerged from the Vatican Council, and eventually reached the Carthusian desert. Such emphasis was put on this idea that one of my fellow monks remarked, "How much formation can we take? When we're completely formed, we'll be ready to die!"

When I left Spain in 1971, I had yet to complete my theological studies. In Vermont I finished the studies under the able tutelage of Dom Philip, earning the equivalent of a Master's Degree in Theology. I was particularly interested in Church history and did some extra studies in this area. I also began a semester study of Hebrew, but did not absorb much. In lieu of writing a thesis, I was asked to answer several elaborate test questions in writing. In addition, I was given an oral exam on general theological and moral questions before the Prior and Dom Philip, who was also the Prefect of Studies. I passed *cum laude*!

Having finished the prescribed program of studies, I was in a position to devote more of my time to being Assistant Novice Master. Dom Raphael had been acting as Novice Master since the opening of the Charterhouse as a temporary solution until someone could take his place. I was destined to take his place. In the meantime I began answering requests for information, scheduled vocational retreats, and interviewed retreatants.

Dom Raphael kept a close eye on my work, offering valid criticisms and suggestions. In all this he probably was trying to exercise his own position as Prior by closely following the letter of the Statutes, ensuring that "the younger monks be not left to themselves and too much to the bidding of their own wills." Experience had taught that those were the crucial years of our vocation and that on them the character of our whole subsequent life depended. And so, during my first weeks in Vermont, and especially after he had appointed me to assist him in the selection and training of novices, he visited me in my cell to talk, striving to give me fatherly and even brotherly help.

On my part, I was initially pleased with his visits and the attention I received, but I did not feel that I needed his advice or brotherly help. If I did need advice or help, I usually asked for it. I had been my own counselor since my Dad had passed away, and I tended to resent anyone trying to give me unsolicited advice. I was accustomed to "marching to my own drummer," always within the context of what I knew to be the authentic Carthusian way.

After a few of his weekly visits to my cell, I told him that I really didn't feel that I needed any further help, and requested that he not come so often to my cell. Perhaps to show that he was "the boss," he continued to come, but less frequently, once a month for a time, and then he stopped altogether. Later on it was he who would call me aside to ask my opinion on various matters that concerned his life or the community. And for my part, I sometimes felt that I had unnecessarily and prematurely pushed him out of my "private life."

Dom Raphael's office as Prior required no small degree of self-denial. Everyone in the community had all come from different houses, each one with its peculiarities of formation. Our little community, as many other Carthusian communities, was made up of monks of different nationalities and cultural backgrounds. Since I had been trained in Spain and returned to the United States with a very strict and somewhat inflexible Carthusian mentality, the Prior sometimes referred to me as "a square peg in a round hole." Comparing my background with his liberal Jewish background and his Carthusian training in France and England, I sometimes saw him as "round peg in square hole."

At first I was concerned more with the letter of the law than with the spirit, and openly criticized Dom Raphael and his leadership for what I perceived to be less "authentically Carthusian." I did this openly to him, and not to any of the members of the community. When I brought the issue before the Visitors on one occasion, they gently reminded me of the words of St. Paul, that *there was no difference between Jews and Gentiles*, that we were all one in Christ Jesus. But that did not resolve my problem immediately. I did not feel entirely comfortable with Dom Raphael as Prior. Later on, I began to accept what I knew was never to change. But the damage had been done.

Being very sensitive by nature, Dom Raphael accused me of trying to intimidate him. This was never my intention, although I admit that I did see him as indecisive and inefficient. He had a variety of physical ailments that sometimes interfered with his office of Prior, and this also influenced my impression of him. He readily admitted to some of my criticisms, but rarely did anything to improve the image. To his credit, I believe that he made efforts to govern us as sons of God, attempting to develop in each of us a spirit of voluntary submission, so that we might more fully conform ourselves to the obedient Christ. If necessary, he admonished us in his own charitable way, and on more than one occasion he confided that this was difficult for him.

Some of the monks had problems that were sporadic and whose origins were largely unknown. Dom Raphael was always concerned with those problems of individual monks in relation to their effect on the rest of the community. At times he seemed to act as if good external order were his sole concern. Indeed, the peace and concord of the house depended on everyone striving to be in full accord and of one mind; but I believe that his concern for peace and accord within his small and fragile community sometimes led him to exaggerated conclusions.

Dom Raphael must have been pleased with my work as Assistant, and wanted me to take as active a role as I could. Before deciding anything of importance concerning the Novitiate, he consulted with me and we tried to reach a decision by common consent. I normally found myself ready to accept his final decisions with filial submission. He kept a watchful eye on the novices and would visit them frequently, something that I never experienced from the Prior when I was a novice in Spain.

I began answering letters requesting information about our life and the Charterhouse; I started to schedule vocational retreats, and I began to interview retreatants. I took the position very seriously and after a time began to resent Dom Raphael's visiting with the retreatants. I began to think that he was meddling in my affairs by his checking on my work. Perhaps he noticed this resentment, because he told me that he had decided to pay less frequent visits to any retreatants or novices.

Dom Raphael felt the time had come for me to transfer from cell G to cell M, which had been especially planned for the Novice Master. I was pleased with the transfer, since I had never quite adapted to cell G. It was much smaller than the cell I had in Spain, and it didn't have a good view of the mountains or the woods. Cell M, on the other hand, was warm and cozy, with windows opening toward the south so as to take advantage of the winter rays of the sun. From the window I had an unobstructed view. I could look down the long valley toward the mountains beyond.

I could watch the mountainsides turn from white and brown in spring to green when the leaves appeared, to bright red and yellow and orange in the fall. I could sit for hours watching the white clouds darken with heavy rain. Frequently deer would be playing at suppertime outside the garden enclosure. Sometimes I saw owls in the trees beyond the walls and called to them and they would answer me. I sometimes just sat for hours watching the hills, the sky, and the changing patterns of the clouds, all the while thanking God for the beauty that surrounded us.

My prayer was one of joyous and silent adoration. Sometimes I would recite the "Our Father" slowly, relishing every word, meditating on each phrase. I learned this prayer and also the "Hail Mary" in Greek. I would recite both prayers slowly in English, Latin, Spanish, and Greek. God was my Father; Mary was my mother. I was their son.

Cell M was larger than cell G. It had an extra room upstairs, which was planned for Novitiate conferences. When I entered cell M, I could go down a few steps to the wood storage and garden area, or I could go up a few steps to reach the *Ave Maria*. The conference room was off to the left, and the *cubiculum* was to the right. The *cubiculum* was laid out in a slightly different manner. The greatest difference was that the oratory was in a small closed-in area by itself. The oratory felt cozy and warm with the kneeler facing a window of opaque glass.

The daily schedule I followed in Vermont was basically the same as I had followed in Jerez. It conveyed both the simplicity and the rigor of the Carthusian life, and could differ slightly according to the location and needs of each monastery or of the individual monk.

Early on in my Carthusian career I had realized that knowing what to do at all times of the day kept the mind from wandering. The schedule helped me *to be* -- to be alert and prayerful -- without being distracted by thoughts of wondering what *to do* next. From the Prior to the last Brother, we all had an individualized schedule, all the while keeping to the major outline:

11:30 p.m.	-	rise, Matins of Our Lady
12:15 a.m.	-	Matins and Lauds in the church
2:00-3:00 a.m.	-	Lauds of Our Lady's Office in the cell, then return to bed
6:30 a.m.	-	rise, Prime, prepare for Mass
7:45 a.m.	-	community Mass; then Mass alone in a chapel
9:00 a.m.	-	prayer in cell, Tierce, spiritual reading, manual work or study
11:30 a.m.	-	Sext, main meal of the day
2:00 p.m.	-	None, manual work or study, spiritual reading, Vespers of Our Lady
5:00 p.m.	-	Vespers in the church
5:30 p.m.	-	prayer in the cell, light supper
7:30 p.m.	-	Compline, retire

Day after day, week after week, from the beginning of one year to the next, I followed that basic outline during the week. As soon as I woke up, both at night or in the morning, I first blessed myself with the Sign of the Cross. Then I went to the little bathroom sink, sprinkled some cold water on my face, dressed in my robe, cincture and scapular, and knelt at the kneeler of the tiny oratory, listening for the bell that signaled the start of prayers. In winter I checked my wood stove, stirred the embers and put a fresh log on.

It took me a little while to learn the art of using the small cast iron stove. But I learned quickly which types of wood burned longest, which burned hottest, how to keep the fire banked at night, and -- most importantly -- what to do if the fire went out. Pine shavings were good to start the fire, but pine logs didn't last long. They burned quickly and put out good heat. Hard wood like oak and maple burned longest and produced a more steady and easily regulated heat. I had a variety of everything in the small storage area in the cubiculum.

To my great surprise, soon after moving into cell M, one of the white doves that had been living in the garden of cell G showed up on the window sill of my new cell, making itself right at home. I had acquired a loyal friend and companion in my solitude! Because of the almost continuous cooing that it made, I named her Coo-coo. I thought the bird was a male until one evening I discovered that "he" had laid an egg. I sent the egg to the kitchen with the request that the Brother cook fry it for me, which he did. The fried egg was about the size of a half-dollar with a tiny yellow yoke in the center!

I set up a coat hanger perch in my cell with a box under it for droppings; and I constructed a crude birdhouse in the garden for her. But she never used it, preferring to stay in the *cubiculum* with me. Later on I moved the birdhouse into my basement wood storage area. She liked this arrangement and went there to roost. She was free to come and go. I would call her and she flew to my shoulder or landed on my hand. When the food box came she would jump up and down on top of it, waiting for peas or rice, which she took one by one from my fork. She especially liked graham cracker crumbs, which she would suck up with her little beak.

I soon established a garden in my new cell that Dom Raphael called "the best garden" in the cloister. He was so proud of it that on one special occasion he brought the Governor of the State of Vermont to my cell to view the garden. As I had done in cell G, I used pieces of rock together with rocks I brought in during the weekly walks to outline garden plots.

I even planted grass seed, created a lawn, and acquired an old push lawn mower to cut the grass. I had created an oasis in the desert!

Dom Raphael provided me with an extra allotting of plants and shrubs. When Mom came for a visit, she brought lilies, tulip bulbs, and other annuals for me to plant in the garden plots. I planted wild climbing roses and wired them to the garden wall. In my workshop I made a rustic wood bench and set it out under one of the trees. Once I asked the Prior if I could work in the garden naked in imitation of Adam in the Garden of Eden; but we agreed that the gnats and flies would quickly drive me to cover if ever I tried it!

The first snowstorm I experienced in Vermont took place on Thanksgiving Day. It wasn't celebrated as a religious holiday. It was a day like any other. Out of respect for the national holiday, however, we had a complete holiday dinner, with cranberry sauce and mashed potatoes, but without the turkey. At around dinner time Mom called that first year to wish me a happy day. I was eating my dinner when the Prior called me on the intercom. Mom was always very thoughtful about those things, and she appreciated my being closer to her distance-wise and in a safe environment.

On that first Thanksgiving Day and all through my first winter in Vermont, I never tired of contemplating the bright snow on the roofs of the other cells. My cell felt even cozier as I watched the smoke rising slowly from the chimneys. I always knew that the occupant was still alive if smoke was coming from his chimney!

In the spring of 1973, we had our first canonical Visitation. Having a canonical Visitation was something decided early on by the Carthusian Order, moved by concerns for peace and love, and the faithful observance in the houses of the Order. The General Chapter appointed several Visitors who were to visit each house of the Order. Their main concern was to manifest the solicitude of the Order in regard to each community; and they were endowed with the necessary powers to resolve any problems in the house they were delegated to visit.

Ironically, just the thought of an official Visitation caused uneasiness among many of the monks. I had experienced at least two Visitations while I was in Jerez, but I too had jitters about the whole thing. Someone from the outside was coming into the community to inspect what was going on. Everyone was exhorted to help the Visitors in the accomplishment of their duty in a climate of mutual trust. The chief duty of the Visitors was to offer everyone a fraternal welcome in the name of the General Chapter, and listen to each of the monks "with the greatest attention" with the goal of enabling each one "to give to God and his brothers the best of himself."

Besides talking to each monk separately, the Visitors met with the entire community assembled in the chapter room at the opening and closing sessions of the Visitation. They were advised to perform their task "not as judges, but as brothers," to whom the tempted and the afflicted could open their minds freely and without fear of any breach of confidence. Still, there was a certain reluctance to bare everything, and sometimes the Prior would warn his community members not to mention certain things.

One of the Visitors that year was my former Prior from Jerez, Dom Luis. I was happy to visit with him, and he enquired about my adaptation in Vermont. I talked freely about my occupations as Assistant Novice Master, and with slightly less freedom, mentioned my reservations about Dom Raphael and the way he led the community. I was happy to be in Vermont; I had nothing purely negative to say about by brethren.

When the Visitors were in my cell, they noticed that I kept a white dove in my quarters. Coo-coo had made her appearance known by flying onto the head of Dom Luis, who wasn't happy about it. He thought it might "do something" on his head. Even though she didn't "do anything," both Visitors later reminded the Prior that Carthusian monks were not to keep pets in their cell.

Neither the Prior nor I had really thought of the dove as "a pet." After the Visitation had ended, Dom Raphael told me that he considered the unofficial recommendation as just a recommendation; but he also made the decision to give the little white dove to someone who would take good care of her. I ended up keeping the bird for another year, until Dom Raphael eventually felt obliged to follow the Visitors' recommendation. I had become attached to Coo-coo. I loved that little bird, and it took a firm act of my will to accept giving her up. I had been taking care of her for almost two years.

One of the momentous decisions coming from the Visitation was my official appointment as Novice Master. Both the Visitors and Dom Raphael thought I was ready for the task. At thirty-two, I was one of the youngest Novice Masters ever appointed in the Order. Dom Luis was especially pleased because I had been "formed" in his house. Although some thought I was too young and inexperienced, later they would see that I took to the job with enthusiasm and a certain amount of wisdom. One of the doubters later remarked that I was worth my weight in gold!

In a wise move, the Prior had already prepared the community by first making me his assistant. And in another wise political move, so as not to disappoint anyone who might secretly have wanted the job, he recommended that the Visitors make the appointment official with the announcement of their determination. When the announcement was made to the assembled community in the Chapter room, there was an audible gasp of surprise and approval.

The office of Novice Master carried with it the implicit duty of Vocation Director as well. To attract and recruit new members we did not advertise through the common channels that were available. We prayed to the Lord to send vocations, and relied entirely on Him to increase our number. In His own way, He found young men who were willing to travel all around the world to find a Carthusian monastery.

When they came to try their vocation, we called them "retreatants" or "aspirants." As a rule, they were the only ones outside the Order allowed to participate at the offices or the community Mass. Those who neither were not, nor aspired to become, members of the Order, were not allowed to stay in the monastery cells. In order not to attract attention, and to avoid drawing crowds of visitors, the Order has insisted on keeping the monasteries small and hidden from view, ever maintaining a distaste for all publicity.

Unlike some other contemplative orders, we did not run a bookstore, nor did we encourage lay people to visit our chapels. We did not offer retreats in the strict sense of the term. The only people who entered the Charterhouse were young men who felt a call to the Carthusian way of life. They were invited to experience our life to test a possible calling.

One of my first tasks as Novice Master was to compose an informative brochure that I could send to prospective candidates. The Prior asked everyone in the community to write something appropriate and give it to me for editing. Several of the monks contributed something, and I put it all together, adding photos, and preparing the work for printing. I used an older brochure from the 1950s for much of the material, integrating excerpts from the *Renewed Statutes* with photos of the land, the monastery, and some of the monks. Before being published, it required the approval of the local Bishop and the Reverend Father General.

The Reverend Father made the comment that a part of the brochure seemed "too triumphal," something not in step with the Church's soul-searching apologetics after the Vatican Council. I had written: *Today Jesus has chosen a group of monks and led them up a high mountain in...Vermont. There they contemplate Jesus' glory...and listen and meditate on His words. While they listen and pray, they...are transfigured into other Christs.* Eventually the Reverend Father and Bishop Marshall gave their approval.

Each week Dom Raphael passed five or six letters of inquiry to me from men who wanted to explore our life of solitude and silence. I responded to each of them in a different way, depending on the tone and content of the letter I had received. To most individuals I sent a copy of our informative brochure with a cover letter and a detailed preliminary questionnaire. The promise of a vocation could be ascertained from the answers given to the questionnaire.

In response to some letters of inquiry I merely sent a brochure and cover letter. To still others, I sent a detailed and individualized letter, either asking them to come for a visit, or pointing out that their reception as a candidate would be impossible. We could not receive anyone over the age of forty. Some were married and obviously could not be received. One spouse actually called me pleading that we not accept her husband! One married man could be received if he had a divorce and an annulment. Another had physical problems that would definitely eliminate him because of the rigor of the life.

Dom Raphael initially read the letters that I wrote and gave helpful criticism. He thought many of them were too harshly worded. I had tried to be as succinct and direct as possible, writing more than once, "You don't have a calling, so forget it." Sometimes I used Spanish phrases, twisted sentences, or improper English prepositions.

The Prior corrected me in a gentle way and asked me to rewrite the letters. Having lived in Spain and used nothing but Spanish and Latin for such a long time, my English definitely needed some improvement. My spoken English wasn't much better either. Mom remarked when she saw me that I spoke with a "foreign accent." Some retreatants even asked if I was American!

If the preliminary correspondence seemed promising, we invited the candidate to come to the Charterhouse for a retreat of a few days to thirty days. I asked the candidate to arrive on a Tuesday if possible, and most of them were able to accommodate me. I didn't want them to arrive on a weekend or on a Monday, since these days were taken up with community activities. I would not have been able to devote enough initial time to the arrivals on those days. Nor did we receive retreatants during the cold winter months.

Part of my job as Novice Master and Vocation Director was to prepare the cells. Several empty cells were set aside for exclusive use by retreatants. I kept them clean, made up the bed, and took care of the towels and other linen. I also prepared a detailed schedule for the retreatant to follow, and left specifically chosen reading and meditation material.

When the retreatant arrived at the gatehouse, the people there called Dom Raphael to advise him. He then called me on the intercom. Sometimes I met the retreatant at the door of the enclosure and took him to the cell he was to occupy. Once in a while one of the Brothers met the retreatant and brought him to my cell. I then took him to the cell I had prepared. I spent a few minutes talking with each of them and then left for a time, giving the new arrival a chance to look around the cell and to form any questions for me.

Before returning to see a candidate, I prayed to the Holy Spirit for discernment; and I tried to interview the candidate with this in mind. After a while I could discern the presence of a calling from my first conversation with the candidate with ninety-nine percent accuracy. I think part of this was due to experience; but I also think the major part was due to the grace of discernment I received with the office of Novice Master.

After he had settled into the cell, I visited the retreatant for a longer interview. If I were reasonably sure that a calling might be there, I spent more time speaking with the candidate to further discern the calling; but if I felt otherwise, I would leave the candidate retreatant to the cell, and reported back to Dom Raphael with my first impressions. He would ask, "Does he have a vocation?" I would answer, "Maybe," or "No, I don't think so," and explain briefly why I thought so.

To experience a little of what life in the Carthusian monastery was all about, the retreatant followed a modified novitiate schedule. Most of the candidates were familiar enough with the Divine Office to recite it in cell on their own at the appointed times. I saw to it that they assisted at Mass and Vespers and the night office, usually placing them in choir next to me. I strictly regulated their reading in cell, and I suggested what work they might do. My advice was that they should try to enjoy the solitude -- give themselves to it in total confidence. I told them that if they remained in peace, they would begin to understand what Jesus said about the Spirit and the peace that the world could not give.

I advised the retreatants that there was "free time" after dinner, but the free time was generally not for taking a nap. The Brother cook advised me if the retreatant was not eating well, and other monks would from time to time advise me of what they observed. I looked in on each one at unannounced times as I saw fit; but I wanted them to become aware that while in the cell you were pretty much left to your own devices. Self-discipline was essential.

The cell was the water, and the monk was the fish. The monk could not live for long away from the cell, either physically or spiritually. My procedure was to test the candidate in the cell, to let the cell decide whether the candidate was capable of living in it. I felt that this was the only fair way to test a calling, fair to all parties involved. As the old monks said, "The cell will teach you all things." Life in the cell could be frightening to an outsider, but the one who was called to this unique way of life would find that he came to love the hermitage.

We wanted candidates to spend time with us so that we might together discern if they had that one most essential element for a vocation: the calling from God. Some candidates would have been able to live the life reasonably well for a time; but if they truly lacked the calling, we knew that they would leave sooner or later. More than one young enthusiast lasted less than twenty-four hours before fleeing from Mt. Equinox! They may have had an idealized vision of contemplative life, and their illusions were quickly shattered by the stark realities of the everyday solitude and silence of the Carthusian existence.

An extraordinary twist of events occurred once during my first year in Vermont when a young man who had been wandering in the mountains wandered into the monastery complex. He entered a cell one evening through the wood storage area. The usual move was for a retreatant to break out as from a prison! Though he did no damage to the cell, he didn't want to leave when he was found in the morning. The Vermont State Police had to physically remove him from the enclosure.

Retreatants came from a wide variety of backgrounds and experiences. Some were well educated, including college professors and other professional men. Others had a few years of college, or no college at all. Some aspirants were members of other religious orders who felt a call to a life of greater austerity; others were single laymen, and still others were diocesan priests. After a while we decided that candidates should have at least two years of college behind them before being accepted, although they were sometimes invited to come for a retreat in the meantime. Many were gifted and talented, but that was not a prerequisite.

Having few guidelines or procedural directives to follow, I had to make them up on my own under the Prior's direction. I had been trying to be a good silent and solitary monk while at the same time attempting to relate to and understand the young men who came to us. I had to lead something of a double life for a time before becoming integrated. I wanted to understand each and every individual: who they were and where they were coming from. I was out of touch with the cultural milieu of the country where these young men were coming from.

I was trying by trial and error to be the best Novice Master and Vocation Director that I could. My first encounters with aspirants were awkward. Some of the candidates seemed to appreciate my being new on the job, while others probably thought I was rather weird -- more weird than they had expected. One retreatant suggested to me that I should smile more. Another told me that when he shook my hand he had the feeling that I was "a dead man." Eventually I realized that I was taking the whole interviewing and discernment process much too seriously. I began to loosen up, to smile more, and to spend more time chatting with the retreatants.

On Sundays and holidays the retreatants did not eat with the community or go to the chapter. I explained that things were different for the monks, who found stimulation for the mind through the community recreations as well as through reading and study. The only community exercise the retreatants attended was the weekly walk, which many of them would have preferred to miss. Occasionally a retreatant would be invited to the novitiate recreation if I thought it was fitting.

Each and every retreatant seemed to appreciate the time I spent with them. On the other hand, I felt absolutely terrified when Dom Raphael suggested that I frequent the guest parlor to accompany the postulants and novices when their families came. Ever mindful of my calling to solitude and silence, I had very little to say, and usually sat there smiling and answering questions in as few words as possible. I felt extremely awkward, and the visitors must have wondered what I was doing in their presence, merely smiling and saying very little!

Once I was appointed Novice Master and we had postulants and retreatants, we began to take our walks separately from the professed. As leader of the group I had to be careful to avoid pairing certain individuals together for too long a time. One or another of my charges would sometimes meddle in the affairs of the others, trying to give advice on matters that were out of their jurisdiction. It also prevented disagreements from arising.

The Prior was aware that certain professed monks should not walk with the novices for the same reason. In a small and developing community like ours, it was not always easy to avoid hurting feelings or making others feel that they were somehow unappreciated or being discriminated against. While I was the Novice Master, Dom Philip was the only professed Father who was permitted to walk with the members of the novitiate. He was always discreet and deferred to my judgment, even though he was more senior than I was in profession.

Since we were a younger group, I normally took the novices for longer walks than the professed. I planned it beforehand and advised the Prior of our general route in the event that we were late in getting back. In the very beginning we were late in getting back several times due to poor planning on my part. I finally learned to plan the walks in such a way that we either traveled in a circular route, or else in one direction for half of the allotted time and then returning back on basically the same route. We rested for a few minutes about every forty-five minutes, sometimes to recite a decade of the rosary during the rest period, just as we had done in Spain.

I tried to avoid going to inhabited places, and we never talked to anyone beyond simple greetings, unless there was some extreme need, and then I was the one who would do the talking. Although I carried a topographical map and a compass, we sometimes became disoriented. At those times I had to ask for directions. When it was necessary to walk along a public highway or come close to a town or village, we simply passed through without detaining ourselves at any one place. Except in an emergency situation, we were not permitted to enter the houses of seculars, nor hold conversation with strangers.

Once I was walking across a frozen stream in the valley when I fell through. The temperature was around fifteen degrees, my habit became frozen stiff as a board after thirty seconds, and we were more than five miles from the monastery. We had to stop at a house and telephone the monastery for transportation. Dom Marianus came to our aid with a car. On several occasions, we wandered so far from the monastery that it would have been impossible to return on time. I had to find a telephone to notify the Prior that we would be late for Vespers, lest he be worried.

In an attempt to be more democratic in the selection of walking routes, I sometimes asked the novices where they would like to go. If I thought it could be done, and if it did not clash with a plan I had already worked out in my mind, we voted on the suggestion. The General Chapter with the advice of the Visitors normally laid out the bounds for the walks. Our boundaries were pretty liberal. We could easily walk a total of seven to ten miles up and down the hills if we so desired. Sometimes we walked down into the valley; sometimes we walked to the top of Mt. Equinox. During the winter we sometimes used snowshoes, and some of the monks used skies.

We did not give anything like rosaries or holy cards to anyone we might meet along the way; nor were we permitted to eat anything or drink anything except plain water. If we came across apples or berries along the way, we were not permitted to taste them. In accordance with a very old custom of the Order, we took an exceptionally long walk once a year. On this walk, we were permitted to go beyond the limits assigned by the Visitors and General Chapter. Each of us was given a picnic lunch which we were told to consume "well removed from strangers."

I found that the weekly walk was sufficient to dispel any "hermit fever" that might have built up during the week. Yet whenever the walk day was delayed or put off because of rain or some other reason, the delay caused a blip in the ordinary regime so much so that you actually felt that something was wrong. Sometimes I felt depressed, sometimes worse; and this affected different monks in different ways. Those of our brothers who were inclined toward depression felt this most deeply.

One week the walk had to be delayed for two days because of a heavy snowstorm. On this particular walk day before we departed, the Prior called me on the intercom and told me that one of the Fathers was "missing," and asked me to keep an eye out for him as we hiked. I communicated this to my two novices, and we decided that the best course of action would be to climb through the snowdrifts to the top of Mt. Equinox.

There was a rumor that our brother intended to literally climb over the mountain and head north on Rt. 7 toward Canada. We trudged through the snow and climbed to the top; and, sure enough, when we reached the top, we saw him. He had walked with us at different times, so we called to him to see if he wanted to join our group. When he replied negatively, I went to speak with him privately. With some reluctance and embarrassment, he told me what I already knew: that he was headed toward Montreal and intended to fly to France.

I don't know how he intended to walk to Montreal, purchase a ticket without any money, and board a plane for France without any passport. But I told him I was going with him. He was touched by the reply, but declined my offer. I went back to the novices and instructed them to return to the monastery to inform Dom Raphael that my brother monk and I were headed down the other side of the mountain and would come out somewhere along the main road.

It was quite an experience to descend the east side of the mountain, slipping and sliding down the steep slope that was covered in snow and ice. By the time we reached the main highway it was already dark and cold. At times I lost sight of him as we made our way through the trees down the steep mountain; from time to time I saw him look back to see if I was still following.

In the meantime, having received news from the two novices, the Prior had sent a vehicle out on the highway to intercept us. We met the vehicle and drove back up the mountain. My brother monk had asked to be driven into town to speak to our dentist, I think in the hope of receiving funds for his trip to France; but he resigned himself without a fight to be returned to the monastery.

Dom Raphael was relieved to see us when he met us at the door. He took the disturbed monk to his office for a talk. I reported the good news to the two novices and then went to the shower room for a hot bath. He told the Prior that his relationship with me had become much closer because of our experience. I hadn't seen it exactly that way; but I was happy to have performed an act of fraternal charity that was appreciated.

Retreatants came and went through the years. I kept a notebook with the dates of their arrival and departure, with a few notations that would help me remember them. All of them had their unique story, and the more I dealt with them the more I began to appreciate my own privileged position of having contact with each and every one of them. When they left and I had to prepare the cell for the next one, I almost always felt a pang of disenchantment and melancholy. I wanted all of them to have a calling; but at the same time I was learning by experience that the calling was given to very few. I wondered to myself if I could have done more to foster a possible calling.

Each and every one of the retreatents made an impression on me, and most of the impressions were favorable. I began to enjoy spending time with them, even though few of them had a Carthusian calling. I prayed that they would do well, that each one would have the grace, the strength, and the courage to follow his particular path toward the truth. Of the fifty to eighty letters of inquiry that I received each year, less than a third of those who had written the letters actually came for a retreat. Of those who came, I expected no more than one or two to have an authentic calling.

Some retreatants came out of curiosity or out of some necessity that had not been mentioned in their original letter. There was, for example, the brother of a young woman who wanted to join the Carthusian Nuns. She thought there was some kind of entrance process that began with Dom Raphael at the Charterhouse of the Transfiguration. Her brother came with her under the pretext of testing a calling to the monastery, whereas in reality his intention was solely to accompany his sister. She stayed in the guesthouse for a day or two, while her brother suffered in a cell, vowing never to return to any monastery.

One of the first retreatants was so stressed after a day in the cell that he had something of a seizure or nervous breakdown in the choir during the night office. Dom Philip and several of the more corpulent monks had to sit on him to subdue him. We sent him away the following morning. When I expressed a sense of culpability, Dom Raphael assured me that I had no fault in his being stressed. Another young man from Philadelphia wanted to try our life, but because of kidney problems, could not be accepted.

Many of the young men who came as retreatants tried the Brothers' life for a week or two, finding it too busy or not solitary enough. They came to the Fathers' side of the cloister for another week or two, and though we tried to accommodate them as best we could, none of them had a calling to our life. One of these that I remember well also went to the Camaldolese foundation in Ohio, where he persevered to become Prior of the hermitage. Another young Trappist Brother returned to his abbey, where he belonged. Most of those who found they did not have a Carthusian calling expressed gratitude for the experience of living our life for a time. They had gotten the Carthusian "bug" out of their system.

A young man from Oregon who had been in the movie *Goodbye Mr. Chips*, that I had seen on my flight from Spain thought he had a Carthusian calling. Ironically, his one line in the movie, which he repeated several times to my delight, had to do with learning Latin! He didn't really know Latin, nor did he have a calling. However, he saw my dove, and on his returning home, sent me a white dove as a companion for Coo-coo. He sent a female, because at that time I thought my bird was a male. The two females were unable to live in my cell together, and we had to return the dove after a few weeks.

Anyone interested in entering the Carthusian Order had to undergo rigorous psychological screening before he could enter the monastery as a postulant. Dom Raphael was particularly adamant and inflexible about this. The psychological testing was carried out in New York City, normally after the candidate had completed a thirty-day retreat at the monastery. If the psychological tests showed no major problems, we invited the candidate to return as a postulant. If the test results were questionable, we made a judgment whether to invite the candidate to return of not.

Only sufficiently mature candidates were encouraged to return. Even so, as Novice Master I had to watch my charges for signs of either spiritual or psychological problems. Some candidates were mature, but less flexible than we would have wanted, and so we decided that they could not be accepted. They would have cracked in time. Several were on the age-limit borderline, and were put him off indefinitely. They would not have adapted to the rigors of the life. Being a young community, the Prior wanted young men who could grow with the community. We sometimes recommended that older men try for admittance at one or another of the established European Charterhouses, since they were more flexible about admitting candidates than we were.

According to the Church's law, any religious could attempt to transfer to the Carthusian Order from another order or congregation. On the other hand, we Carthusians, who were considered to be at the top, were not permitted to transfer to any other religious order. Most Carthusians who became unable to live in the cell applied for either a complete dispensation from their vows, or an "indult of exclaustration." While the dispensation, if it could be obtained, effectively severed all visible and binding ties with the Order, exclaustration meant that the monk was still a member of the Order, but lived outside the monastery.

Of the priests and active religious who came to test their calling to the cloistered life, with one exception, none were admitted, each for his own reason. An Australian missionary priest came to us by way of South America for a month-long testing. He did very well in the cell, and felt very comfortable with our life. Unfortunately the Reverend Father General, whose permission he had to have for the transfer, refused to give it. He felt that the priest was too old at forty-one to begin our austere life. I had the somewhat unpleasant task of taking the negative news to him. All religious from other congregations or orders, and anyone over forty years of age, had to receive permission from the Reverend Father to enter.

In 1973, Father DePaul, a young Benedictine monk from Latrobe, PA, came for a retreat. He had tried the Carthusian life in Italy and France, and had been accepted for the Italian Charterhouse. But he wanted to be closer to his family in the United States. He gave the impression of being an authentically spiritual soul, a true monk searching for God. Although he was very pious and pleasant, he soon recognized that he was called to something other than the Charterhouse. He returned to his abbey, and soon after was sent to France and Rome for further studies, eventually earning a doctorate on the spirituality of Saint Therese of Lisieux.

One month a priest of the Carmelite Order, who had recently escaped from Communist Cuba by hiding in the landing wheel compartment of a plane bound for Miami, came for a retreat. He soon recognized that there was no Carthusian calling. And a pleasant young Dominican priest tried the life, but decided to return to his parish work in New Mexico. Other priests from several dioceses around the country came and tasted our monastic lifestyle, all being greatly impressed, but without a calling to stay.

While he was still the Novice Master, Dom Raphael had arranged for several promising candidates to come for extended retreats. Among them was an intellectually gifted young Jesuit cleric who was in perpetual vows, but not yet a priest. He became the first official postulant and novice of the new Charterhouse, under the direction of both Dom Raphael and me. After I was officially appointed Novice Master, Dom Raphael continued to have a keen interest in Dom Bruno's formation. Perhaps Dom Bruno would rather have continued dealing with Dom Raphael than with me, perceiving him to be more an intellectual than I. Perhaps the Fordham University connection they both shared was also present in the background.

After a brief period of ups and downs, I think Dom Bruno accepted the idea that I was *the* Novice Master. But he still made it plain on more than one occasion that he did not appreciate the simplicity and (what he perceived as) the anti-intellectual quality of my spirituality. I did my best to explain that the Spanish spirituality of "nothingness," in which I was formed as a Carthusian, could seem pretty bleak and forbidding by itself. Nothingness, however, was really the opposite side of the coin that bore the inscription, "everything."

It was not my job to impose any one system of spirituality on anyone, nor did I try. It was my job to form the novice into a Carthusian monk in the image of the Statutes. I made this very clear to my charges, making it equally clear that any novice was always free to go to the Prior with complaints and comments. Dom Bruno did this on occasion. However, as time passed, his complaints and visits to the Prior were fewer and fewer. While he encountered a variety of problems during his first few years in the Charterhouse, he managed to persevere, going on the hold several important and responsible positions in the Order.

During the 1970s we had retreatants who had served in Vietnam, and who perhaps were seeking a refuge where they could recover from the scars of that war. One such candidate completed a thirty-day retreat successfully, but received a questionable psychological report. Dom Raphael accepted him as a postulant anyway. He and Dom Bruno were postulants together, coming to my cell every Sunday afternoon for a novitiate conference. After two or three months, however, he began to experience psychological problems as had been predicted. He left the community of his own accord.

Of all the retreatents who came for a long retreat, only three advanced through the postulancy period into the novitiate. One of these was an especially fervent and eager young man who had been in the army and had spent some time as a postulant in a Trappist abbey. Dom John-Paul was rather on the active side and seemed to have some problems with both the studies and the rule of silence. He was, nevertheless, a sincerely spiritual soul and a very good novice. In time he developed several health problems, and as a consequence had to leave before making solemn vows.

The other excellent novice came all the way from California. A quiet individual, he had spent some time with the Carmelites. Advancing successfully through the postulancy period into the novitiate, Dom Joseph developed a severe health problem and had to leave. I felt a profound sense of disappointment when he left. For a time I wondered if the problem had arisen because of the way the novitiate regime was set up. Maybe it had been too harsh for him. But Dom Raphael reassured me that there was no fault on my part.

The Prior encouraged me to visit the members of the novitiate, and to talk to them with frank simplicity. I came to know their interior dispositions, and tried to give each one the advice suited to his particular needs. It was ever my intention to help each one attain the perfection of his vocation, ever keeping in mind the demands of the Carthusian and monastic traditions. Both demands could at times seem downright brutal to the popular mentality of the day. On the other hand, I found that the postulants and novices were eager and willing to experience the rigors of the tradition in all its strength. At times they had to be restrained from going too far.

After the admittedly difficult months of the postulancy and novitiate, the novice monks generally adapted well to their new world. The weight and permanence of the granite walls reinforced the radical commitment that they wanted to make. They gradually learned, as I had in Spain, that they could not always expect help from outside their cell, or wait for some change in their routine to bring relief from any heaviness of spirit. Our life had only one meaning and one object: God had led us into solitude to speak to our heart.

In solitude one learns to expect nothing and be ready for anything. Within a year of my arrival in Vermont, the American-born Procurator, Dom Louis, informed me one day that he was leaving. The only explanation I ever heard was that he had entered the monastery at too young an age and had never matured. They said it was just a matter of time before he left. As an example of immaturity, Dom Raphael pointed out that Dom Louis had suggested that we form a softball team and play against the Brothers, or perhaps against a neighboring monastery!

Someone, perhaps it was also Dom Louis, suggested that we be allowed to swim in any of the two large ponds or smaller feeder ponds on the property. This idea didn't fly too well either, although we were given permission to "swim," provided we did it in full habit. Following up on this permission, Dom Philip, on returning from a weekly walk one hot summer afternoon, jumped in, shoes and all, and swam across the pond. I also tried it, but the water proved too cold, and I never tried it again.

On entering the Charterhouse, I gave up all idea of participating in sports. It was totally foreign to the contemplative monastic life. The weekly walk provided enough exercise, and some of the Fathers, including myself, did floor exercises and moderate aerobics in the cell to keep toned. In winter we walked with snowshoes, which was quite strenuous at times. Some of the monks went out on skis, and sometimes we used a sled in winter to slide down the snow-covered roads.

One winter I used snowshoes to slide down a steep trail from the top of Mt. Equinox. On reaching the bottom of the trail I hit a small stump and went head over heels into a snow bank. My eyeglasses flew off, and I had to go to town for a new pair. The next spring after the snow had melted, I returned to the spot and found my glasses!

Dom Raphael always placed a great deal of emphasis on psychological and social maturity. Dom Louis and I were about the same age, both of us having entered the Order in our early twenties. He had been trained in France and had been sent to Vermont a year before I was. As I look back on my experiences in the Charterhouse, I understand that I, like Dom Louis, was lacking in maturity. Dom Raphael often commented that what I said or did was "immature." I don't know if I really understood at the time what he was talking about when he mentioned the word.

Dom Louis' departure was a great disappointment to me. I had grown to appreciate his candor and the freshness of his approach to life. Soon after he left, a monk was sent from the only Charterhouse in Germany to be Procurator and Novice Master for the Brother candidates. Dom Marianus was not only German, but also an authentic German Prince. At first he seemed to act the part of a prince and seemed somewhat disdainful of Americans and American culture. In the beginning, he once said that he "wouldn't give two cents" for one of the American Brothers he was in charge of. But he spoke English well, and after a few understandable false starts adapted to the American culture and mentality.

We Fathers didn't see much of Dom Marianus during the week outside of community prayers, the Sunday recreation, and an occasional Monday walk day. If we needed anything that the Procurator was authorized to provide, most of us went directly to the Prior with our request at first. As Dom Marianus adapted more and more to the American mentality and customs, we had more occasion to go to him if we needed something; and the Brothers, on their part, came to respect and love him.

Most of the young American men who contacted the Charterhouse were more inclined toward the Brothers' life than the Fathers'. Both among those who had no experience whatever with the religious life, and also among those who had been in other monasteries, there seemed to be more of an attraction to the Brothers' more active lifestyle. There was a perception of more freedom of movement and more everyday activity.

There was also the perception that the Fathers' life called for great intellectual ability, whereas the Brothers did not have to worry about studies or other intellectual pursuits. Their lifestyle was somehow more humble. All this was basically in keeping with the Order's general view of Americans as more inclined toward activity than contemplative pursuits.

After the renewals initiated after the Vatican Council, however, Fathers and Brothers began to share more of a common family life. We had occasional recreations together, and weekly walks were sometimes taken together. The Brothers could sing among the Fathers in choir, if they wished, and they could act as "deacons" during the sung Mass. Some of the older Fathers resented what they considered the intrusion of the Lay Brothers into their exclusive territory. For a time I was among this number. I had developed a highly conservative attitude, and anything that was not totally traditional was at least suspect in my eyes. I had to accept the changes and bear with them. There was no going back to former customs.

At the same time, monasteries and convents began to empty. Monks started to return from the desert to a world that was no longer a place to flee from. The Council documents stated that the world was "fundamentally good." It was up to the individual to seek and cultivate that goodness for himself and for others. You didn't have to "bury yourself" in a monastery or convent. These winds of change eventually reached the Charterhouse, and they affected my life as Novice Master when fewer candidates wrote for information, or showed up demanding entrance into the monastery.

On the other hand, major changes were taking place in our religious community. The aim of Vatican II had been "to invoke a new Pentecost" in the Church. There was no mention of abandoning the religious life. Religious were exhorted to make greater efforts to dedicate themselves entirely to the loving service of Christ in the Church. We monks were encouraged to adapt ever more perfectly to the continuously changing circumstances of our times. "Renewal" and "adaptation" were buzzwords within the Church.

Renewal meant returning to the sources of the religious life, to the original inspiration of the community. Adaptation meant taking into account the real situation and needs of the world today in shaping one's rule of life, and ministry. Prescriptions toward the adaptation and renewal of the religious life included both the constant return to the sources of all Christian life and to the original spirit of the institutes and their adaptation to the changed conditions of our time.

In response to the general mandate of the Council for renewal, we retreated further into the solitude and silence of the desert. Most of the particular changes were concerned with the liturgical celebrations. Use of the vernacular (language of the country) was permitted under certain spelled-out limitations. There was a reduction of the number of feast days and octaves that took us from our cells and normal daily occupations. Medieval leftovers like "Rogation days" (days of special prayers for specific intentions), the "Minutions" (bleeding for health purposes), and the "Crusader tax" in Spain, were all eliminated.

Although I was accustomed to the former ways, I generally liked the changes, especially those that afforded more solitude in the cell. Latin enthusiast that I was, I wasn't happy with the introduction of the vernacular, even though it was on a limited basis, and not obligatory in the cell or at the private Mass.

While many religious communities suffered a loss of membership and decline in vocations in the years following Vatican II, the Carthusian Order did not suffer as great a loss as many others; but the vocational abundance of former times could no longer be taken for granted. History has shown that religious communities go through a life cycle, and those that remain faithful to their identity, while striving at the same time to carry out the evangelizing ministry of Christ, seem to be able to weather any storm.

More than fifty years ago, an elderly Carthusian monk said that we were "a dying breed." But we had not disappeared, and were confident that young men would continue to experience the unique call to the Carthusian life of prayer and penance. In an age marked by constant activity and competition for material welfare, some young men would find the life of silence and interior prayer even more attractive. We invited them to dare, to go beyond themselves, to enter into the depths of their being, and to aspire for something noble and higher.

Communities entirely dedicated to contemplation like ours retained an honorable place in the Mystical Body of Christ, whose members did not all have the same function. By occupying ourselves with God alone in solitude and silence, with constant prayer and penance willingly undertaken, the Church told us that we offered to God "an outstanding sacrifice of praise." I had always believed this, that we contemplative monks gave a degree of luster to the people of God, that we were a wellspring of heavenly graces for all of mankind.

The Church told us that our lifestyle had to be revised while we preserved our withdrawal from the world and the exercises proper to the contemplative life. As a consequence of this revision, each Charterhouse took on some of the character of the national and local place. In keeping with the letter and spirit of Vatican II, some traditional American customs were introduced into the Charterhouse of the Transfiguration. At Christmas we had a tree, and each of us monks received a present. Most of the presents were given by kind benefactors, and were useful articles like tee shirts and warm socks. The first Christmas I was in Vermont we all received a quilted vest that could be worn under the habit. It was very useful and I wore it often.

Although we spent Christmas Day itself mostly in the silence and solitude of the cell, we had a common recreation with the Brothers on the day following Christmas. It was as authentic a family gathering as you might expect from solitary monks. We sang Christmas carols and talked freely. Brother Anthony crooned his interpretation of *White Christmas*. We had our noon meal in common, and a larger-than-usual supper Christmas night in our warm cell. There were lots of special desserts on that day for the first few years. Then, due to complaints from a few of the more austere monks, the Prior generally cut back on the sweets.

As time passed, and I adapted to living in Vermont and exercising my various responsibilities in the community, I adopted variations to the schedule, all with the knowledge and permission of the Prior. For example, I substituted a decade of the rosary for each hour of the Office of the Blessed Virgin, finding it more helpful to my prayer life to meditate quietly on each mystery of the life of Jesus, rather than recite a number of psalms.

Always nervous about the night office, I began to rise a little later than normal, giving myself just enough time to pray and prepare myself for the Office. When my body began telling me that I needed more rest, I began to get up later in the morning, sometimes rising as late as 7:30, giving myself just enough time to prepare for going to the church for Mass. Nor did I celebrate a private Mass everyday after the community Mass. I did this partly out of humility, considering myself unworthy; and I did it partly out of a desire to spend more time in quiet contemplation after receiving communion at the community Mass.

When I did celebrate Mass in private after the community Mass, one of the novices would be assigned to serve the Mass. While we had permission to celebrate Mass in English, I always celebrated my private Mass in Latin as I had always done. Sometimes I used English for the readings, mostly for the benefit of novices or retreatants.

Outside of feast days when it was obligatory to celebrate the Mass of the day, I normally chose to say the votive Mass of the Blessed Trinity. For me, the mystery of the Trinity was the culmination of revelation and all religion. I felt privileged and proud to celebrate that particular Mass with its moving and relevant texts. *Blessed be the Holy and Undivided Trinity, for He has shown us His mercy.* Although some of my servers grew tired of hearing the same Mass, I never tired of reading the texts and praising the Trinity.

During my first few months in Vermont I had read nothing but the Bible for "spiritual reading," dwelling and meditating on each word as I read the passages. I tried to scrutinize the divine mysteries with that desire to know that had its origin in love of God. I found great nourishment for my soul in the Holy Scriptures. Dom Raphael suggested that I read the works of St. Francis de Sales, a moderate, rational writer, perhaps thinking that my harsh Spanish spirituality needed moderating; but when I tried to read his works, I found little nourishment for my spirit.

The same occurred when I tried to read the works of other "spiritual writers," especially the modern and contemporary ones. With the exception of the early works of Thomas Merton, very little moved me as being worthwhile of the time. In addition to Holy Scripture, however, I did scan through the writings of the Fathers of the Church, and the proved monastic authors every week looking for material that I could use for the novitiate conferences.

I gave a weekly novitiate conference in my cell on Sunday after Vespers. Just as I had been taught in Spain, I followed my Novice Master's lead by concentrating heavily on the study of the Liturgy. I taught the meaning and historical development of the liturgical seasons, and I discussed the saints whose feast days we would celebrate. Every year at Christmas time a liturgical calendar for the following year was sent from the Grand Chartreuse. When I entered the Order, and until the late 1960s, the calendar came in the form of a little book that you could carry in your pocket. Later one sheet was sent that you could hang in your little oratory.

To the novices I pointed out that St. Bruno and his companions had put together a liturgy particularly adapted to their semi-eremitical vocation. Over the centuries, our Fathers had sought to preserve this unique liturgy, characterized by its simplicity and sobriety in terms of external forms. Certain elements of our liturgy were the long periods of silence, the absence of all musical instruments, and a particular version of Gregorian chant that we appropriately called "Carthusian chant." I discussed all these elements at length in their historical and spiritual context.

The spiritual orientation that the Carthusian monk quite naturally developed as he lived the life had always been known for its characteristics of discretion, joy and simplicity, a tender love for Jesus and Mary, and a constant care not to lose sight of the lowly struggles of the purgative way, even in the heights of the contemplative life. I discussed the Statutes in great depth with the novices, and how their faithful and careful observance would lead to the "savoring knowledge of God," which was the basis and end of Carthusian spirituality.

For background information I was fortunate to have an annotated copy of the first draft of the *Revised Statutes*. I pointed out that the *Customs* of the Chartreuse were not committed to writing till 1127, that Bruno had left the world in order to serve God in solitude, and without any intention of founding a religious order. In the earliest days the hermits of Chartreuse had no rule. They strove simply to live after Bruno's example and in accordance with the evangelical counsels.

When regular monastic buildings were erected and vocations began to increase, some sort of rule became a necessity. St. Bruno wrote none, but the customs that he introduced, together with additions born of experience, were put into written form by Guigo, the fifth prior of the Grand Chartreuse. There was, then, no written rule before 1130, when Guigo reduced to writing the body of customs that had been the basis of Carthusian life.

Guigo pointed out that Bruno and his first successors belonged to "the school of the Holy Spirit," letting themselves and their lifestyle be forged by experience. They elaborated a unique eremitical way of life, which was transmitted from one generation to another by example, and not by the written word. Rather than a rule written with authority, it was a record of the usages of the motherhouse of the Order, compiled at the request of the Priors of the associated Charterhouses, and accepted by them as their rule of life.

Much of the text had appeared originally in the writings of Saint Jerome and the writings of other monastic Fathers, including the Rule of the Camaldolese, which had been reduced to writing in 1080. The Rule of St. Benedict gave the norm of those duties that were performed in common, and supplied the arrangement of the Divine Office, the treatment of guests, the wording of the vows.

Departures from St. Benedict's Rule were introduced to meet the essential needs for solitude in the Carthusian life; and from the Fathers of the Desert came the arrangement of the buildings and the solitary life of the cells. In this way, the Western monasticism embodied in St. Benedict's Rule was blended with the eremitical life of the Egyptian solitaries.

The first Carthusians tended to be more purely eremitical; but a cenobitic development was hastened by the necessities of life and by the influence of neighboring Benedictine houses, especially perhaps of Cluny. The union of the two systems only gradually evolved under the pressure of circumstances. The Order grew slowly at first. In the year 1300 there were approximately thirty-nine monasteries; but during the fourteenth century, one hundred and thirteen more monasteries were founded.

During the fifteenth century, forty-four Charterhouses were founded; and by 1521, there were two hundred and six. However, in the turbulent years of the sixteenth century, at least thirty-nine were destroyed by the Protestant Reformation. In 1559 a foundation in Mexico was projected, but fell through owing to the opposition of the King of Spain. Between 1600 and 1667, some twenty-two monasteries were founded, and then no more until the nineteenth century.

Except for a few years during the fifteenth and sixteenth centuries, there have never been many Carthusian monks. The Carthusian community was originally limited to thirteen monks in imitation of Christ and His twelve disciples. In 1607, the Prior General Dom Innocent Le Masson wrote, "We number about two thousand five hundred choir monks and one thousand three hundred Lay Brothers and Donates, with an average of a dozen Fathers and eight or nine Lay Brothers to each house." Later, especially with the influx of more Lay Brothers, the number of choir monks in each monastery also increased. In recent times the number of combined Fathers and Brothers has fluctuated between three and seven hundred worldwide.

Guigo's *Customs* (the *Consuetudines*) were approved by Pope Innocent II in 1133, and are still the basis of the modern statutes. In time, additions and modifications were made to adapt to conditions of new times and locations. Revisions and modifications always had as their end the return to the pristine Carthusian spirit and practice. New editions always added the various ordinances passed by the General Chapters. The Carthusian Rule was printed for the first time in 1510. Various other editions and revisions followed. The largely legalistic 1932 revision was in force when I entered the Order.

After the council of Vatican II, the highly spiritualized *Renewed Statutes of the Carthusian Order* were drawn up in

1973. They were further revised and approved by the General Chapter of 1987. The many formal changes and additions that the original *Customs* have undergone have affected neither their substance nor the spirit of the original foundation of the Order. One Prior has remarked that the revisions "have been like a change of clothing, which adds nothing and takes nothing from the substance of the body."

As Novice Master, I taught the novices the Carthusian path as I had learned it and lived it for more than ten years. The old monks said that it took at least ten years to become a true Carthusian. As I grew in the life, I felt in my heart that a Carthusian monk was, more than anything else, *a poor man who wanted to dedicate himself exclusively to God in a life of solitude and silence.* Our mission in life as Carthusians was before all else *to be there,* alone in God's presence. My Carthusian brothers and I had been singled out "to discover the immensity of God's love" within the confines of the Charterhouse walls, to live as watchmen and defenders on the walls of the City of God.

Guigo had encouraged those desiring to follow Saint Bruno's ideal *to follow the example of the poor man Christ, in order to share in His riches.* As I experienced it, this "dispossession" passed through a complete and entire break with the world, which did not necessarily have to mean contempt for the world, but rather a fresh orientation of one's whole life in a tireless search for God.

The sole end of the Carthusian lifestyle has always been contemplation, to live as continually as possible in the light of God's love for us. Purity of heart and entrance into the contemplative repose of continuous prayer, assume that the monk has traveled a long and sometimes rough road. He will be tested with both interior and exterior trials. He will experience a closeness to the Cross of Christ, and visits of God coming to test him like gold in the fire. Ultimately, the monk will be purified by patient endurance. The Holy Spirit will take the monk into the recesses of his own heart, where he will be able to serve God in truth and adhere to Him in love.

I learned that all monastic life consisted of this journey towards the heart, while the value of the Carthusian monastic life would be measured by how it facilitated the reaching of this goal. We Carthusian monks were distinguished from other contemplative monks by the particular path that we had taken, whose essential characteristics were:

- solitude
- a measure of community life
- the Carthusian liturgy

We most certainly shared certain monastic values with other contemplatives: silence, work, poverty, chastity, obedience, listening to Scripture, prayer, and humility. Drawing from the writings of Thomas Merton and some of the Eastern Fathers, I expounded on the monastic values that we shared with other monks. I pointed out that the first essential characteristic of the Carthusian life, the one that distinguished our calling from other callings, was the vocation to solitude. I could not repeat enough that the essence of our vocation was to give ourselves to the silence and solitude of the cell.

The cell was the holy ground where God and His servant could hold frequent conversations. In the cell the soul could unite itself to the Word of God as the bride to the groom, the earth to the sky, man to the divine. The human being became divine by becoming what he already was. I had experienced a long journey through a dry and barren desert. It demanded of me the strong faith that God was leading me through the desert, finally to attain "the fount of water" as He had promised.

Each one in his own way learned, as I had learned years earlier, that one's particular solitude was lived on three levels: separation from the world, faithfulness to the cell, and interior solitude. Each monk might feel an urge to concentrate on a particular aspect of this solitude more than on the others; and it might occur that one would concentrate on one aspect at different times in his life.

I concentrated on the physical solitude of the enclosure and cell at first. Later, when I had more activities outside of my cell, on interior solitude. In any case, I had felt in my innermost being that this solitude, together with the life of asceticism as ordained by the Statutes, joined us with the work of Christ who surrendered Himself to the Father for the salvation of souls. By doing penance I took part in the redemptive role of Christ, who saved mankind, captive and burdened by sin, through His prayer to the Father and by His death on the Cross.

Separation from the world was made possible by the monastic enclosure, which was usually a physical barrier that surrounded the monastery. It was the wall that closed us off from the world, and the world was likewise closed off from us. Whether in actuality we were confined within, or whether the world was closed out, was part of a continual debate. In any case, it was the cell within the enclosure that assured that we had a solitude that was as complete as possible.

Within the cell we lived alone for most of the day, for the entire duration of our life, if such were God's will. The most important interior solitude, "purity of heart" as it was often called, meant keeping one's spirit from any and all things not of God or leading towards God, through the habit of a tranquil listening of the heart, a stillness which allowed God to enter in.

It has ever been the mind of the Carthusian Order that absolute dedication to God be expressed and sustained by a great strictness of enclosure. Indeed, the Prior of the Grande Chartreuse never went beyond the boundaries of the desert of Chartreuse. And since all who professed it in a uniform and like manner should observe one and the same rule of life, it followed that those who had adopted the Carthusian ideal did not readily admit exceptions.

Among us Carthusian monks there has always existed a solitary communion, both within the same monastery, and also between monasteries of the Order. The unique balance of solitude and brotherly coexistence was an essential of the Carthusian lifestyle. The Holy Spirit had gathered together those who lived in solitude into a communion of love in the image of the Church, which was one and extended to all ends of the earth. We Carthusians, like all contemplatives, consciously lived in the heart of the Church. We accomplished an essential function in the ecclesiastical community and the world, namely, the glorification of God.

Our community life consecrated itself around the daily liturgy and in the weekly community reunions; but the celebration of the daily Eucharistic sacrifice was always the center and summit of our communal life. Novices and postulants were quick to realize this. My explaining it to them was a way of confirming what they already knew, that we had withdrawn to the desert to worship God, to praise Him, to admire Him, to be seduced by Him, to give themselves to Him, in the name of all mankind.

By our presence on this earth, we witnessed that God lived and could take over the hearts of men. Separated from all, we were truly and consciously united to all, for it was in the name of all that we presented ourselves to the living God. In spite of our apparent lack of outside activity, we exercised a very real apostolate in a most immediate way. By our monastic profession we were witnesses to the existence and priority of God before a world engrossed in the earthly and material realities.

During my early years in the Charterhouse, I had practiced different techniques and methods of prayer, arriving in time at what suited me best. I pointed this out to the novices and encouraged them to seek their particular way within the Carthusian context. A prayer of praise, a life of intercession, and a radical witness to the Gospel message, expressed the reason of the Carthusian's existence.

By teaching the novices about the different methods of prayer, I too learned a great deal, especially the Eastern and Orthodox traditional methods. I taught the novices about *hesychia*, a sense of peace coming from a contemplative prayer. *Hesychasm* transcended the ordinary conditions of life in the world leading the spirit into the spiritual world. Associated with this was the notion of *anachoresis*, the complete withdrawal from the world. The *anchorite* abandoned the ties of home, family, friends, and possessions to retreat from the world and communicate solely with God. All this was perfectly adaptable to our Carthusian calling.

I practiced the *Jesus Prayer*, a kind of mantra used in connection with *hesychasm*. Continuous repeating of the prayer, *Lord Jesus Christ, Son of God, have mercy on me*, provided a practical means for achieving a personal experience of the divinity, another means of entering into the heart. It was similar to a method of prayer that had become popularly known as *Centering prayer*. I was also especially

235

fond of the Spanish mystics who had developed imaginative techniques that transcended the ordinary limits of space and time. They were able to find the sacred anywhere and everywhere, because it was experienced in the interior places of the soul.

Both as a community and as individuals we received specific prayer requests from all over the world. The intentions mentioned in these petitions ranged from the health of a family member who had been in an automobile accident or was about to undergo surgery, to the evangelization of Africa or the Arab world. While we honored all prayer requests, we were conscious that our witness and our role in the universal Church went far beyond responses to particular appeals for intercessory prayer.

Our contemplative prayer could not be tied down to, or in any way confined by, particular causes. Prayer intentions were posted on the community bulletin boards and mentioned in the Sunday liturgical celebrations, and we often talked of them in more detail in our Sunday recreation periods. In community I remembered all the intentions; but as an individual I prayed that the Lord's will be done. That was the Carthusian way of approaching requests for prayer as I had learned it.

In contemplating God and God's creation, I saw the Reality that was the basis of all things. I got into the habit of seeing beyond the physical things that the eyes beheld. I once said that I looked right through the mountains when I gazed out my cell window in contemplation. One of the novices mentioned it to the Prior, who asked me if I could see any gold in the hills! I don't think he understood the meaning of my words. It was all a question of self-transcendence, transpersonal identification, and perhaps the hint of mysticism that Carthusians have tried to avoid.

While I was explaining these things in the weekly novitiate conferences, I was living my own personal journey. I continued to have continuous and severe headaches. On some days the headaches were worse than on others. Whatever I tried had no effect on taking them away. It wasn't just a little headache that would come and go. While still in Spain I had thought that if I ever returned to the States, I would have my health checked with doctors I knew I could trust. I mentioned this health problem to Dom Raphael.

As a true father to his community, he was always particularly solicitous concerning the sick, knowing from his own experience how harsh solitude could become at times. He wanted to explore all possibilities toward finding the root of the headaches. We thought it might be my teeth, or eyes, or perhaps a neurological problem. The dentist found nothing. The optometrist gave me a new prescription for the glasses that I now wore continuously; and I went to a hospital in Rutland for a series of neurological tests, which also showed nothing.

I had learned to live with the constant pain, and even considered it a blessing in as much as it slowed me down, making me less competitively active. Whenever I did something that caused stress on my body, my headaches became worse. My body gave a signal to back off and loosen up. Whenever I felt a headache coming on I knew that there was stress somewhere in the air. Being an "A-type" personality, I sometimes had problems controlling my emotional reactions in stressful situations. The headaches helped me keep things in perspective and under control.

Everything in the Carthusian life encouraged the sick to bear in mind the sufferings of Christ. Most of my brothers had some physical ailment. All of us drew strength to suffer patiently from the Lord's example. Sickness and illness provided opportunities for our souls to grow. It was positive contact with the Lord. The sick were also reminded that they were not to ask for superfluous or impossible things, or even grumble in any way. Mindful of the religious state we had adopted, we were well aware that, just as healthy monks differed from healthy laypersons, so too sick monks should differ from sick laypersons.

We were advised not to use medicines in an abusive way, possibly adding to the financial burden of the house. This was merely a caveat, since I never heard of anyone in the Order abusing drugs or medicines. The community in Vermont had health insurance coverage, and Brother Anthony, who was in charge of its administration, was happy when we used it. He always said that we paid too much into the system not to use it at all.

We had good and sufficient medical care from the local doctor in Arlington. We could go to a specialist in a neighboring town, provided we returned to the monastery on the same day. In my case, however, because none of the doctor visits or tests indicated a cause for my headaches, I continued to endure the pain patiently with little hope of improvement.

Several of the monks, including the Prior, consulted with an osteopathic physician in Manchester. He seldom prescribed medicines, which merely alleviated symptoms as he later told me; rather he tried to attack the root of the problem through manipulative techniques similar to chiropractic medicine. One of the monks suggested that my headaches might have something to do with an organic misalignment of the bones, and could be corrected.

Having nothing to lose, I went to see this doctor. He took one look at me as I walked into his office, and told me that I had a serious problem. Brilliant utterance on his part, as if I didn't already know it! He diagnosed that I had dislocated the bones of my skull at the temple suture, either from some physical blow, or from a moment of abnormal stress. The neck and spinal bones had adapted to the situation in my skull, and the misalignment was causing stress on the nerves and muscles of my neck and back, thus causing the headaches.

Dr. Barney told me that he could partially correct the situation at the very least, but that I would have to see him several times a week for a while. He gave me a neck adjustment that day which threw my system into a state of shock. I felt worse than when I had walked into his office. He told me he had to see me in two days, and probably several times a week for the next few weeks. Although I was not in favor of leaving the monastery several times a week for an hour or two, Dom Raphael was in favor of the arrangement.

Eventually I went once a week for treatment for a period of about three years. I began to feel much better, almost as well as I had felt when I entered the Order. I suspect that the stress of living in Europe coupled with the stress of being chanter in the choir had caused my body to react. The headaches never completely left me, but the severity of the pain diminished greatly. Not having to fight against pain continuously, my personality seemed to change. I started to feel even more enthusiastically fervent in my Carthusian life.

Besides the headaches, I had a problem breathing through my nose. There was considerable "post-nasal drip." I didn't think much of this problem while in Spain, but in the cold and sometimes damp environment of Vermont, it became worse. Particular difficulties showed themselves during the night office. The inner drainage from my nose would build up in my throat so much that my voice did not come out as clear as I would have wanted; and I tried to avoid continuously clearing my throat so as not to disturb my brethren. The whole thing proved very annoying to my brethren and me.

Having to intone a psalm, or to begin the Office with the *Deus in adjutorium meum intende* (*Oh God, come to my assistance*) sometimes made me self-conscious because of the quality of my voice. I started taking *Actifed* when I retired in the evening, and the antihistamine helped keep my voice clear for the night office. It also served to calm my nerves when I knew I had to sing an especially difficult solo part.

When I mentioned the breathing problem to Dom Raphael, he sent me to a specialist in Bennington, who diagnosed a deviated septum. I would have to have an operation to correct the problem. If the operation did not solve the problem, he was prepared to try acupuncture. We were encouraged to receive any necessary treatment in our own cells, and not to attach much importance to the counsels of certain doctors who might advise going outside. We alone would have to give an account to God as to how we had observed our vows. However, the Prior could permit a monk to be admitted to the hospital; and so I went into the hospital for an operation.

The operation proved painful and I offered my pain to God. I was locally sedated and conscious for only part of the procedure. The surgeon literally stuck a chisel up one nostril and hammered away at the cartilage that was out of place. I don't remember what happened next; but I do remember receiving a lot of attention from the nursing staff when I finally woke up; and not only from the staff, but from other patients and visitors as well. The news that a solitary and silent hermit monk was in the hospital made me something of a celebrity. And I could not say that I did not enjoy the attention. Several of the other patients and visitors came to visit me, and some to seek my advice.

One man, for example, approached me with the question of weather his mother, who was in another room at the hospital, should be given more medication. He told me that without the medication she would most likely feel a lot of pain; but with the medication, she might go into a coma. I was reluctant to offer any advice, but he insisted. I remember saying that suffering was not bad, and that I thought less medication would be the safest way to go. The next day that same man came to my room and thanked me. He had followed my suggestion, and that morning his mother was awake and feeling much better. On my part I thanked the Holy Spirit for putting words in my mouth.

Although I was in some pain and under sedation, I liked being in the hospital, and began to hope that I could remain there as long as possible. The food was good, the nurses were attractive and attentive, and there was time to read and to rest. Although I did not fully understand my reaction, I enjoyed being away from the monastery. Dom Raphael came to visit me, as did Dom Marianus, who celebrated Mass in my hospital room. Harvey visited me with a gift -- actually two: a book of Thomas Jefferson's writings, and one of Abraham Lincoln's. One was his favorite and one was mine.

My stay at the Bennington Hospital "resort" could not last forever, and I finally returned to the monastery with a black and blue nose, three times the normal size. Within a few weeks the swelling was gone and everything returned to normal. Most of all, I was thankful that I could breathe better. Memories of my pleasant hospital experience gradually faded into the background, eventually to disappear. Although I did not attend the night office at first, I had resumed my everyday schedule and occupations almost immediately on returning to the cell.

I was conscious of my responsibilities in the community, and conscientious to keep up with them. I looked for ways to serve the community while keeping occupied in a contemplative way. And the Prior could always impose some task or service for the common good. Work was a service that united us to Christ who came "not to be served but to serve." The idea of service was always in the forefront of my mind. I could never be accused of being lazy or shirking responsibility. The Prior once said to me, "You do more for the community than anyone else."

Following the example of the Desert Fathers, I was bound by the divine law of work, the law imposed upon Adam and Eve. The ancients had told us to flee from idleness, the enemy of the soul. Did this mandate give me an excuse for becoming too engrossed in my work? I tried to do only that work approved by the Prior; and there were other tasks that a poor and solitary life demanded. I tried to do my work in such a way that everything was ordered to prayer. It wasn't difficult to pray as I worked, since there were few distractions grabbing at my attention. But I had to be careful not to become so engrossed in my work that I forgot to transcend it in a prayerful spirit.

As a normal thing, we Fathers were not asked to work outside their cells. As many as three times a year, however, we could have "*opera communia.*" This "work in common" could continue for three days at a time if necessary. As well as work that the Sacristan might require, like cleaning the church or the chapels, the Prior could enjoin something that might be of assistance to the Brothers, or any other job that was too big for any one monk by himself. On such occasions, we were allowed to speak briefly among ourselves, but only concerning matters useful for the work. It was not time for idle chatter.

Those days of common work were not well appreciated by some of the monks (including me), because they took away from our solitude and silence. Undoubtedly, there could be something of selfishness in all this. During my first year in Vermont we had the "opera communia" twice, although there was enough common work in the nascent community for more working in common. The Brothers, on the other hand, did a very good job of taking care of the ordinary work. On one occasion we gathered in the Prior's garden and were assigned various tasks like preparing the soil and planting trees. I wheeled cartloads of good topsoil through the cloister into the Prior's garden on one of the days. The Prior was always proud of his little garden. On another common work day we trimmed some of the pine trees that had been planted around the monastery walls.

For my work in cell, I continued to exercise the bookbinding skills I had learned in Spain. Dom Raphael obtained a book press and several smaller pieces of equipment. Under my direction Brother Conrad put together a sewing machine for me. I ordered book cover cardboard of different sizes, and covering materials of different colors, from a catalogue. Father Raphael bought me a small paper cutter. I bound some library books and repaired the bindings of some of the choir books. I bound some in leather and embossed the spines with gold lettering. Besides adding and correcting musical notations in the choir books, I supplied the books with ribbons, which made turning to different parts of the books much easier.

I found an old mimeograph machine and set it up in my cell. Besides printing a questionnaire for those interested in our life, I printed schedules for the retreatants and Novices. At Christmas time I produced a set of simple greeting cards that the monks could send out. The cards were appreciated, and I continued making them for several years, sending out samples from which the brethren could choose. The first year I made the cards, I had a design with a drawing of the Charterhouse against the mountains. A large star was overhead, and the inscription read, *We have seen His star in the East and have come to adore Him.* Dom Raphael liked the design so much that he had it put on the Charterhouse's stationery. He thought it expressed the peacefulness of our life.

The Prior entrusted other small projects to my care, and I took upon myself even other projects with the Prior's approval. Everything I did was with the understanding that I could do it with a certain liberty as far as arranging my work. There was no anxiety to meet a deadline or produce a profit. No one looked over my shoulder or otherwise kept tabs on my work. My attention was fixed not so much on the work itself, as it was on keeping my heart ever watchful. I tried to allow my activity to spring always from a source within me, after the manner of Jesus, who worked with the Father in such a way that the Father dwelt in Him and Himself did the works. I wanted to faithfully follow Jesus in the hidden and humble life of Nazareth, both by praying to the Father in secret and by obediently laboring in His presence.

In addition to manual labor, my quota of work comprised all the duties related to the divine worship, and to the study of theology and the Word of God. I continued to devote myself to studies befitting a Carthusian monk, not from an itching desire for learning, but because I truly believed that wisely ordered reading endowed the mind with greater steadiness. This "steadiness of the mind" was a necessary foundation for the contemplation of heavenly things. The mind had to be at peace, saturated to the point of losing that innate and itching desire to know. It was another expression of the call "to be" rather than "to do."

Although Carthusian monks have had their works published, we were not allowed to write with the intention of publication. The cell could do strange things to the monk, and some fell into the illusion that their writings would make a difference if published. Manuscripts found in the cells of deceased monks were normally destroyed. Many of the writings were personal notes or journals for private use only. The thought of writing for present or future publication never occurred to me. There really was not enough time to do a good job composing any manuscript. I saw no need for doing this.

After completing my course of theological studies, I continued to read the several theological publications that were passed through the cloister. I was interested in keeping abreast of the latest studies, and was particularly interested in the book review sections. I took notes in case I wanted to request that the Prior purchase certain books for the monastery library. I took up the study of Hebrew, but never got to the point of learning any more than the alphabet and a few simple words.

In addition to other duties, Dom Raphael appointed me Professor of Theology. I had a special interest in moral theology and Church law, so that, while Dom Philip taught dogmatic theology, I taught moral theology and Church law. This fit in very well with my work as Novice Master, since it dealt with "ascetical and mystical theology," which was the study of prayer and our relation with the Divinity. I don't remember being either pleased or displeased with this new appointment. The new job fit in well with the rest of my career activities; and besides, I was in the habit of doing what I was asked to do, whether I liked it or not.

At the Prior's request I volunteered to make a translation of the short form of the Carthusian Day Prayer Book -- the *Diurnal* -- from Latin to English, mainly for the benefit of the Brothers who wanted to join with the choir monks in reciting the office in cell. Previous to the early 1970s, the Brothers' liturgical office consisted of a certain number of 'Hail Mary's and 'Our Father's. Even though there had been highly educated men who had preferred to be named among the Carthusian Converse Brothers, they generally had the unfair reputation of being uneducated workers, unable to read or write, and certainly unfamiliar with the Latin that was used in the Office.

I enjoyed the translating work. I used a copy of the *New American Bible* for direct Biblical texts and a copy of the recently translated *Liturgy of the Hours, Christian Prayer* for the psalms and prayers. Many of the prayers used in the Roman rite corresponded to those we used in our Carthusian books. I also translated from Latin to English some of the readings that were used in the night office for the benefit of both Brothers and Fathers. The project took me about three months to complete. After the copies were printed, I bound them and distributed them to the Brothers. The Prior told me that the Brothers were very pleased with the outcome. We also sent copies to St. Hugh's Charterhouse in England for their use.

When I returned to my cell after Mass during the week, I sometimes started doing some work almost immediately. When it was especially cold, I would first sit warming myself in front of a fire. In the warmer spring and summer months, I did a few tasks in my garden, while in the fall and winter, I cut some wood for the fire. I sometimes gave more time to work on some days than I did to reading or study. Sometimes I was so engrossed in my morning work projects that I waited until 1:00 or 1:30 to eat my dinner. The food was already cold, but it didn't matter to me.

I loved being in my cell. In a purely human way I felt that I that my whole Carthusian existence was a continuous vacation. I liked the solitude and the fact that I could work alone at my own pace. I came to know my needs and myself very well. I was a contemplative monk living in an enclosed environment. Everything in my being told me that that was my place in this world. I truly experienced what the Statutes said in such a beautiful way about living in the cell:

> *Here strong men can return into themselves as much as they wish, and abide there; here they can with eager earnestness cultivate the seeds of virtue, and with gladness eat of the fruits of paradise. Here is acquired that eye, by whose serene gaze the Spouse is wounded with love; that eye, pure and clean, by which God is seen. Here the solitary is occupied in busy leisure, and at rest in tranquil activity. Here God rewards His athletes with the longed-for prize: peace that the world does not know, and joy in the Holy Spirit.*

The longer I lived in the cell, the more gladly I did so, as I occupied myself in it usefully and in an orderly manner, reading, writing, reciting psalms, praying, meditating, contemplating and working. I had learned to make a practice of resorting, from time to time, to a tranquil listening of the heart, which allowed God to enter through all its doors and passages. Not that I was always successful, but generally with God's help, I avoided the dangers that often lie in wait for the solitary, such as following too easy a path in cell and meriting to be numbered among the lukewarm.

I always knew that I had to be diligent and careful about contriving or accepting occasions for leaving the cell, more than ever in Vermont. Since my days in Spain I had diligently and carefully guarded against going out of the cell for unnecessary reasons. I thought of the cell as necessary for my life, just as water was for fish and the sheepfold for sheep. Every detail of my life in and out of the cell was determined by what the Statutes said. In my striving to be as perfect a Carthusian as possible by observing the rule, the rule had molded my thinking and being.

I did have to leave the cell from time to time to visit my novices, the Prior, and the retreatants. I tried to make these visits at times that were compatible with our solitude, either immediately before, or immediately after, Mass in the morning or Vespers in the late afternoon. As Novice Master, I had an intercom telephone in my cell, so that I could communicate with the Prior, Procurator, kitchen, and guest parlors without leaving my physical solitude.

I was alone for most of the day and night, and sometimes I experienced a sense of loneliness and even fear. When the wind blew, the rains came, and the lightning lit up the dark night, I felt so completely alone that I sometimes "locked" the inside door of the *cubiculum* by putting a pair of scissors in the latch. I did this too on calm and peaceful nights when I watched the snow falling on the hills in large flakes. I became a very light sleeper and rarely slept for more than three or four hours at any time. Any small noise woke me. Because I was usually disoriented when I woke, I used this as another excuse for locking the inside door.

I did not like others coming into the *cubiculum*. It was holy ground for me. For the Novitiate conferences and Theology classes, I moved a desk into the *Ave Maria*. I set up a portable kerosene heater there, and also left the *cubiculum* door open for extra warmth. The third room, which had been intended for use as a conference room, became my bookbinding workshop. I used it only in warm weather because it had no heating source.

Besides the keeping of the cell, our rule prescribed that we not to speak to one another without the Prior's permission, unless there was a case of extreme emergency. In the early stages of my Carthusian life I may have found silence a burden at times. It was one thing to be silent when you did not have anything to say, but it was something else to live under a rule that commanded you to keep silent at all times. As I remained faithful in keeping to the rule of silence, however, I noticed that something was gradually born within my soul that drew me on to a still greater silence. I lost the need to speak. I gradually felt that my being silent would be of more use to both myself and others.

As the months and years passed in rapid succession, Dom Raphael continued to exercise a profound influence on my life. Early on he had reached the conclusion that my intellect and spirit needed "broadening," and he wanted to hasten the process. Some in the community had the impression that he was grooming me to take over as Prior.

Through some of our benefactors and his family, he supplied me with books of sound quality, carefully selected for their usefulness in broadening my spirit. He asked around town for someone who might be interested in tutoring me in English and in literature. An English professor from the local high school was highly recommended, and it was arranged that I meet with him once a week for several weeks.

Harvey introduced me to some of the world's best literature, which we discussed during our weekly meetings in the guest parlor. I was hesitant at first about all this, but after a few visits, I began to look forward to our meetings and discussions. He made me think about things of a non-spiritual nature; and he proposed additional ideas to compliment mine, all in a respectful and gentle way.

He listened to me and affirmed my thoughts. Sometimes we would agree to disagree; but after having time to reflect on his side of the disagreement, I more often than not agreed with his evaluations of plots or characters. More than anything else, I was pleased that we became friends. My spirit and intellect were developing in a human and worldly way. No one at that time made any judgment whether this was good or bad.

After this introduction to literature, I took it upon myself to go to the *Encyclopedia Britannica* in the monastery library and make a list of all the English and American literature that was worth reading. I read every one of the books on the list. In addition, Dom Raphael had me read some of his favorites, especially the classics of Russian literature. I read through the great religious writers, the Hindu *Vedas*, the Buddhist writings, the *Koran,* and the works of Confucius.

Then I started on an historical theme, asking for and receiving books through the local public library. I read all I could about colonial New England, about the rise of the Catholic Church in the Americas, and about the Spanish explorers in the South and Southwest. I was extremely interested in knowing what had happened in the United States during the years I had been in Spain and into the 1970s. After that I devoured as many scientific books as I could. I became interested in astronomy and historical geology. Medical books and clinical psychology manuals came into my cell. I was fascinated by everything I read.

I gained a great amount of knowledge and broadening of spirit, sometimes reading three or four books at any one time. I would have a stack of books in front of me, and read five or ten pages of one and then go to the next, and so on, passing two or three hours each morning in this way. Much of what I read helped me understand the spirit of the times so that I could better interact with the candidates who presented themselves. And I began to understand myself both from readings in psychology, sociology, and history.

I kept in mind the principle that my faith should be nourished and prayer life fostered, even through works of fiction. I wasn't really interested in being informed about the latest opinions or fads that came and went. Rather, I wanted to gain more understanding of the basic human condition. While the Prior could prohibit me from reading any book, I don't remember his ever doing so. He sometimes questioned me about certain books, and read parts of them; but he never prohibited me from reading anything. We had always been allowed to read "secular books," and our library had a number of them. Such reading material was intended to be a good distraction from too much spiritual and intellectual activity.

The Prior generally exhorted us monks to be rather circumspect in the matter of secular reading. Although there was sometimes a question over exactly what was considered secular reading, everyone agreed that the exhortation was intended to encourage the formation of a mature mind that would be master of itself. Some of my brethren criticized the Prior for letting me read just about anything I wanted; but he kept to his plan when he saw that the readings did not interfere with my solitary and silent Carthusian life, or with my functioning as Novice Master.

And then one day I began to feel that I had learned too much -- that I had read too much. I had read so much and so fast during a period of two or three years that I began to feel "read out." There wasn't anything I was interested in reading. I had learned to "speed read," skimming across the pages and scanning for important words and phrases. It tired me and took the enjoyment out of the reading.

I think I became cynical of other opinions, and thought I knew most, if not all the answers. I was able to see through everything into hidden and secret meanings. The fact is that I could find no enjoyment in anything, except perhaps the liturgy and the beauty of nature. For reasons beyond my understanding, I had become incapable of enjoying anything for what it was. I thought that that was the way it was supposed to be as I advanced in the spiritual life toward complete union with God. Art, food, people, places...it didn't matter. From then on, outside of Scripture, I rarely read anything; if I did read anything, it was a non-fiction work.

I began to retreat once more into the intellectual and spiritual desert from whence I had come. Before I started Dom Raphael's "enrichment program" I had read nothing but the Bible for my spiritual and intellectual nourishment. I had never tired of reading and re-reading the prophets, the Wisdom books, and John's Gospel. I had read every word and chewed the meaning out of each of them. I didn't have time to waste reading fiction anymore. And when I read non-fiction, I rarely read every word. I continued to skim and scan through the pages of a book or religious periodical, looking for something that I knew a little about to see if that information was correct.

Such was my life as a Carthusian monk to that point in time. And then, one Sunday morning in the late summer, everything suddenly changed. It all started with a choir incident, just as many of my previous issues had. It was customary, every Sunday morning, to bless holy water for use during the coming week. The principal celebrant of the Mass blessed the water and intoned the verse, *Asperges me, Domine*. The rest of the choir was supposed to take up the verse, following the lead of the weekly chanter.

According to the *Method of Chant*, the pace of the verse was meant to be lively, in fact, much livelier than it was going that Sunday morning. And so, in accord with my position of Chanter, I tried to speed the pace. In a small community most of the monks will let the Chanter bear the load of the singing, but in this case, everyone else stopped singing and looked at me. I gestured with my hands that the pace should be speedier; but the singing resumed at the original slow pace, and once again I resigned myself to business as usual.

After Mass the Prior asked me what had happened, and voiced his concern that I might have a deeper "emotional problem." Dom Raphael was ever obsessed with identifying and eliminating emotional problems in his community. I told him that I was okay. But he had already spoken by phone to the Reverend Father General in France, and that he was making arrangements for me to go to New York City to talk with the monastery's psychologist. He would make arrangements for me to stay with the Paulist Fathers for a few days while I underwent a series of psychological tests.

After that, I was to remain in New York until he returned from Europe, where he had to go on business for the Order. He did not want me to return to Vermont while he was absent, ostensibly to avoid any further "disturbance" in the community. I didn't like the idea at all; but there was no persuading Dom Raphael to the contrary. Perhaps he didn't realize what a powerful effect my being in the world would have on my spiritual life. As one of the Visitors of the Order, he had traveled from one house to another on numerous occasions, and was accustomed to making concessions and adaptations. Going out, staying overnight with his family in New Jersey, traveling to Europe: none of this seemed to affect his own spiritual life.

I gathered into a suitcase some secular clothing that was kept in the tailor shop. It was the first time in almost twenty years that I left the monastery not wearing the habit. For a long time I felt naked without my monastic robes. With a few dollars in my pocket, I took the bus that passed by the tollhouse into New York City. It was a crisp September morning. I was thrust into the world that I felt I did not belong in.

I did it with simplicity of heart, trusting that the Lord was with me. I didn't have any apprehension, nor was there fear in my heart. I knew I would not be away from the monastery indefinitely; and in fact, after reading so much about what was out there, I welcomed the opportunity to see a little of it for myself.

I was amazed by the number of cars on the road since the early 1960s. I went into the supermarkets just to see the variety of foods that were now available. I started to watch television and learned to make telephone calls. While in New York I visited with some of my relatives: aunts and uncles and cousins, many of whom I had not seen in years.

I took long walks around Manhattan Island and rode the subway to Brooklyn. I walked around the neighborhood where I had stayed with Nana, and I walked as far as where Aunt Mae had lived. I never thought I would ever again see those places. One morning I took the Long Island Railroad to Hempstead and rented a car and drove around the neighborhood where I had grown up.

So many memories flooded into my mind and heart! I wondered what I had missed, if anything important, during those twenty years I had been away in the monastery. With each new experience I felt an increase of self-confidence and satisfaction. I was surprised with the sense of freedom and even fulfillment I felt, and I began to like it.

The freedom and satisfaction that I felt in my monastic life was different from this new experience. It felt good, like a return to a former self that I thought had long since died. I began to realize that the freedom of the monastic life was more of an inner spiritual freedom; this was a liberty to do more or less what I wanted to do physically whenever I wanted to do it. I was no longer directly and immediately responsible to a superior for every move I made.

I began to have thoughts of remaining in the world, and the thoughts frightened me. At the same time, I didn't know how I would survive on my own at forty years of age. While in New York, I passed hours before the Blessed Sacrament. Were these thoughts of leaving the monastery temptations from the devil? I did not want to sin by rejecting God's grace. I didn't know what to do other than await Dom Raphael's return from Europe and the results of the psychological tests.

I consulted with different people seeking an answer. Most of them agreed with the opinion of a priest psychiatrist I had spoken to, that by remaining in the monastery I was destroying my personality. Apparently, my spirituality of nothingness was leading to a destruction or disappearance of my human personality. I had always thought of this as a positive thing, a losing of one's self in the divinity -- a kind of "divinization." Now I began to understand another point of view. Perhaps what I was consciously attempting might not be the best thing.

When Father Raphael finally returned from Europe after almost a month, I returned to the Charterhouse. Because of a long-standing agreement between Father Reinhold (not his real name) and Dom Raphael, the person undergoing the testing was not allowed to see the final report with its recommendations. However, in a sort of debriefing after the testing, Father Reinhold, had mentioned words and phrases such as "intellectualization, need for a daily schedule, expediency, opportunism." Supposedly I was "uncomfortable" outside of familiar surroundings. I showed signs of "feeling overworked."

All this was not a big revelation, and most of it only served to confirm what Dom Raphael and I already knew. Father Reinhold recommended that I be relieved of all duties in the community, and that I visit with a priest psychologist in Albany once a week for a "counseling" session. It was Dom Raphael's wish that I not associate with the community outside of prayer times. There would be no Sunday recreations or weekly walks.

Dom Raphael always had great confidence in the testing service and the resulting recommendations. He and I talked about the findings and recommendations on several occasions. I told him that I didn't think there was anything extraordinary in the report, and for the most part he agreed. I didn't particularly relate to Father Reinhold well on a personal level, and I certainly did not like, or agree with, the recommendations that originated from the testing.

For better or for worse, however, Dom Raphael was inflexible about carrying out the recommendations. He made arrangements for me to obtain a driver's license so that I could drive to Albany once a week. My New York driver's license had expired years ago, and I had to take a written and road test in Rutland before getting a new license.

Having been out of the cell for almost a month, I found it very difficult, both emotionally and physically, to remain in the solitude of the cell. Without any contact with the community, I had been stripped of all that had been my life for the past six or seven years. With Dom Raphael's permission, I left my cell during the day to pass time before the Blessed Sacrament, speaking heart to heart with Jesus about my situation, seeking light and guidance. I took long walks through the forest I had loved, but found no consolation there either.

I anguished in my heart and mind over whether I was being faithful to my God. I applied to myself the words of the poet Francis Thompson, *I fled Him, down the night and down the days; I fled him, down the labyrinthine ways of my own mind.* I did not want to flee from Him or be unfaithful to Him. I wanted to remain faithful to my calling, to renew my life in solitude and silence, and at the same time be submissive to the recommendations of my Superiors.

To my dismay and confusion, the solitude I loved so deeply had become an empty shell. The silence I had been so attached to had become empty of all repose and consolation. I felt abandoned, isolated as I was from my Carthusian brothers. Had Jesus abandoned me? Was I losing my faith? Was I losing my mind?

All of this came to a head when Dom Raphael suggested that it might be better if I went on a leave of absence rather than anguish in the cell. My first reaction was one of feeling betrayed by my Superiors, the Order, and even God, who had called me to live with Him in solitude. I felt drawn in conflicting directions. Perhaps I did need time away from the monastery to sort things out.

Though I did not feel that I belonged in "the world," neither did I feel that I could remain in the monastery. I had seen so much, and done so much, in the weeks that I had been out of the cell, that in my conscience I felt too contaminated to continue in the pristine purity and sacredness of the Carthusian cell.

That I should leave my beloved monastery ultimately was a decision reached by my Carthusian Superiors to whom I could only give my resigned acquiescence. Dom Raphael gave me money to buy a suit and a pair of shoes. With my Vermont driver's license, I launched out into the deep with three thousand dollars in checks in my pocket.

In October, 1978, I began a temporary leave of absence. I was on my own for the first time in almost twenty years, on an adventure. I felt again that strange sense of freedom. My health was good. After a while my headaches started to disappear. I was not scared or frightened. Maybe I was a bit naïve, but I felt challenged. I was a fish out of water; but I also felt that I could adapt if necessary.

I knew that I might never return to the monastic cell; but I trusted in the Lord, knowing He was close by my side at every step of the way. I was on an officially sanctioned leave of absence, which could last up to six months. I was between two worlds. At any time I could return to the monastic enclosure, or I could remain in the world indefinitely. I was in a unique position. I didn't know how long my unique situation would last.

Six months would be extended for another six months, and eventually I broke all ties with the Carthusian Order. At my request, and with the support of the Order, the Pope released me from the obligations both of my vows and of the priesthood.

in retrospect

Whoever does what is true comes to the light in order that the light may show that what he did was in obedience to God. (John 3:21)

I have always tended to be a loner, drawing apart from others, content to be with myself. Solitude is part of my personality, my mode of being, the way I reveal myself to the rest of creation. As I thought about my experiences as a monk -- the calling, my training in Spain, and my life in Vermont -- and put them into writing, the threads of my life began to form a woven fabric, a personal and unique creation. I journeyed along a path in my own particular way, the way I thought I was supposed to do at the time.

I like to be with others, and have many acquaintances; but I have made only a few close friends over the years. My closest friends are scattered around the country and the world. My friends and family have been aware of that certain solitary dimension to my personality. They recognize this as an expression of who I am, how I relate to the material world. I cannot tolerate a lot of noise around me or in my life, be it exterior or interior. I do not like crowds. I am not a city dweller. One of these friends once summed it up in this way: "You like to be with people when you want to be with people."

Fortunately, most of my friends can accept how I am and remain friends with me; although more than once have I heard the words, "You should go back to the monastery," the "monastery" being a place of refuge, quiet, and hiddenness, and sometimes just anywhere else. But at this point in my life, attractive as it sometimes may appear, I believe that my returning to the silent isolation of the desert would be a regression to a former self that has since disappeared. I would not recommend such a course of action to anyone else in a similar situation.

Although I feel that I have remained a monk in my heart and soul, I no longer have the inner need to live in a monastic setting. A monastery sometimes becomes a beckoning attraction when one faces the fright of the real world and thinks that he has been mistakenly deposited on the wrong planet. The feeling of being alienated from almost everything that is happening around him can sometimes supply the necessary motivation to go into the desert and live as a hermit. I originally felt that way, and at times the feeling returns. At those times, however, instead of returning to the monastery, I seek out my "special places," places that have a relaxing effect on my body, mind, and soul.

I think it would be wrong to look as my decision to enter the monastery as either a mistake or an escape. I followed what I knew without any doubt to be a calling. With and by God's grace I undertook my own specific pre-planned journey. The whole of life is a journey for those who do not stand still. The journey toward and through the Carthusian monastic experience was an important part of my total journey through life. And my life has not yet come to an end. Perhaps if I had remained in Spain, I would still be in the Charterhouse. But that was not the case. Then again, the twenty years that I was in the monastery was often a whole lifetime in the Middle Ages, when people often did not live beyond forty years.

And so, my conclusion has been that I was called to leave the monastery because I basically outgrew the life. Perhaps I was too young when I entered. In any case, I was ready for a change; but in the end, it was not I who initiated the change. God spoke through my Superiors and through occurrences that were outside of my control. After that I took another leap of faith, struggled through the change, and eventually found peace.

So what had been answered? What do I have to show for those twenty years of living in the Charterhouse? Negatively speaking, I do not consider them wasted years, though at times I have felt that the world "passed me by." Even so, if such were the case, I doubt that I missed much, if anything. There are few regrets about that part of my journey. Perhaps my biggest regret would be that I did not have the maturity to truly love my monastic brethren in a deep enough way while I lived with them.

On the other hand, I think I attained a personal spiritual maturity that has enabled me to live with God -- in silent communion with God -- the same now in the midst of the noise of today's world as I lived with Him then in the monastery. I have acquired a great and deep knowledge of my own self. In my high school yearbook under my photo was the quotation from Plato: "*Full wise is he who can himself know.*" Through the years lived in solitude and silence I came to the fulfillment of those words beyond my wildest expectations, reaching a level of wisdom and maturity that very few humans can reach in a lifetime.

In retrospect, I entered the monastery to search for and attain wisdom and spiritual maturity. When it started to happen I was ready to leave. I had been cooked enough in the pressure cooker of the monastic life. At the time I left the monastic life I did not fully understand this -- but that is neither here nor there. What is important is that I answered a need in the first place by entering the monastic life and persevering in it. If I had not done what I did, I would not have reached that spiritual maturity. I would not be the person before God and man that I am now.

I have reached the awareness of who I am, with my good and not so good qualities. Long ago I relinquished any sense of self-importance without giving up any respect for my true self. And I am very much aware of the good and bad qualities in others, which prompts me to accept others for what they really are, and not for what they may pretend to be.

Though I no longer dwell in "the house of the Lord," I continue to be a monk in my innermost being. For several years after I had officially severed my ties with the Carthusian Order, I visited with Dom Raphael in Vermont. I expressed my feelings that I still belonged in the Charterhouse; but he replied that I had "put my time in," or that I would never have grown to what I was had I not left. He gave me the opportunity to spend some days in cell on at least three occasions. I attended the night office, and even the weekly walk. I remember kneeling in the oratory of the cell and asking God to "please take me back."

Dom Raphael confessed to me that he had been severely criticized by some of the brethren for the way he had "handled my case." Less than a month before he passed away, he telephoned me and repeated more or less the same thought. He wanted to know how I was doing. I told him that I was reconciled to living outside of the Charterhouse. He knew that I had tried living with several other religious communities, but none of them measured up to the Carthusians. They were excellent communities, but not for me.

In my heart, I knew I did not belong anywhere but in a Charterhouse. At one point, Dom Raphael asked the Reverend Father if I could return to the Order; but the Reverend Father and the General Chapter refused the request. I was not allowed to return "under any circumstances." Both Dom Raphael and I came to the conclusion that all that had happened was in God's design. *All things work toward the good for those who love Him.*

For a long time I kept a notebook of reflections on the details of my journeys, and to help me keep to a straight course. I set certain principles as guidelines:

I would strive to live in the present moment, in the here and now.

My attention would be focused on the One.

Before Him I would continuously empty myself in adoration, humility and simplicity of spirit.

I would try to remain faithful to my inner calling, keeping my intention focused on the calling to know, love, and serve God in this world.

I continued to believe that I had an eremitical vocation, a calling to a life of silence and solitude in the heart of the Church. At the same time, I felt strongly that my calling was to be lived outside of the traditional Benedictine or Cistercian monastic structure. My needs included a time for prayer, time for study, and time for adoration before the Blessed Sacrament. I needed spiritual guidance from time to time from mature men.

Nowadays I do not always have enough free time to dedicate to prayerful contemplation. Without this time for prayer on a regular basis I sometimes feel that my deepest needs are unanswered. But, have I become less spiritual? To the contrary, I hope I have matured in the spiritual life. Like most mature Carthusians, I rarely pray in words. If I do pray in words, the words are simple: *I believe in You, I hope in You, I love You.*

Mostly, I pray in silence and by silences. I try to make my entire life, every conscious moment of the day and night, a silent and living presence before the Supreme Being. I lose myself in Him. Sometimes I become impatient with distractions. But I try to abandon myself consciously and habitually into the hands of the Spiritual Being who is my Father in every sense of the word. I try to place all my trust in Him, that He will lead me and guide me and take care of those who are closest to me.

For the most part God is silent with me too, though He sometimes surprises me with something good that was totally unexpected. By His grace, I have kept the faith. I trust in Him, though I sometimes feel abandoned. If God *were* to abandon me, I would still trust in Him, for He is God. I do not think in terms of salvation, or perfection, or merit, but rather in terms of gratefulness for God's mercy and goodness in my life. I hope to rely solely on His mercy at the end of my life. I have little else to rely on.

Have I have remained true to my calling? I often tell people, "I used to be a monk." In actuality the monastic calling was burned into my personality in such a way that I am still a monk. I think of it as a *living calling* -- born in eternity and continuing for eternity, never to die. I was a monk from birth. My journey has taken me through the spiritual and physical deserts. And I am still seeking God in my life.

With St. Paul I can say that by the grace of God I have kept the faith (at least so far). True faith has to be tested by a silence in which we listen for the unexpected, in which we are open to what we do not yet know, and in which we slowly and gradually prepare for the day when we will reach out to a new level of being with God. True hope is tested by that silence in which we have to wait on the Lord in the obedience of unquestioning faith.

Isaiah recorded the word of Yahweh to His rebellious people who were always abandoning Him in favor of worthless political and military alliances. *In silence and hope shall your strength be* (Is 30:15). Faith demands the silencing of questionable deals and strategies. Faith demands the integrity of inner trust, which produces wholeness, unity, peace, and genuine security. Here we see the creative power and fruitfulness of silence. It helps us to concentrate on a purpose that really corresponds not only to the deepest needs of our own being but also to God's intentions for us.

Whether there is a reward waiting for me at the end of my earthly journey is not my concern. In the end, I have nothing to rely upon but God's mercy, knowing that my monastic journey was a gift of love and that I responded to it with love in return. I can say to the Lord, "Jesus, I trust in You." I did the best I could.

Meanwhile, in the retreat of their monasteries, in the solitude of their cells, my brother Carthusians spin Holy Church's wedding garment *beautiful as a bride decked out for her bridegroom* (Rev. 21:3). Untiring sentinels of the coming kingdom, seeking "to be" before doing, they continue to give strength and courage to the Church in her mission. Every day they offer the world to God and invite all mankind to the wedding feast of the Lamb.

The emblem of the Carthusian Order is a globe representing the earth, surrounded by a cross and seven stars, with the motto *Stat crux, dum volvitur orbis*: The world turns while the cross stands firm.

DISCLAIMER

What I have written are the personal memories and reflections of a former Carthusian monk. I tell of my calling, training, and life as a Carthusian priest and choir monk. I also relate the *whys* and *wherefores* of my eventual departure from the Carthusian monastery.

These reflections are in no way either officially sanctioned or authorized by the Carthusian Order. They are not intended as an authorized promotion of the monastic life, the Carthusian Order, or the Roman Catholic Church in general; nor, on the other hand, are they intended to be a criticism of the Carthusian Order, or of any persons therein, whether living or deceased.

Any direct or indirect quotations from, or paraphrasing of, the Carthusian Statutes, are not to be taken as official translations of the original Latin or French versions of the *Renewed Statutes of the Carthusian Order.*

ACKNOWLEDGMENTS

I am indebted primarily to the Carthusian Order for giving me the opportunity to journey into the Carthusian desert.

Several of the photographs, including the one on the cover, were taken from *angel fire.com*. The excerpt from Ernest Dowson's poem was found at *ELCore.net*.

I wish to thank my good friends, Father Jacques Daley, O.S.B. and Father Basil, e.c. for their encouragement and valuable suggestions. During the year and a half since I started my writing, my friends and associates at the Norton, including Jane Watick, Bob and his wife Maryann, John, Ron, Clem, Beverly, Herb, Matt, and Peter, among others, all contributed valuable critical input and encouragement.

Harvey, Marcella, and Monie, read my manuscript with great interest, each of them contributing valuable ideas and suggestions. Bernard Banks labored through my manuscript with a fine toothcomb, finding and correcting errors that I had overlooked, while at the same time offering very valuable suggestions. I thank our neighbors, including Darlene, Jacky, and Anne, for their continual interest in my story.

I am also grateful to my loving wife, Nettie, for her understanding, patience, and support while I worked alone on my manuscript.

Printed in the United Kingdom
by Lightning Source UK Ltd.
132738UK00001B/390/A